ENGLISH–
EGYPTIAN ARABIC
EGYPTIAN ARABIC–
ENGLISH

Dictionary & Phrasebook

Also by Mahmoud Gaafar and Jane Wightwick:

Arabic Compact Dictionary
Arabic Dictionary & Phrasebook
Emergency Arabic Phrasebook
Mastering Arabic 1 with 2 Audio CDs
Mastering Arabic 2 with 2 Audio CDs
Mastering Arabic 1 Activity Book

ENGLISH–
EGYPTIAN ARABIC
EGYPTIAN ARABIC–
ENGLISH

Dictionary & Phrasebook

Mahmoud Gaafar
Jane Wightwick

HIPPOCRENE BOOKS, INC.
New York

For information, address:
HIPPOCRENE BOOKS, INC.
171 Madison Avenue
New York, NY 10016
www.hippocrenebooks.com

Design and typesetting by:
g-and-w PUBLISHING, UK
www.g-and-w.co.uk

Library of Congress Cataloging-in-Publication Data
Gaafar, Mahmoud.
 English-Egyptian Arabic Egyptian Arabic-English dictionary
& phrasebook / Mahmoud Gaafar, Jane Wightwick.
     pages cm.
 ISBN-13: 978-0-7818-1317-4 (pbk.)
 ISBN-10: 0-7818-1317-4 (pbk.)
1. English language—Dictionaries—Arabic. 2. Arabic
language—Dictionaries—English. 3. Arabic language—
Dialects—Egypt. 4. Arabic language—Conversation and
phrasebooks—English. 5. English language—Conversation
and phrasebooks—Arabic. I. Wightwick, Jane. II. Title. III.
Title: English-Egyptian Arabic Egyptian Arabic-English
dictionary and phrasebook.

 PJ6640.G33 2013
 492.7'70962--dc23

                                            2013029765

CONTENTS

INTRODUCTION

Egyptian Arabic, informal and spontaneous, has been released from the shackles of grammar. It is constantly updating itself with words and expressions from a variety of sources. This includes foreign words that morph into Arabic verbs and adjectives, and then fit right in as if they had been Arabic words all along. Nowhere is this more evident than in the area of computers. *dallit*, *shayyir*, and *sayyev* are actually "delete," "share,' and "save" being used as if they were Arabic.

Egypt is the most populous Arab country and human resources are one of its top exports to its neighbors. Egypt exports doctors, school teachers, builders, accountants, salesmen, pilots, and so on. It also supplies most of the popular culture. That is why Egyptian Arabic is widely understood and your new Hippocrene *Egyptian Arabic Dictionary & Phrasebook* will be useful in most Arabic-speaking countries.

Whenever I travel to a country where they speak a language I don't understand or a language I am trying to learn it always seems to me that the locals are speaking too quickly and too loudly. I rather expect you to feel the same when you go to Egypt. Think of this book as a taster of the language and culture. Help yourself to the real deal when you visit Egypt. We've included lots of cultural tips to make it more informative and enjoyable.

PRONUNCIATION GUIDE

The pronunciation guidance in this phrase-book is designed to be intuitive, and to reflect what you may actually hear Egyptians saying. Pay attention to how particular phrases are pronounced in Egypt, even if you can read the Arabic script. Be aware, also, that you will hear variations in pronunciation within Egypt, and even within a single city.

Many Arabic sounds are familiar and similar to their English equivalents. However, there are some sounds that benefit from additional explanation:

Arabic letter	*Pronunciation*
خ *khaa*	throaty **h** as in the Yiddish **ch**utzpah or the Scottish lo**ch**
ث *thaa*	soft **th** as in **th**in, often pronounced as **t** in Egypt
ذ *dhaal*	hard **th** as in **th**at, often pronounced as **z** in Egypt
غ *ghein*	throaty **r** as in the French **r**ue
ح *Haa*	breathy **h**, as if breathing on glasses to clean them
ج *geem*	Almost always pronounced **g** as in **g**ate in Northern Egypt, but pronounced as a soft **j** in Modern Standard Arabic and in Southern Egypt

Arabic letter	Pronunciation
ص Saad	emphatic **S** ("s" pronounced with the tongue touching the roof the mouth)
ض Daad	emphatic **D**
ط Taa	emphatic **T**
ظ DHaa	emphatic **DH**, usually pronounced as an emphatic **D** in Egyptian Arabic
ع 9ein	The letter 9ein (ع) takes time to master. It is a strangulated **ah** sound. We have used the number **9** to show the 9ein in the pronunciation.
ق qaaf	Pronounced as a throaty **q** in Modern Standard Arabic, but usually dropped in Egyptian Arabic, producing a glottal stop similar to the sound when English-speakers drop a "t" (for example "be'er" instead of "better").

THE ARABIC ALPHABET

Opposite you will find the Arabic letters in alphabetical order. The script is written from *right to left* and most Arabic letters join to the following letter in a word. This usually affects the shape of the letter. The chart shows how the letters look at the beginning, in the middle, and at the end of a word.

letter sound	beginning	middle	end
alif *a/e/i/o/u/aa*	ا	ـا	ا
baa *b*	بـ	ـبـ	ب
taa *t*	تـ	ـتـ	ت
thaa *t/th*	ثـ	ـثـ	ث
geem *g/j*	جـ	ـجـ	ج
Haa *H*	حـ	ـحـ	ح
khaa *kh*	خـ	ـخـ	خ
daal *d*	د	ـد	د
dhaal *z/dh*	ذ	ـذ	ذ
raa *r*	ر	ـر	ر
zaa *z*	ز	ـز	ز
seen *s*	سـ	ـسـ	س
sheen *sh*	شـ	ـشـ	ش
Saad *S*	صـ	ـصـ	ص
Daad *D*	ضـ	ـضـ	ض
Taa *T*	طـ	ـطـ	ط
DHaa *D/DH*	ظـ	ـظـ	ظ
9ein *9*	عـ	ـعـ	ع/ع
ghein *gh*	غـ	ـغـ	غ/غ
faa *f*	فـ	ـفـ	ف
qaaf *'/q*	قـ	ـقـ	ق
kaaf *k*	كـ	ـكـ	ك
laam *l*	لـ	ـلـ	ل
meem *m*	مـ	ـمـ	م
noon *n*	نـ	ـنـ	ن
haa *h*	هـ	ـهـ	ـه/ه
waaw *w/oo/oh*	و	ـو	و
yaa *y/ee/ei*	يـ	ـيـ	ي

ABBREVIATIONS

adj	*adjective*
adv	*adverb*
fem	*feminine*
masc	*masculine*
n	*noun*
pl	*plural*
pron	*pronoun*
v	*verb*

A BRIEF LOOK AT THE LANGUAGE

Standard Arabic and Egyptian Arabic

Modern Standard Arabic is the shared, formal language of the Arab world. It has rather a lot of rules and its parentage is clearly identifiable in its religious roots. Egyptian Arabic, on the other hand, is primarily a spoken language. It was born on the street and continues to live there until today. Egyptian Arabic follows "pointers" rather than "rules."

Egyptian Arabic is written mainly in cartoon captions, lyrics of popular songs, contemporary novels, advertisements, movie scripts, and so on. It is written phonetically rather than following strict grammatical rules, which accounts for the fact that it has few friends amongst the traditional highbrow linguistic establishment.

Egyptian Arabic takes short cuts in pronunciation and grammar. So be prepared for variations and inconsistencies. Having said that, here are some basic pointers.

Genders and Articles

Arabic has two genders: masculine and feminine. Everything you'll meet is either a *he* or a *she*, nothing is an *it*.

Feminine nouns are words that either refer to females, or words that end in **-a** (ة), e.g. بنت **bint** *(girl)*; مدرسة **madrasa** *(school)*; غرفة **ghurfa** *(room)*.

Almost all other nouns are masculine, e.g. ولد walad (boy); درس dars (lesson); صابون Saboon (soap). Exceptions are rare.

There is no indefinite article (a/an) in Arabic. ولد walad means both "boy" and "a boy."

The definite article (the) is el (ال), which is added to the beginning of nouns:

ولد walad (a boy) → الولد el walad (the boy)

بنت bint (a girl) → البنت el bint (the girl)

If a noun begins with certain letters of the alphabet, these letters take over (assimilate) the l sound of el:

صابون Saboon (soap) becomes...

الصابون eS-Saboon (the soap)

درس dars (lesson) becomes...

الدرس ed-dars (the lesson)

This assimilation applies to approximately half the letters of the alphabet, but is something you need only recognize.

If el- comes after a word ending in a vowel, the e is dropped:

الولد el walad (the boy)

والولد wi l-walad (and the boy)

المتحف el matHaf (the museum)

في المتحف fi l-matHaf (in the museum)

Personal Pronouns

Arabic	English
أنا **ana**	*I*
أنت **enta**	*you* (masc.)
أنت **enti**	*you* (fem.)
هو **howwa**	*he*
هي **heyya**	*she*
إحنا **eHna**	*we*
أنتو **entu**	*you* (pl.)
هما **humma**	*they*

Possessive pronouns (*my, your,* etc.) are added to the end of words:

Ending	Example	English
ي- **-i**	كتابي **kitaabi**	*my book*
ـك **-ak**	كتابك **kitaabak**	*your* (masc.) *book*
ـك **-ik**	كتابك **kitaabik**	*your* (fem.) *book*
ـه **-uh**	كتابه **kitaabuh**	*his book*
ـها **-ha**	كتابها **kitaabha**	*her book*
ـنا **-na**	كتابنا **kitaabna**	*our book*
ـكو **-ku**	كتابكم **kitaabku**	*your* (pl.) *book*
ـهم **-hom**	كتابهم **kitaabhom**	*their book*

Note: Modern Standard Arabic has a plural form especially for groups of females, and another for two people. Egyptian Arabic largely ignores these.

Simple sentences and questions

There is no verb *"to be"* (am/are/is) in Arabic and no special question form. This means you can make simple statements and questions without using complicated structures. Here are some examples:

Arabic	English
ana Edward أنا ادوارد.	I [am] Edward.
ana amreekaani أنا أمريكاني.	I [am an] American.
entu Talaba? أنتو طلبة؟	[Are] you (pl.) students?
el matHaf fein? المتحف فين؟	Where [is] the museum?
el bint Taweela البنت طويلة.	The girl [is] tall.

Adjectives

Adjectives come *after* the word they are describing, and will also have **el** if the word described does:

matHaf kebeer متحف كبير *(a large museum)*

el matHaf el maSri المتحف المصري
(the Egyptian Museum)

Adjectives will also have the feminine ending -a if the word they describe is feminine:

bint Taweela بنت طويلة *(a tall girl)*

el ghorfa ek-kebeera الغرفة الكبيرة *(the big room)*

Notice the difference between the previous two phrases and the following sentences:

البنت طويلة. **el bint Taweela** *(The girl [is] tall.)*

الغرفة كبيرة. **el ghorfa kebeera** *(The room [is] big.)*

Because there is no verb "to be" in Arabic, the difference in meaning is determined only by where you put the article **el**.

Plurals

Arabic forms the plural in many different ways. The simplest is adding plural endings **-een** or **-aat** to the singular:

Singular	Plural
مدرس **modarris** *(teacher)*	مدرسين **modarriseen**
اجتماع **igtimaa9** *(meeting)*	اجتماعات **igtimaa9aat**

However, many words have plurals that are irregular and need to be learned individually:

Singular	Plural
ولد **walad** *(boy)*	أولاد **awlaad**
بنت **bint** *(girl)*	بنات **banaat**
غرفة **ghorfa** *(room)*	غرف **ghoraf**
كتاب **kitaab** *(book)*	كتب **kutub**

The dictionary section of this book gives the plural of common words after the singular.

Verbs

The person carrying out the action (*I, you, he, she, it,* etc.) is shown by the addition of different prefixes and suffixes around a stem.

Here is the verb **yektib** *(to write)*. The prefixes and suffixes are underscored:

Pronoun	Present	Past
ana *(I)*	**a**ktib أكتب	katab**t** كتبت
enta *(you,* masc.)	**te**ktib تكتب	katab**t** كتبت
enti *(you,* fem.)	**te**ktib**ee** تكتبي	katab**ti** كتبتي
howwa *(he)*	**ye**ktib يكتب	katab كتب
heyya *(she)*	**te**ktib تكتب	katab**it** كتبت
eHna *(we)*	**ne**ktib نكتب	katab**na** كتبنا
entu *(you,* pl.)	**te**ktib**u** تكتبوا	katab**tu** كتبتوا
humma *(they)*	**ye**ktib**u** يكتبوا	katab**u** كتبوا

Verbs are shown in the dictionary under the present tense "he" form, e.g. **yektib, yel9ab**. Use the table above to change the verb to refer to another person or people.

To show that something will take place in the future, **Ha-** is sometimes added before the present verb:

حنكتب **Ha-nektib** *(we will write)*

In addition, to show that something takes place routinely, **b-** is sometimes added before the present tense:

بنكتب **b-nektib** *(we write routinely)*

It is not usually necessary to use a pronoun (*I, you*, etc.) with the verb as the ending shows who is carrying out the action:

امبارح رحنا المتحف المصري.
embaariH ruHna l-matHaf el maSri
(Yesterday we went to the Egyptian Museum.)

كتبت إيمايل لماما.
katabt eemayl li-mama
(I wrote an email to my mom.)

بيلعبوا تنس كل يوم.
b-yel9abu tennis koll yohm
(They play tennis every day.)

REFERENCE

Numbers

one
واحد
waaHed

two
اثنين
itnein

three
ثلاثة
talaata

four
أربعة
arba9a

five
خمسة
khamsa

six
ستة
sitta

seven
سبعة
sab9a

eight
ثمانية
tamanya

nine
تسعة
tis9a

ten
عشرة
9ashra

eleven
حداشر
Hedashar

twelve
اثناشر
itnashar

thirteen
ثلاتاشر
talatashar

fourteen
أربعتاشر
arba9tashar

fifteen	twenty-three
خمستاشر	سبعة وعشرين
khamastashar	*talaata wi-9eshreen*

sixteen	thirty
ستتاشر	ثلاثين
sittashar	*talateen*

seventeen	forty
سبعتاشر	أربعين
sab9atashar	*arbe9een*

eighteen	fifty
ثمانتاشر	خمسين
tamantashar	*khamseen*

nineteen	sixty
تسعتاشر	ستين
tis9atashar	*sitteen*

twenty	seventy
عشرين	سبعين
9eshreen	*sab9een*

twenty-one	eighty
واحد وعشرين	ثمانين
waaHed wi-9eshreen	*tamaneen*

twenty-two	ninety
ستة وعشرين	تسعين
itnein wi-9eshreen	*tes9een*

one hundred

مية

miyya

one hundred and one

مية وواحد

miyya wi-waaHid

one hundred and forty

مية وأربعين

miyya w-arbe9een

three hundred

ثلاث مية

tolto meyya

one thousand

ألف

alf

ten thousand

عشرة آلاف

9ashar talaaf

ninety thousand

تسعين ألف

alf tes9een

one million

مليون

milyohn

Ordinal Numbers

first
أول
awwil

second
ثان
taani

third
ثالث
taalit

fourth
رابع
raabi9

fifth
خامس
khaamis

sixth
سادس
saadis

seventh
سابع
saabi9

eighth
ثامن
taamin

ninth
تاسع
taasi9

tenth
عاشر
9aashir

Days of the Week

Monday
الأثنين
el itnein

Friday
الجمعة
eg-gum9a

Tuesday
الثلاثاء
et-talaat

Saturday
السبت
es-sabt

Wednesday
الأربعاء
el arba9

Sunday
الأحد
el Had

Thursday
الخميس
el khamees

Seasons of the Year

Spring
الربيع
er-rabee9

Fall
الخريف
el khareef

Summer
الصيف
eS-Seif

Winter
الشتاء
esh-shitta

Months of the Year

January
يناير
yanaayir

July
يوليو
yoolyo

February
فبراير
febraayir

August
أغسطس
aghusTus

March
مارس
maaris

September
سبتمبر
sebtambir

April
أبريل
abreel

October
أكتوبر
oktohbir

May
مايو
maayo

November
نوفمبر
nofambir

June
يونيو
yoonyo

December
ديسمبر
deesambir

Times of the Day

What's the time?

الساعة كام؟

es-saa9a kaam?

twelve o'clock

الساعة اثناشر

es-saa9a itnashar

five past one

واحدة وخمسة

waHda wi-khamsa

ten past two

اثنين وعشرة

itnein w-9ashra

quarter past three

ثلاثة وربع

talata wi-rub9

twenty past four

أربعة وثلث

arba9a wi-tilt

twenty-five past six ("half past six minus five")

ستة ونصف إلا خمسة

sitta wi-noSS illa khamsa

half past seven

سبعة ونصف

saba9a wi-noSS

twenty to eight

ثمانية إلا ثلث

tamanya illa tilt

quarter to nine

تسعة إلا ربع

tis9a illa rub9

ten to ten

عشرة إلا عشرة

9ashra illa 9ashra

five to eleven

حداشر إلا خمسة

Hidashar illa khamsa

ENGLISH-ARABIC DICTIONARY

This English–Arabic dictionary is arranged in alphabetical order. The Egyptian Arabic pronunciation is designed to make it as easy as possible for you to say a particular word.

Notes for using the dictionary:

- The Arabic plural is shown after the singular, e.g.

    house *beit, beyoot.*

- English verbs are shown with (v). Arabic verbs are listed in the present tense, third person masculine ("he" form), e.g.

    visit (v) *yezoor.*

- The Arabic script is included to improve your reading skills, or to confirm the word with a native speaker.

- Where there are common alternative Arabic translations for an English word or phrase, these are shown on separate lines. (See entry for **age** on the opposite page).

- For Arabic numbers, months, days of the week, and times see the **Reference** section (page 18).

- Some common foods are included in the dictionary. For more food items and dishes see Chapter 5 (**Food Shopping**) and Chapter 6 (**Eating Out**) in the phrase book.

A

abbey	deir, adyera	دير
abdomen	baTn, boToon	بطن
ability	odra, odraat	قدرة
above	foh'	فوق
absent	ghaayib	غائب
accent (n, speech)	lahga, lahgaat	لهجة
accept (v)	ye'bal	يقبل
accident (road, etc.)	Hadsa, Hawaadis	حادثة
accommodation	iqaama	إقامة
according to	Hasab	حسب
account (n, bank)	Hisaab, Hisabaat	حساب
accountant	moHaasib, moHasbeen	محاسب
ache (n)	alam, aalaam	ألم
acidity	HumooDa	حموضة
across (sideways)	bil-9arD	بالعرض
active	nasheeT	نشيط
activity	nashaaT, anshiTa	نشاط
add to (v)	yezawwid	يزوّد
address (n, street, etc.)	9inwaan, 9anaween	عنوان
adjust (v)	ye9addil	يعدل
administration	idaara	إدارة
adolescent	muraahiq, murahqeen	مراهق
adult	raashid, rashdeen	راشد
advanced (adj)	met'addim, met'addimeen	متقدّم
adventure	mughamra, mughamaraat	مغامرة
adversity	shidda, shadaayed	شدّة (وقت)
advertising (n)	i9laan, i9lanaat	إعلان
advice (n)	naSeeHa, naSaayeH	نصيحة
Afghan (adj)	afghaani, afghaan	أفغاني
Afghanistan	afghaanistaan	أفغانستان
afraid	khaayef, khayfeen	خايف
after (prep)	ba9d	بعد
afternoon	ba9d eD-Duhr	بعد الظهر
again (adv)	taani	تاني
against	Didd	ضد
age (in years)	9omr, a9maar;	عمر
	sinn	سن
agency (n)	wikaala, wikalaat	وكالة
aggression	9idwaan	عدوان
agree (v)	yewaafi'	يوافق
agriculture (n)	ziraa9a	زراعة
aim (intention)	aSd	قصد

air (n)	*hawa*	هواء
air conditioning	*takeef (el hawa)*	تكييف (الهواء)
air raid	*ghaara*	غارة
airmail (n)	*bareed gawwi*	بريد جوي
airplane	*Tayyaara, Tayyaraat*	طائرة
airport	*maTaar, maTaraat*	مطار
airport terminal	*mabnal maTaar*	مبنى المطار
alcohol	*el kuHool*	الكحول
alcoholic drinks	*khamra, khomoor*	خمرة
algebra	*gabr*	جبر
Algeria	*eg-gazaayer*	الجزائر
Algerian	*gazaa'iri, gazaa'ireyyeen*	جزائري
alimony	*nafa'a*	نفقة
alive	*Hayy*	حي
all	*koll*	كل
all day long	*Tool en-nahaar*	طول النهار
all my life	*Tool 9omri*	طول عمري
allergic	*Hassaas*	حساس
alley	*zo'aa'*	زقاق
allow	*yesmaH*	يسمح
almonds	*lohza, lohz*	لوز
almost	*ta'reeban*	تقريبا
alone	*lewaHdo*	لوحده
(and) also	*wi-kamaan*	وكمان
altered (to improve)	*mo9addal*	معدّل
altitude	*irtifaa9, irtifa9aat*	ارتفاع
always	*dayman*	دائما
ambassador	*safeer, sufara*	سفير
amber	*kahramaan*	كهرمان
ambergris	*9anbar*	عنبر
ambulance	*el-is9aaf*	الإسعاف
ambush	*kameen, kamaayin*	كمين
America	*amreeka*	أمريكا
American	*amreekaani*	أمريكاني
amiable	*laTeef, loTaaf*	لطيف
amicable	*widdi*	ودّي
amid	*wisT*	وسط
amusing	*Zareef, Zoraaf;*	ظريف
analysis	*taHleel*	تحليل
ancient	*9atee'*	عتيق
angle (n)	*zawya, zawaya*	زاوية
angry	*ghaaDbaan*	غضبان
anklet (bangle)	*kholkhaal, khalakheel*	خلخال

animal	Hayawaan, Hayawanaat	حيوان
annoying	sakheef	سخيف
another	taani	تاني
answer (n)	radd, rodood	رد
ant	namla, naml	نمل
anthem	nasheed, anasheed	نشيد
antique	anteeka	أنتيكا
antiseptic	muTahhir	مطهر
anxiety	hamm;	همّ
	ala'	قلق
any	ayy	أي
anybody; anyone	(ayy) Hadd	(أي) حد
anything	ayy Haaga	أي حاجة
anywhere	ayy Hetta	أي حتة
apartment	sha''a, shu'a'	شقة
apartment block	9imaara, 9imaraat	عمارة
aperture	fatHa, fatHaat	فتحة
apologize	ye9tezir	يعتذر
apparent	zhaahir;	ظاهر
	baayin	باين
appetizers	fawaatiH esh-shaheyya	فواتح الشهية
apple	tufaaHa, tufaaH	تفاحة
appliance	gihaaz, aghiza	جهاز
appointment (date)	me9aad, mawa9eed	موعد
apricot	mishmishaya, mishmish	مشمش
apricot-colored	mishmishi	مشمشي
April	abreel	ابريل
Arab(ian)	9arabi	عربي
Arabian Jasmine	foll	فل
Arabic language	9arabi; el 9arabi	العربي
archbishop	moTraan, maTarna	مطران
architect	mohandis mi9maari	مهندس معماري
architecture	el 9imaara;	العمارة
	handasa	هندسة
arm (n, anatomy)	deraa9, dera9aat	ذراع
Armenians	armann	أرمن
army	geish, goyoosh	جيش
around	Hawalein	حوالين
arrange (v)	yerattib	يرتب
arrive (v)	yewSal	يوصل
arrival	wuSool	وصول
art	fann, fonoon	فن
artery	shoryaan, sharayeen	شريان

artichoke	*kharshoof*	خرشوف
artificial (man-made)	*Sinaa*	صناعي
artist	*fannaan, fannaneen*	فنان
ashtray	*Ta'Too'a, Ta'aTee'*	طقطوقة
ask (v)	*yes'al*	يسأل
asleep	*naayim*	نايم
assist (v)	*yesaa9id*	يساعد
assortment	*tashkeela*	تشكيلة
asthma	*rabu*	ربو
astronomical	*falaki*	فلكي
astute	*naaSiH;*	ناصح
	Hidi'	حاذق
at all: (none) at all	*(mafeesh) khaaliS*	(ما فيش) خالص
atheist	*kaafir, koffaar*	كافر
athletic	*riyaaDi*	رياضي
atom	*dharra, dharraat*	ذرة
attack	*hegoom*	هجوم
attorney	*moHaami, moHaamiyeen*	محام
attract (v)	*yeshidd*	يشد
attractive	*gazzaab*	جذّاب
auction (n)	*mazaad, mazadaat*	مزاد
audience	*gomhoor, gamaheer*	جمهور
aunt (maternal)	*khaala, khalaat*	خالة
aunt (paternal)	*9amma, 9ammaat*	عمة
authentic	*aSli*	أصلي
author (n)	*kaatib, kottaab;*	كاتب
	mo'allif, mo'allifeen	مؤلف
autumn	*el khareef*	الخريف
available	*motaaH*	متاح
average	*mutawassiT*	متوسط
award (n)	*gayza, gawaayiz*	جائزة
axe	*balTa, bolaT*	بلطة
azure (sky blue)	*azra' samaawi*	أزرق سماوي

B

bad	*weHish*	وحش
bad luck	*naHs*	نحس
bachelor	*9aazib, 9uzzaab*	عازب
back (adj, rear)	*warraani*	وراني
back (n)	*Dahr, Duhoor*	ظهر
backgammon	*Tawla*	طاولة
bag	*shanTa, shonaT*	شنطة
baggage (n)	*shonaT*	شنط

Baghdad	baghdaad	بغداد
Bahrain	el baHreyn	البحرين
Bahraini	baHreyni	بحريني
bail	kafaala	كفالة
baker	khabbaaz, khabbazeen	خباز
bakery	makhbaz, makhaabiz; furn, afraan	مخبز فرن
balance (n, scales)	mezaan, mawazeen	ميزان
balcony	balakohna, balakohnaat	بلكونة
bald	aSla9	أصلع
bald patch	Sal9a	صلعة
ball	kohra, kowar	كرة
balloon	ballohna, ballohnaat	بالونة
bamboo	kharazaan	خرزان
bamboo cane	booSa, booS	بوصة
bamboo flute (traditional)	naay	ناي
banana	mohza, mohz	موزة
band (e.g. musical)	fer'a, fera'	فرقة
bangle (ankle)	kholkhaal, khalakheel	خلخال
banister	darabzeen, darabzeenaat	درابزين
bank	bank, bunook	بنك
bank interest	fayda, fawaayid	فائدة
banquet	9ezooma, 9azaayem	عزومة
barber	Hallaa', Halla'een	حلاق
barber shop	Saloon Helaa'a	صالون حلاقة
bargain (n, adj)	lo'Ta, lo'aT	لقطة
barley	she9eer	شعير
barrel	barmeel, barameel	برميل
base (adj)	waaTi, waTyeen	واطئ
base (n, foundation)	asaas, asasaat	أساس
basic	asaasi	أساسي
basil	reeHaan	ريحان
basket	sabat, sebeta	سبت
bat (baseball, etc.)	maDrab, maDaarib	مضرب
bathroom (WC)	Hammaam, Hammamaat; dort el mayyah	حمام دورة المياه
battery	baTTareyya, baTTareyyaat	بطارية
bay	sharm	شرم
bay leaves	wara' el ghaar	ورق الغار
beach	belaaj, belajaat	بلاج
beans (French/green)	faSolya khaDra	فاصوليا خضراء
beard	da'n, do'oon	ذقن
beat (n, tempo, music)	eeqaa9	إيقاع

beat (v, hit)	*yeDrab*	يضرب
beautiful	*gameel*	جميل
because	*9alashaan;*	علشان
	la'an	لأن
become	*yeb'a*	يبقى
bed	*sereer, saraayir*	سرير
bedouin	*badawi*	بدوي
bedroom	*ghorfit nawm*	غرفة نوم
bee	*naHla, naHl*	نحلة
beech (wood)	*khashab ez-zaan*	خشب الزان
beef	*laHma kandooz*	لحم كندوز
beef steak	*bofteik*	بفتيك
beer	*beera*	بيرة
beer belly	*kersh, koroosh*	كرش
beetle	*khonfessa, khanaafis*	خنفسة
beetroot	*bangar*	بنجر
before	*abl*	قبل
beggar	*shaHHaat, shaHHateen*	شحات
begin	*yebtedi*	يبتدي
behind	*wara*	ورا
belief (faith)	*eeman*	إيمان
believe (v)	*yeSadda'*	يصدق
belonging to	*taba9*	تبع
below	*taHt*	تحت
belt	*Hizaam, Hizema*	حزام
benefit (n)	*fayda, fawaayid*	فائدة
berries	*toota, toot*	توت
beside	*ganb*	جنب
best	*aHsan*	أحسن
bet (n)	*rahaan, rahanaat*	رهان
Bethlehem	*beit laHm*	بيت لحم
better	*aHsan*	أحسن
between	*bein*	بين
bible	*ingeel*	انجيل
bicycle	*9agala, 9agal;*	عجلة
	beskeletta, beskelettaat	بسكليتة
big	*kebeer*	كبير
big spender	*fangari, fangareyya*	فنجري
bigger	*akbar*	أكبر
bilingual	*bi-lughatein*	بلغتين
bill of lading	*boleeSit shaHn*	بوليصة شحن
bird	*Teir, Teyoor*	طائر
birth (n)	*wilaada, wiladaat*	ولادة

birthday	*9eed meelaad*	عيد ميلاد
biscuit	*baskohta, baskoht*	بسكوت
bitter (taste)	*morr*	مَر
black (color)	*eswid*	أسود
blackboard	*sabboora*	سبورة
blacksmith	*Haddaad*	حدّاد
bladder	*mathaana*	مثانة
blank check	*sheek 9ala bayaaD*	شيك على بياض
blanket	*baTTaneyya, baTaTeen*	بطّانية
bleed (v)	*yenzif*	ينزف
blend (n)	*khalTa*	خلطة
blender	*khallaaT, khallaTaat*	خلاط
blessing	*baraka, barakaat*	بركة
blessing (from God)	*ni9ma, ni9am*	نعمة
blind (adj, without sight)	*a9maa, 9imyaan*	أعمى
blocked	*masdood*	مسدود
blonde (adj)	*ash'ar*	أشقر
blood (n)	*damm*	دم
blood group	*faSeelet ed-damm*	فصيلة الدم
blood test	*taHleel damm*	تحليل دم
blood transfusion	*na'l damm*	نقل دم
blouse	*bilooza, biloozaat*	بلوزة
blue	*azra'*	أزرق
boat	*markib, maraakib*	مركب
body	*gism, agsaam*	جسم
boil (v)	*yeghli*	يغلي
boiling	*ghalayaan*	غليان
bolt (n, for door)	*terbaas, tarabees*	ترباس
bomb (n)	*qonbela, qanaabil*	قنبلة
bone	*9aDma, 9aDm*	عظمة
book (n)	*kitaab, kutub*	كتاب
book (v)	*yeHgiz*	يحجز
booklet	*kutayyib, kutayyibaat*	كتيب
bookshop	*maktaba, maktabaat*	مكتبة
border guards	*Haras el Hodood*	حرس الحدود
borders	*Hodood*	حدود
bore (of)	*yemill*	يملّ
boring (adj, tedious)	*mumill*	ممل
borrowing	*salaf*	سلف
bottle (n)	*ezaaza, azaayez*	إزازة
box (n)	*Sandoo', Sanadee';*	صندوق
	9ilba, 9ilab	علبة
boy	*walad, awlaad*	ولد

boy scouts	ek-kash-shaafa	الكشّافة
bracelet	gheweisha, ghawaayish	غويشة
brain	mukh, emkhaakh	مخ
brakes (n, vehicle)	farmala, faraamil	فرامل
branch	far9, faroo9	فرع
brand (n)	marka, markaat	ماركة
brass	naHaas aSfar	نحاس أصفر
brass coffee pot (traditional)	kanaka, kanak	كنكة
brassiere	sotyaan, sotyanaat	سوتيان
brave (person)	garee'; shagee9	جريء؛ شجيع
bread	9eish	عيش
break (n, interval)	istiraaHa	استراحة
break (v, smash)	yekassar	يكسر
breakdown (n, malfunction)	9oTl	عطل
breakfast	feTaar	فطار
breakfast cereal	Huboob el fiTaar	حبوب الفطار
breast	Sidr, Sudoor	صدر
breath (n)	nafas, anfaas	نفس
breed (n)	sulaala, sulalaat	سلالة
breed (v)	yerabbi	يربي
breeze	nesma, neseem	نسيم
brick	Tooba, Toob	طوبة
bridal dowry	mahr	مهر
bride	9aroosa, 9araayes	عروسة
bridegroom	9arees, 9irsaan	عريس
bridge (n)	kobri, kabaari	كوبري
bring (v)	yegeeb	يجيب
bring (me)!	haat!	هات!
bring up (children)	yerabbi	يربي
Britain	biriTaanya	بريطانيا
British (adj)	biriTaani, biriTaaneyyeen	بريطاني
broken down (not working)	baayeZ	بايظ
broker	simsaar, samasra	سمسار
brother	akh, ekhwaat	أخ
brother-in-law	9adeel	عديل
Brotherhood (the Muslim)	el ekhwaan	الإخوان
brown	bonni	بنّي
bucket	gardal, garaadel	جردل
budget (adj, cheaper)	iqtiSaadi	اقتصادي
budget (n, fiscal)	mezaneyya, mezaneyyaat	ميزانية

building	mabna, mabaani	مبنى
bulb (light)	lamba, lomuD	لمبة
bull	tor, teraan	ثور
bullet	roSaaSa, roSaaS	رصاصة
bureau de change	Siraafa	صرّافة
bureaucracy	beeroqraTeyya	بيروقراطية
burglar	Haraami, Harameyya	حرامي
burn (v)	yeHra'	يحرق
burst (v)	yenfegir	ينفجر
bus (n)	otobees, otobeesaat	أوتوبيس
bus stop	maw'af el otobees	موقف الأوتوبيس
busy (adj)	mash-ghool	مشغول
but	bass;	بس
	laakin	لكن
butcher (n)	gazzaar, gazzaareen	جزار
butter	zebda	زبدة
butterfly	faraasha, faraash	فراشة
button (n)	zoraar, zaraayer	(زر) زرار
buy (v)	yeshteri	يشتري
by (car, force, etc.)	bi...	ب...

C

cab (n)	taksi, takaasi	تاكسي
cabbage	koromb	كرنب
cabin (n)	kabeena, kabaayen	كابينة
cable (n)	silk, aslaak	سلك
cactus	Sabbaar	صبّار
Caesarean (delivery)	qaySareyya	قيصرية (ولادة)
cage	afaS, e'faaS	قفص
Cairo	el qaahira	القاهرة
calamity	balwa, balaawi;	بلوة
	dahya, dawaahi	داهية
calculate (v)	yeHsib	يحسب
calendar (e.g. wall)	nateega, nataayeg	نتيجة
calf	9igl, 9ogool	عجل
caliph	khaleefa, kholafaa'	خليفة
call (n, phone)	mukalma, mukalmaat	مكالمة
call (v, summon)	yenaadi	ينادي
call to prayer	adaan	أذان
calligrapher	khaTTaaT, khaTTaTeen	خطّاط
calligraphy	fann el khaTT	فن الخط
camel	gamal, gimaal	جمل
campaign	Hamla, Hamlaat	حملة

camping (n)	*takhyeem*	تخييم
canal (fresh water)	*ter9a, tera9*	ترعة
canal (n, channel)	*qanaah, qanawaat*	قناة
cancellation	*ilghaa'*	إلغاء
candle	*sham9a, sham9*	شمعة
candy	*bonboni*	بنبوني
cannabis	*Hasheesh*	حشيش
canvas	*khaish*	خيش
capital (city)	*9aaSima, 9awaaSim*	عاصمة
captain (of a ship)	*obTaan, abaTna*	قبطان
car	*9arabeyya, 9arabeyyaat*	عربية
carafe	*dohra', dawaari'*	دورق
card	*kart, koroot*	كارت
cardamom	*Habbahaan*	حبّ الهال
care (n)	*9inaaya*	عناية
carpenter	*naggaar, naggareen*	نجار
carpet (n)	*siggaada, sagageed*	سجادة
carrot	*gazara, gazar*	جزر
carry (v)	*yesheel*	يشيل
cartilage	*ghaDroof, ghaDareef*	غضروف
Casablanca	*ed-daar el beyDa*	الدار البيضاء
case (n, state)	*Haala, Haalaat*	حالة
case (n, court)	*aDeyya, aDaaya*	قضية
cash payment	*na'dee*	نقدي
cashier	*Sarraaf, Sarrafeen*	صرّاف
castle	*al9a*	قلعة
cat	*oTTa, oTaT*	قطة
catacomb	*sirdaab, saradeeb*	سرداب
catch (v, e.g. fish)	*yeSTaad*	يصطاد
catch (v, e.g. ball)	*yemsik*	يمسك
cauliflower	*arnabeeT*	قرنبيط
caution (n, warning)	*taHzeer, taHzeeraat*	تحذير
caution (n, prudence)	*iHtiraas*	احتراس
cave (n)	*kahf, kuhoof*	كهف
cavity	*tagweef, tagweefaat*	تجويف
ceiling	*saqf, es'of*	سقف
celebration	*iHtifaal, iHtifalaat*	احتفال
celery	*karafs*	كرفس
cell (tissue)	*khaleyya, khalaaya*	خلّية
cell (prison)	*zinzaana, zanazeen*	زنزانة
cell phone	*mobaayel, mobaylaat*	موبايل
cement	*asmant*	أسمنت
central (adj, main)	*markazi*	مركزي

certainly (definitely)	akeed	أكيد
certainly (I'll do it)	HaaDir	حاضر
certificate	shahaada, shahadaat	شهادة
chair	korsi, karaasi	كرسي
chameleon	Herbaaya, Herbayaat	حرباء
chance	Sudfa, Sudaf	صدفة
chandelier	nagafa, nagaf	نجفة
change (n, alteration)	taghyeer, taghyeeraat	تغيير
change (n, coins)	fakka	فكّة
change (v, clothes, etc.)	yeghayyar	يغيّر
chaos	darbaka	دربكة
character	shakhSeyya, shakhSeyyaat	شخصية
charcoal	faHm	فحم
charge (n, fee)	ogra	أجرة
charge (n, accusation)	tuhma, tuhamm	تهمة
charge (v, battery, etc.)	yesh-Hin	يشحن
charge card	kart el bank	كارت البنك
charitable donation	Sada'a, Sada'aat	صدقة
charity (good deed)	Hasana, Hasanaat	حسنة
charity organization	munaDH-DHama khaireyya	منظمة خيرية
charter flights	Tayaraan 9aariD	طيران عارض
chatter (v)	yedardish	يدردش
chatterbox	ghalabaawi, ghalabaawiyeen	غلباوي
cheap	rekheeS	رخيص
cheat (v)	yeghish	يغش
cheating	ghish	غش
check (n, bank)	sheek, sheekaat	شيك
check (n, invoice)	fatoora, fawateer	فاتورة
check, the (restaurant, etc.)	el Hisaab	الحساب
check-up (at doctor)	kashf, koshoofaat	كشف
checked (adj, pattern)	murabba9aat	مربعات
cheese	gibna, giban	جبنة
chemistry	kemya	كيمياء
cheque (bank)	sheek, sheekaat	شيك
cherries	kereiza, kereiz	كرز
chess	shaTarang	شطرنج
chewing gum	lebana, lebaan	لبان
chicken (meat)	feraakh	فراخ
chicken (hen)	farkha, feraakh	فرخة
chickpeas	HummuS	حمص
child	9ayyil, 9yaal	عيل

chin	da'n, do'oon	ذقن
China	eS-Seen	الصين
chit-chat (n)	dardasha	دردشة
choice	ikhtiyaar, ikhtiyaraat	اختيار
choicest	na'aawa	نقاوة
choose (v)	yekhtaar	يختار
chop (lamb, veal, etc.)	kostaleita	كستليتة
Christian	meseeHi, meseeHiyeen	مسيحي
Christianity	el maseeHeyya	المسيحية
chronic	muzmin	مزمن
church	keneesa, kanaayis	كنيسة
cigarette	segaara, sagaayer	سيجارة
cilantro	kozbara	كزبرة
circle (n)	dayra, dawaayer	دائرة
circumcision	Tohoor	طهور
circumstance	Zarf, Zoroof	ظرف
citadel	al9a	قلعة
civilian (not military)	madani	مدني
civilization	HaDaara, HaDaaraat	حضارة
class (n, society)	Taba'a, Taba'aat	طبقة
classroom	faSl, fuSool	فصل
clean (adj)	neDeef	نظيف
clear (adj, unambiguous)	waaDiH	واضح
clear (adj, unclouded)	Saafi	صاف
clerk	kaatib, kottaab	كاتب
clever	shaaTir;	شاطر
	zaki	ذكي
cleverness	shaTaara	شطارة
client	zuboon, zabaayen	زبون
climb (v)	yeTla9	يطلع
climbing	Teloo9	طلوع
clinic (doctor's)	9iyaada, 9iyaadaat	عيادة
cloak	9abaaya, 9abayaat	عباءة
clock	saa9a, sa9aat	ساعة
closed	ma'fool	مقفول
closet (cupboard)	dulaab, dawaleeb	دولاب
clothes	hedoom	هدوم
cloud	saHaaba, saHaab	سحابة
clove	oronfil	قرنفل
clown	moharrig, moharrigeen	مهرج
club (sporting, etc.)	naadi, nawaadi	نادي
co-operative organization	gam9eyya, gam9eyyaat	جمعية

coach (n, bus)	otobees, otobeesaat	أوتوبيس
coach (n, trainer)	modarrib, modarribeen	مدرّب
coal	faHm	فحم
coast (n, shore)	saaHil, sawaaHil	ساحل
coat (clothing)	balTo, balaaTi	بالطو
cock (rooster)	deek, deyook	ديك
cockroach	Sorsaar, SaraSeer	صرصار
coconut	gohz el hind	جوز الهند
coffee (beans)	bunn	بنّ
coffee (beverage)	ahwa	قهوة
coffee boy (in office)	farraash, farraasheen	فرّاش
coincidence	Sudfa, Sudaf	صدفة
cold (adj)	baarid	بارد
cold (weather)	bard	برد
cold refreshments	Haaga sa'-9a	حاجة ساقعة
colleague	zemeel, zomala	زميل
collection (n)	magmoo9a, magmoo9aat	مجموعة
college	kolleyya, kulleyyaat	كلية
colloquial language	el 9aameyya	العامية
colon	qawloon	قولون
color (n)	lohn, alwaan	لون
comb	mishT, emshaaT	مشط
come (v)	yeegi	ييجي
comfortable	mureeH	مريح
comma	faSla, faSlaat	فاصلة
commercial district	Hayy tigaari	حي تجاري
commission (percentage fee)	9omoola, 9omoolaat	عمولة
commitment (to someone)	irtibaaT, irtibaTaat	ارتباط
committee	lagna, legaan	لجنة
common (adj, normal)	9aadi	عادي
companion	refee', refaa'	رفيق
company (n, business)	sherka, sherikaat	شركة
compensation	ta9weeD	تعويض
complain (v)	yeshteki	يشتكي
complaint	shakwa, shakaawi	شكوى
complete (v)	yekammil	يكمل
complex (n)	9o'da, 9o'ad	عقدة
compliment (v)	yemdaH	يمدح
complimentary (free)	bebalaash; maggaani	ببلاش؛ مجاني
compromise (n)	Hall wasaT	حل وسط

conceited	*maghroor*	مغرور
concern	*ala'*	قلق
concert (n)	*Hafla museeqeyya*	حفلة موسيقية
concussion	*irtigaag*	ارتجاج
condition (n, state)	*Haala, Haalaat*	حالة
condition (n, stipulation)	*sharT, shurooT*	شرط
condom	*9aazil Tibbi*	عازل طبي
confidential	*sirri*	سري
confirm (v)	*ye'akkid*	يؤكد
congestion (nose)	*zokaam*	زكام
congestion (people, traffic, etc.)	*zaHma*	زحمة
connect (v)	*yewaSSal*	يوصل
conscience	*Dameer, Damaayer*	ضمير
conscript	*dof9a*	دفعة
consent (n)	*taraaDi*	تراض
constant	*dayem;*	دائم؛
	saabit	ثابت
constipation	*imsaak*	إمساك
construct (v)	*yebni*	يبني
consulate	*onSuleyya, onSuleyyaat*	قنصلية
consultant	*istishaari, istishaariyeen*	استشاري
contact (v, phone, etc.)	*yetteSil*	يتصل
contagion	*9adwa*	عدوى
contagious	*mo9di*	معد
contemporary	*9aSri*	عصري
contract	*9a'd, 9o'ood*	عقد
contradictory	*mutanaaqiD*	متناقض
convenient	*munaasib*	مناسب
cook (n, chef)	*Tabbaakh, Tabbaakheen*	طباخ
cook (v)	*yeTbukh*	يطبخ
cooked food	*Tabeekh*	طبيخ
cooking pot	*Halla, Hilal*	حلة
copper	*naHaas aHmar*	نحاس أحمر
Copt (n)	*ebTi, a'baaT*	قبطي
copy (n)	*noskha, nosakh*	نسخة
coral	*sho9aab morganeyya*	شعاب مرجانية
coriander	*kozbara*	كزبرة
cork	*fill*	فل
corner (n)	*rukn, erkaan*	ركن
corridor	*Tor'a, Tor'aat*	طرقة
corrupt	*faasid*	فاسد
corruption	*fasaad*	فساد
cost (n)	*taman, atmaan*	ثمن

cotton (n)	*quTn*	قطن
cotton wool	*fatla, fitall*	فتلة
couch (sofa)	*kanaba, kanab*	كنبة
cough	*koHHa*	كحة
count (v, add)	*ye9idd*	يعدّ
country (n, state)	*dawla*	دولة
countryside	*reef*	ريف
couple (n)	*gohz, egwaaz*	جوز
courgette	*kohsaaya, kohsa*	كوسة
cover (n, lid)	*ghaTa, ghoTyaan*	غطاء
cover (of book, etc.)	*gholaaf, aghlefa*	غلاف
cover (v)	*yeghaTTi*	يغطّي
cow	*ba'ara, ba'ar*	بقرة
coward	*gabaan, gobana*	جبان
crab	*kaboria*	كابوريا
craft	*Hirfa, Hiraf*	حرفة
craftsman	*Sanai9i, Sanai9eyya*	صنايعي
crash (n, car, etc.)	*taSaadum*	تصادم
crazy	*magnoon, magaaneen*	مجنون
cream (n, dairy)	*eshTa*	قشطة
cream (n, cosmetic)	*kereim, keremaat*	كريم
crease (in clothes)	*karmasha, karameesh*	كرمشة
creativity	*el ibtikaar*	الابتكار
crescent	*hilaal*	هلال
crime	*gareema, garaayem*	جريمة
criminal (n)	*mugrim, mugrimeen*	مجرم
criminal offence	*genaaya, genayaat*	جناية
crisis	*azma, azamaat*	أزمة
crocodile	*timsaaH, tamaseeH*	تمساح
crook	*naSSaab, naSSaabeen*	نصاب
cross (n, crucifix)	*Saleeb, Solbaan*	صليب
cross (v, e.g. road)	*ye9addi*	يعدّي
crow	*ghoraab, gherbaan*	غراب
cruise (n)	*gawla baHareyya*	جولة بحرية
crumbs	*fatafeet*	فتافيت
cry (v, weep)	*ye9ayyaT*	يعيط
cry (v, yell)	*yesarrakh*	يصرخ
cucumber	*khiyaara, khiyaar*	خيار
cul-de-sac	*shaari9 sadd*	شارع سدّ
culture	*thaqaafa*	ثقافة
cultured (erudite)	*muthaqqaf, muthaqqafeen*	مثقف
cumin	*kammoon*	كمون

cunning	la'eem, lo'ama	لئيم
cup (for drinks)	fingaan, fanageen	فنجان
cup (trophy)	kaas, kasaat	كأس
cupboard (closet)	dulaab, dawaleeb	دولاب
cure (n)	9ilaag	علاج
currency (money)	9omla, 9omlaat	عملة
currency exchange	Siraafa	صرافة
current (electric)	tayyaar ek-kahraba	تيار الكهرباء
current (water)	tayyaar el mayya	تيار المياه
current account	Hisaab gaari	حساب جار
curse (n, evil spell)	la9na, la9naat	لعنة
curse (v, abuse)	yeshtim	يشتم
curtain	setara, sataayer	ستارة
curve	dawaraan	دوران
customer service	khidmit el 9umalaa	خدمة العملاء
customs (n, import duties)	gomrok, gamaarik	جمارك
customs (n, traditions)	taqaaleed	تقاليد
cut (v, tear)	ye'aTTa'	يقطع
cutlet	kostaleita	كستليتة
cycling	rukoob el 9agal	ركوب العجل
cylinder	osTowaana, osTowanaat	اسطوانة

D

dagger	khangar, khanaagir	خنجر
dairy products	muntagaat el albaan	منتجات الألبان
dam	sadd, sudood	سد
damage (n)	talaf, talafeyyaat	تلف
Damascus	dimesh'	دمشق
dance (v)	yor'oS	يرقص
dancer (f)	ra'-'aaSa, ra'-'aaSaat	راقصة
dancing	ra'S	رقص
dandruff	eshra	قشرة
dangerous (adj)	khaTeer	خطير
dark (unlit)	dalma	ظلمة
darkness	dalma	ظلمة
date (calendar)	tareekh, tawareekh	تاريخ
date (fruit)	balaHa, balaH	بلحة
daughter	bint, banaat	بنت
dawn (n)	fagr	فجر
deaf	aTrash	أطرش
death	wafaah, wafeyyaat	وفاة
debauchery	fogr	فجر

debt	*dein, deyoon*	دين
decide (v)	*yeqarrar*	يقرر
decision (official)	*qaraar, qararaat*	قرار
decorations	*zeena*	زينة
deduct (v)	*yekhSim*	يخصم
deep (adj)	*ghaweeT*	غويط
deer	*ghazaala, ghizlaan*	غزالة
defense	*defaa9*	دفاع
degree (extent)	*daraga, daragaat*	درجة
delegation (n)	*wafd, wofood*	وفد
delicate	*ra'ee'*	رقيق
deliver (v)	*yewaSSal*	يوصل
den	*wakr, awkaar*	وكر
dentist	*doctohr sinaan*	دكتور أسنان
dentures	*Ta'm senaan*	طقم أسنان
department	*ism, e'saam*	قسم
departure	*raHeel*	رحيل
deport (v)	*yeraHHal*	يرحل
dervish	*darweesh, daraweesh*	درويش
describe (v)	*yewSif*	يوصف
desert (n)	*SaHra*	صحراء
desk	*maktub, makaatib*	مكتب
design (v)	*yeSammim*	يصمم
despicable	*Haqeer*	حقير
dessert	*el Hilw*	الحلو
detailed statement	*bayaan mufaSSal*	بيان مفصل
details	*tafaaSeel*	تفاصيل
detergent	*munaDH-DHif,*	منظف
	munaDH-DHifaat	
devil	*eblees, abalsa;*	ابليس
	sheTaan, shayaTeen	شيطان
dew	*nada*	ندى
diabetes	*maraD es-sukkar*	مرض السكّر
diagnosis	*tash-kheeS*	تشخيص
dial (v)	*yeTlub bit-tilifoon*	يطلب بالتليفون
dialect	*lahga, lahgaat*	لهجة
dialing tone	*Haraara*	حرارة (تليفون)
dialogue	*Hewaar*	حوار
diamonds	*almaaz, almaazaat*	الماس
diaper	*HaffaaDa, HaffaDaat*	حفاضة
diarrhea	*is-haal*	إسهال
dictionary	*qaamoos, qawaamees*	قاموس
diet	*rejeem*	ريجيم
difference	*far', furoo'aat*	فرق

difficult	*Sa9b*	صعب
digit (number)	*9adad, a9daad*	عدد
dill	*shabat*	شبت
dining room	*oDit sofra, owaD sofra*	أوضة سفرة
dining table	*tarabeizit sofra, tarabeizaat sofra*	ترابيزة سفرة
dinner	*9asha*	عشاء
diplomacy	*deblomaaseyya*	دبلوماسية
diplomat	*deblomaasi, deblomaasiyeen*	دبلوماسي
diplomatic	*deblomaasi*	دبلوماسي
direct (adj, non-stop)	*mobaashir*	مباشر
direct (v, movies, etc.)	*yekhrig*	يخرج
direct (v, give directions)	*yedill*	يدل
director (movie)	*mokhrig, mokhrigeen*	مخرج
director (n, senior executive)	*modeer, modeereen*	مدير
dirt	*wasaakha, wasakhaat*	وساخة
dirty (adj)	*wisikh*	وسخ
disability	*9agz*	عجز
disabled (adj)	*9aagiz, 9agaza*	عاجز
disabled (n)	*mo9aaq, mo9aqeen*	معاق
disappointment	*kheibit amal*	خيبة أمل
discount (n)	*khaSm, khuSumaat*	خصم
disease	*maraD, amraaD*	مرض
dish (n)	*Taba', eTbaa'*	طبق
dishwasher	*ghassaalit eTbaa'*	غسالة أطباق
disinfect (v)	*yeTahhar*	يطهر
disinfectant	*muTahhir*	مطهر
dissolve	*yedoob*	يذوب
distance (n)	*masaafa, masafaat*	مسافة
divide (v)	*ye'assim*	يقتسم
divider	*faaSil*	فاصل
divorce (n)	*Talaa'*	طلاق
divorce (v)	*yeTalla'*	يطلق
dizziness	*dohkha*	دوخة
doctor	*doktohr, dakatra*	دكتور
dog	*kalb, kilaab*	كلب
doll	*9aroosa, 9araayes*	عروسة
dolphin	*darfeel, darafeel*	درفيل
dome	*obba, obab*	قبة
don't know	*mish 9aarif*	مش عارف
don't understand	*mish faahim*	مش فاهم
donkey	*Homaar, Himeer*	حمار

door	baab, bebaan	باب
doorbell	garas el baab	جرس الباب
doorstep	9ataba, 9atabaat	عتبة
dosage	gur9a, gur9aat	جرعة
doubt (n)	shakk, shokook	شك
dough	9ageena	عجين
down (n, feathers)	zaghab	زغب
down river (with the current)	ma9 at-tayyar	مع التيار
downwards	letaHt	لتحت
dozen	dasta, desat	دستة
drag (v)	yegorr	يجز
drain	ballaa9a, balla9aat	بلاعة
draw (v, illustrate)	yersim	يرسم
drawer	dorg, edraag	درج
drawing (n)	rasm, rosumaat	رسم
dream (n)	Hilm, aHlaam	حلم
dream (v)	yeHlam	يحلم
dress (n, women's)	fustaan, fasateen	فستان
drink (n)	mashroob, mashroobaat	مشروب
drink (v)	yeshrab	يشرب
drip (n)	tan'eeT	تنقيط
drive (v, car, etc.)	yesoo'	يسوق
driver	sawwaa', sawwa'een	سائق
drown (v)	yeghra'	يغرق
drowning	ghara'	غرق
drug (medication)	dawa, adweya	دوا
drugs (narcotics)	mukhaddaraat	مخدرات
drum	Tabla, Tobal	طبلة
drum (traditional)	darabokka	دربكة
drunk (adj)	sakraan, sakraneen	سكران
dry (adj)	naashif	ناشف
duck (n, bird)	baTTa, baTT	بطة
duplicate (n)	noskha, nosakh	نسخة
during (prep)	khilaal	خلال
dust (n)	turaab	تراب
duty (n, obligation)	waagib, wagibaat	واجب
dye (n)	Sabgha, Sabghaat	صبغة
dye (v)	yeSbogh	يصبغ

E

| each | koll | كل |
| eagle | nisr, nisoor | نسر |

ear	wedn, wedaan	ودن
early	badri	بدري
Earth (planet)	ek-kohra l-arDeyya	الكرة الأرضية
earthquake	zilzaal, zalaazil	زلزال
east (n)	shar'	شرق
eastern	shar'i	شرقي
easy	sahl	سهل
eat (v)	yaakul	يأكل
economic	iqtiSaadi	اقتصادي
edge (outer tip)	Tarf, aTraaf	طرف
education	ta9leem	تعليم
effective	fa9-9aal	فعال
effort	guhd, guhood	جهد
egg	beiDa, beiD	بيضة
eggplant	betingaan	بتنجان
Egypt	maSr	مصر
Egyptian	maSri, maSriyeen	مصري
Egyptology	9ilm el maSreyyaat	علم المصريات
eject	yeTrud	يطرد
elbow	koo9, ke9aan	كوع
elder (e.g. brother)	akbar	أكبر
elderly	9agooz, 9awageez	عجوز
electricity	kahraba	كهرباء
elegant	sheek	شيك
elephant	feel, feyela	فيل
elevator	asanseyr, asanseyraat	أسانسير
embalming (n)	taHneeT	تحنيط
embarrassment	Harag	حرج
embassy	sifaara, sifaraat	سفارة
embellished (adj)	man'oosh	منقوش
embossed	baariz	بارز
embroidered	meTarraz	مطرز
emerald (n)	zumurrud	زمرد
emergency (n)	Tawaari'	طوارئ
emigration	higra	هجرة
emir	ameer, umara	أمير
Emirates, the UAE	el imaaraat	الإمارات
employee	muwaDH-DHaf, muwaDH-DHafeen	موظف
empty	faaDi	فاضي
end (n)	aakher	آخر
energetic	nasheeT	نشيط
engagement (to be married)	khuTooba	خطوبة

engagement (appointment, etc.)	irtibaaT, irtibaTaat	ارتباط
engine	motohr, mawateer	موتور
engine overhaul	9amrit motor	عمرة موتور
engineer	mohandis, mohandiseen	مهندس
engineering	handasa	هندسة
England	ingeltera	انجلترا
English (person)	ingeleezi, ingeleez	انجليزي
English language	ingeleezi	انجليزي
enjoy (v)	yeHibb; yetmatta9	يحب يتمتّع
enmity	9adawa, 9adawaat	عداوة
enough	kefaaya	كفاية
Enough!	bass!	بس!
enter (v)	yodkhol	يدخل
entertainment	tasliya, tasaali	تسلية
entire	gamee9	جميع
entrance	madkhal, madaakhil	مدخل
entry fee	rasm ed-dokhool	رسم الدخول
envelope (n)	zarf, ezrof	ظرف
environment	bee'a, bee'aat	بيئة
envy	Hasad	حسد
epilepsy	Sara9	صرع
equal (adj)	musawi	مساو
equestrian (adj)	betaa9 el kheil	بتاع الخيل
era	9aSr	عصر
erase (v)	yemsaH	يمسح
error	ghalTa, ghalaTaat	غلطة
escape (v)	yehrab	يهرب
essential (adj)	asaasi	أساسي
essential (item)	Daroori, Darooriyaat	ضروري
estimate (n)	ta'deer	تقدير
estimate (v)	ye'addar	يقدّر
Euphrates	el furaat	الفرات
Europe	orobbaa	أوروبا
European	orobbi, orobbiyyeen	أوروبي
even (adj, level)	metsaawi	متساو
even (even you?!)	Hatta	حتّى
even though, even if	walaw	ولو
evening	mesa	مساء
evening event	sahra, sahraat	سهرة
every	koll	كل
exact	mazbooT	مضبوط

exactly	biz-zabT	بالضبط
examination (n, medical)	faHS, fuHooSaat	فحص
examination (n, school, etc.)	imtiHaan, imtiHaanaat	امتحان
examination score	magmoo9	مجموع
example	mithaal, amthila	مثال
excavation	tanqeeb	تنقيب
excellence	imtiyaaz	امتياز
except	illa; ma9aada	إلا؛ ما عدا
exchange (n)	mobadla; badal	مبادلة؛ بدل
exchange (v)	yebaadil	يبادل
excitement	hayagaan	هيجان
excursion	gawla, gawlaat	جولة
excuse (n, pretext)	9ozr, a9zaar; Higga, Higag	عذر؛ حجة
excuse me	lau samaHt	لو سمحت
exempt	ma9fi	معفي
exercise (n)	tamreen, tamreenaat	تمرين
exhaust (n, fumes)	9aadim	عادم
exhausted (tired)	halkaan	هلكان
exhibition	ma9raD, ma9aariD	معرض
exit (n)	makhrag, makhaarig	مخرج
exit (v)	yekhrog	يخرج
expenses	maSareef	مصاريف
expensive	ghaali	غال
experience (n)	khibra, khibraat	خبرة
expert	khabeer, khobara	خبير
expedite (v)	yesta9gil	يستعجل
explain (v)	yeshraH	يشرح
explanation	sharH	شرح
explode (v)	yenfegir	ينفجر
explore (v)	yestakshif	يستكشف
explosion	enfigaar, enfigaraat; far'a9ah, far'a9aat	انفجار؛ فرقعة
expression (phrase)	ta9beer, ta9beeraat	تعبير
extent	daraga, daragaat	درجة
exterior	barraani	براني
extinguish (v)	yeTfi	يطفئ
extra	zeyada	زيادة
extraction (n, tooth, etc.)	khal9	خلع
eye (n, anatomical)	9ein, 9uyoon	عين

eyebrow	Haagib, Hawaagib	حاجب
eyelash	rimsh, rumoosh	رمش
eyesight	naZar	نظر (ال)

F

face (n, anatomy)	wish, weshoosh	وش
fact	Ha'ee'a, Haqaa'iq	حقيقة
factory	maSna9, maSaani9	مصنع
failure	kheiba;	خيبة
	fashal	فشل
faint (v, pass out)	yughma 9aleih	يغمى عليه
fair (just)	9aadil	عادل
faith	eeman	إيمان
fake	falSo;	فالصو
	muzayyaf	مزيّف
falafel	Ta9meyya	طعمية
falcon	Sa'r, Su'oor	صقر
fall (n, season)	el khareef	الخريف
fall (v, tumble)	yo'a9	يقع
family	usra, usarr	أسرة
famous	mash-hoor	مشهور
fan (n, cooling)	marwaHa, maraawiH	مروحة
far	be9eed	بعيد
fare	ogra	أجرة
farewell!	il wadaa9!	الوداع
farm (n)	9ezba, 9ezab	عزبة
fashion	moDa	موضة
fashion show	9arD azyaa'	عرض أزياء
fast (adj)	saree9	سريع
fast (v)	yeSoom	يصوم
fasting (n)	Siyaam	صيام
fat (n)	dihn, dohoon	دهن
fatal	mumeet	مميت
father	ab	أب
father of	abu	أبو
father-in-law	Hama	حم
faucet	Hanafeyya, Hanafeyyaat	حنفية
fault (n)	khalal	خلل
fava beans	fool	فول
fear (n)	khohf	خوف
fear (v)	yekhaaf	يخاف
feast (n)	9eed, a9yaad	عيد
fee (charge)	rasm, rosoom	رسم

feed (v)	ye'akkil	ياكل
feel (v)	yeHess	يحس
female	untha, inaath	أنثى
fence (enclosure)	soor, aswaar	سور
ferry (n)	me9addeyya, me9addeyyaat	معدّية
festival	mahragaan, mahraganaat	مهرجان
fever	Humma, Hummyyaat	حمى
few (adj)	olayyil	قليل
fez	Tarboosh	طربوش
fiancé (male)	khaTeeb	خطيب
fiancée (female)	khaTeeba	خطية
fig	teena, teen	تينة
fight (v, in war, etc.)	yeHaarib	يحارب
fill, fill out (v)	yemla	يملأ
filth	wasaakha, wasakhaat	وساخة
final	nihaa'i	نهائي
find (v)	yelaa'i	يلاقي
fine (n)	gharaama, gharaamaat	غرامة
finger	Sobaa9, Sawaabi9	صباع
finish (v)	yekhallaS	يخلّص
finished (adj)	khalaaS	خلاص
fire (n, flame)	naar	نار
fire (n, uncontrolled)	Haree'a, Harayi'	حريق
fire (v, terminate employment)	yerfid	يرفد
firm (fixed)	saabit	ثابت
first	awwil	أوّل
fish (n)	samaka, samak	سمك
fish (v)	yeSTaaD samak	يصطاد سمك
fish bones	shohk samak	شوك سمك
fishing	Seid es-samak	صيد السمك
fishing rod	sinnaara, sananeer	سنّارة
fitting (convenient)	munaasib	مناسب
fitting (trying on)	eyaas	قياس
fix (v)	yeSallaH	يصلّح
;maal9a ,mala9	**galf**	علم
	raaya, rayaat	راية
flat (adj, even)	mefalTTaH	مفلطح
flavor	Ta9m	طعم
flea	barghoot, baragheet	برغوث
flight (n, air journey)	reHlit Tayaraan	رحلة طيران
flight attendant (m./f.)	moDeef/moDeefa	مضيف / مضيفة
float (v)	ye9oom	يعوم

flood	seil, seyool	سيل
flood (river)	fayaDaan, fayaDanaat	فيضان
floor (n)	arDeyya, arDeyyaat	أرضية
flop (n, failure)	kheiba	خيبة
florist	maHall ward	محل ورد
flour	de'ee'	دقيق
flower (n, rose, etc.)	warda, ward	وردة
flush (n)	sefon, sefonaat	سيفون
fly (n, insect)	debbaana, debbaan	ذبابة
fly (n, zipper)	sosta, sosat	سوستة
fly (v)	yeTeer	يطير
fog	Dabaab	ضباب
folkloric	sha9bi	شعبي
food	akl	أكل
foot	adam, a'daam	قدم
on foot	mashyy	مشي
forbidden (religion)	Haraam	حرام
forbidden (law)	mamnoo9	ممنوع
foreigner	agnabi, agaanib; khawaaga, khawagaat	أجنبي خواجة
forget (v)	yensa	ينسى
fork (n)	shohka, shuwak	شوكة
formal (adj)	rasmi	رسمي
formal opinion/advice	fatwa, fataawi	فتوى
fortress	al9a	قلعة
foundation stone	Hagar el asaas	حجر الأساس
fountain	nafoora, nafooraat; fas'eyya, fas'eyyaat	نافورة فسقية
fox	ta9lab, ta9aalib	ثعلب
fracture (n)	kasr, kosoor	كسر
fragile	ra'-ee'	رقيق
frank (honest)	SareeH, SoraHa	صريح
free (at large)	Horr, aHraar	حر
free (gratis)	bebalaash; maggaani	ببلاش مجاني
free public faucet	sabeel	سبيل
frequency (radio, etc.)	zabzaba, zabzabaat	ذبذبة
fresh	Taaza	طازه
Friday	eg-gom9a	الجمعة
Friday prayer	Salat eg-gom9a	صلاة الجمعة
fridge	tallaaga, tallagaat	ثلاجة
friend	Sadeeq, aSdiqaa'; SaaHib, aS-Haab	صديق صاحب

front (adj)	*oddamaani*	قدماني
frozen (adj)	*mogammad*	مجمّد
fruit	*fak-ha; fawaakih*	فاكهة
frustration	*kabt*	كبت
fry (v)	*ye'lee*	يقلي
frying pan	*Taasa, Tasaat*	طاسة
fugitive	*harbaan, harbaneen*	هربان
full (not empty)	*malyaan*	مليان
full (not hungry)	*shab9aan, shab9aaneen*	شبعان
full (whole)	*kaamil*	كامل
full moon	*badr*	بدر
funeral	*ganaaza, ganazaat*	جنازة
funny (humorous)	*muD-Hik*	مضحك
funny (peculiar)	*ghareeb*	غريب
furniture	*9afsh;*	عفش
	mobilia, mobiliaat	موبيليا، موبيليات
future (n)	*musta'bal*	مستقبل

G

galabeyya (traditional robe)	*galabeyya, galaleeb*	جلابية
gallant	*shahm*	شهم
gallery	*ma9raD, ma9aariD*	معرض
gallon	*galoon*	جالون
gambling	*omaar*	قمار
game	*le9ba, le9ab*	لعبة
gang	*9iSaaba, 9iSabaat*	عصابة
garden	*geneina, ganaayin*	جنينة
garishly bright	*faa'i9*	فاقع
garlic	*tohm*	ثوم
gas (for cars, etc.)	*banzeen*	بنزين
gastric	*ma9awi*	معوي
gate	*bawwaaba, bawwabaat*	بوّابة
gazelle	*ghazaala, ghizlaan*	غزالة
gecko	*borS, ebraaS*	برص
gem	*gawhara, gawaahir*	جوهرة
generation	*geel, agyaal*	جيل
generous	*kareem*	كريم
genie	*genn*	جنّ
genius	*9abqari, 9abaqra*	عبقري
gentleness	*ensaneyya*	انسانية
genuine	*aSli*	أصلي
geography	*goghrafia*	جغرافيا

germ	garthooma, garatheem	جرثومة
ghee	samna	سمنة
ghost	shabaH, ashbaaH	شبح
gift	hedeyya, hadaaya	هدية
ginger (n, herb)	ganzabeel	جنزبيل
giraffe	zarafa, zaraaf	زرافة
girl	bint, banaat	بنت
give (v)	yeddi	يدّي
give (me)!	haat!	هات!
gland	ghudda, ghuddad	غدة
glass (n, for mirrors, etc.)	ezaaz	إزاز (زجاج)
glass (n, for drink)	kobbaaya, kobbayaat	كباية
glasses (eye)	naDDaara	نظارة
gloves	gewanti	جوانتي
glue	Samgh	صمغ
gluttonous	fag9aan, fag9aaneen	فجعان
go (v)	yerooH	يروح
goat	me9za, me9eez	معزة
goat meat	neefa	نيفة
God	allaah	الله
gold (n)	dahab	ذهب
goldsmith	Saayigh, Soyyaagh	صائغ
good	kewaiyis, kewaiyiseen	كويس
Good for you!	hanyyaalak!	هنيئا لك!
good deed	Hasana, Hasanaat	حسنة
goose	wizza, wizz	وزة
governance	Hokm	حكم
government	Hokuma, Hokumaat	حكومة
grace (n, elegance)	rashaaqa	رشاقة
graduate (adj)	khirreeg, khirreegeen	خريج
grandchild	Hafeed, aHfaad	حفيد
grandfather	gidd, godood	جدّ
grapes	9inab	عنب
gratitude (adj)	imtinaan	امتنان
graveyard	ma'bara, ma'aabir	مقبرة
gray (dark)	roSaaSi	رصاصي
grease (n)	shaHm, shoHoom	شحم
great (adj, marvelous)	9aDHeem	عظيم
greed	Tama9	طمع
greedy	Tammaa9, Tammaa9een	طماع
green beans	faSolya khaDra	فاصوليا خضراء
greeting (n)	salaam, salamaat; taHeyya, taHeyyaat	سلام تحية

grief	Hasra	حسرة
grill (n)	shawwaaya, shawwayaat	شواية
grilled lamb	kabaab	كباب
grocer	ba'-'aal, ba'-'aleen	بقال
grocery	be'aala, be'alaat	بقالة
group (n)	magmoo9a, magmoo9aat	مجموعة
group of friends	shilla, shelal	شلة
grow (v, in size, age, etc.)	yekbar	يكبر
guaranteed	maDmoon	مضمون
guard (n)	Haaris, Haras	حارس
guardian	waSi, awSiyaa'	وصي
guava	gawafaya, gawaafa	جوافة
guest (n)	Deif, Duyoof	ضيف
guidebook (travel)	daleel siyaaHee	دليل سياحي
guilt	zanb, zonoob	ذنب
gulf	khaleeg	خليج
gymnastics	gombaaz	جمباز
gynecology	amraaD nisa	أمراض نسا

H

habitat	mawTin	موطن
haggle (v)	yefaaSil	يفاصل
haggling	feSaal	فصال
hair	sha9r	شعر
haircut	Hilaa'a	حلاقة
hairdresser (women)	kewafeer, kewafeeraat	كوافير
half	noSS, enSaaS	نص
hall	Saala, Salaat	صالة
hallucinations	takhareef	تخاريف
hammer	shakoosh, shawakeesh	شاكوش
hand (n, anatomy)	eed, edein	يد
hand span (measure)	shibr, eshbaar	شبر
handbag	shanTit eed	شنطة إيد
handcuffs	kalabshaat	كلابشات
handkerchief	mandeel, manadeel	منديل
handsome	waseem	وسيم
handwriting	khaTT, khuTooT	خط
happen (v)	yeH-Sal	يحصل
happy	sa9eed	سعيد
harass (v)	yeDaayi'	يضايق
harbor	meena, mawaani	ميناء
harm (n)	Darar	ضرر
harmony	ensigaam	انسجام

hat	borneiTa, baraneeT	برنيطة
hate (v)	yekrah	يكره
have (v, own)	yemlik	يملك
have: I have	9and: 9andi	عند ؛ عندي
hawk	Sa'r, Su'oor	صقر
hay	ash-sh	قش
hazard	khaTar, akhTaar	خطر
head (adj, main, top)	ra'eesi	رئيسي
head (anatomy)	demaagh, demegha; raas, roos	دماغ رأس
headache	Sodaa9	صداع
headlights	Doh' 9aali	ضوء عال
health	SiHHa	صحة
heap (n)	kohm, ekwaam	كوم
hear (v)	yesma9	يسمع
heart	alb, oloob	قلب
heart failure	sakta	سكتة
heat (n)	sukhoneyya	سخونة
heater (domestic)	daffaaya, daffayaat	دفاية
heavy	te'eel	ثقيل
heel (foot, shoe)	ka9b, ko9oob	كعب
help (n)	musaa9da	مساعدة
help (v)	yesaa9id	يساعد
Help!	en-nagda!	النجدة!
hemorrhage	nazeef	نزيف
hen	farkha, feraakH	فرخة
hencoop	9esh-shit feraakh, 9eshash feraakh	عشة فراخ
henna	Henna	حنة
hepatitis	eS-Safra	الصفراء
herbs	tawaabil	توابل
here	hina	هنا
hereditary	wiraathy	وراثي
hero	baTal, abTaal	بطل
hesitant	mela'la'	ملألأ
hieroglyphic	heeroghleefee	هيروغليفي
high (tall)	9aali	عال
higher	a9la	أعلى
hill	tal, tilaal	تل
himself	zaat nafso	ذات نفسه
hire (v)	ye'aggar	يأجر
history	et-tareekh	التاريخ
hobby	huwaaya, huwayaat	هواية

hold (v)	*yemsik*	يمسك
hole	*khorm, ekhraam*	خرم
holiday	*agaza, agazaat*	أجازة
holy	*muqaddas*	مقدّس
home	*beit, buyoot*	بيت
homemade	*beiti*	بيتي
homosexual	*el-mithli, mithliyeen*	المثلي
honey	*9asal*	عسل
honor	*sharaf*	شرف
hood (car)	*kabboot, kababeet*	كبّوت
hoof	*Haafir, Hawaafir*	حافر
hookah	*sheesha, sheyash*	شيشة
hoot (of a vehicle)	*kalaks, kalaksaat*	كلاكس
hope (v)	*yetmanna*	يتمنى
horizontal (adj)	*ufuqi*	أفقي
horn (bull, etc.)	*arn, oroon*	قرن
horn (of a vehicle)	*kalaks, kalaksaat*	كلاكس
hornet	*dabboor, dababeer*	دبّور
horror	*ro9b*	رعب
horse	*HoSaan, HeSena*	حصان
horseback riding	*rukoob el khail*	ركوب الخيل
horsemanship	*feroseyya*	فروسية
horses	*kheil*	خيل
hose	*kharToom, kharaTeem*	خرطوم
hospital	*mustashfa, mustashfayaat*	مستشفى
hospitality	*karam eD-Diyaafa*	كرم الضيافة
hot (weather)	*Harr*	حر
hot chili	*shaTTa*	شطّة
hotel	*fundu', fanaadi';*	فندق
	oteel, otelaat	أوتيل
hour	*saa9a, sa9aat*	ساعة
house	*beit, beyoot*	بيت
houseboat	*9awwaama*	عوامة
how?	*ezzay?*	ازاي ؟
hug	*HoDn, aHDaan*	حضن
humanity	*ensaneyya*	انسانية
humidity	*ruTooba*	رطوبة
hump (n, camel's back)	*sanama*	سنام
hunger (n)	*goo9*	جوع
hunt (v)	*yeSTaad*	يصطاد
hunting	*Seid*	صيد
hurry (v)	*yesta9gil*	يستعجل
hurt (v)	*yewga9*	يوجع

husband	gohz (zohg), egwaaz	جوز (زوج)
hut	9esh-sha, 9eshash,	عشة
hyena	Dab9, Debo9a	ضبع
hypocrisy	nefaaq	نفاق

I

I	ana	أنا
I'm amazed!	9agabi!	عجبي!
ice	talg	ثلج
ice cream	jeelaati	جيلاتي
icon	ayqoona, ayqoonaat	أيقونة
idea	fikra, afkaar	فكرة
identical	Tibq el aSl	طبق الأصل
if	in;	إن
	lau	لو
ignorance	gahl	جهل
ignorant (adj)	gaahil, gahala	جاهل
ill (person)	9ayyaan, 9ayyaneen	عيان
illegal	mish qaanooni	مش قانوني
illness	maraD, amraaD	مرض
imagination	khayaal	خيال
imagine (v)	yetkhayyil	يتخيل
imam (Islamic religious leader)	imaam, a'imma	إمام
imitation (adj, copied)	mish aSli	مش أصلي
immediate	fawri	فوري
immorality	fogr	فجر
imp	9afreet, 9afareet	عفريت
important	muhimm	مهم
imported (adj)	mustawrad	مستورد
impossible	mustaHeel, mustaHeelaat	مستحيل
imposter	affaaq, affaaqeen;	أفاق
	daggaal, daggaleen	دجال
improve (v)	yeHassin	يحسن
in	fee	في
in charge	mas'ool, mas'ooleen	مسؤول
incense (aromatic products)	bukhoor	بخور
inch	booSa, booSaat	بوصة
included (in)	min Dimn	ضمن (من)
includes	yeshmal	يشمل
income	dakhl	دخل
incomplete	naa'iS	ناقص
incorrect	ghalaT	غلط

increase (v)	*yezawwid*	يزود
indebted	*madyoon, madyooneen*	مديون
indecent act	*fi9l faaDiH*	فعل فاضح
independent	*mustaqill*	مستقل
indigestion	*9osr haDm*	عسر هضم
industry	*Sinaa9a, Sinaa9aat*	صناعة
inexpensive	*rekheeS*	رخيص
infant	*9ayyil, 9yaal*	عيل
infectious	*mo9di*	معد
inform (v)	*yeballagh*	يبلغ
information	*ma9loomaat*	معلومات
informer	*mokhber, mokhbereen*	مخبر
ingredients	*mukawwinaat*	مكونات
inject (v)	*yeH'in*	يحقن
injection	*Hu'na, Hu'an*	حقنة
injury	*iSaaba, iSabaat*	إصابة
injustice	*zolm*	ظلم
ink	*Hibr, aHbaar*	حبر
inner	*gowwaani*	جواني
innocent (adj)	*baree'*	بريء
inoculation	*taT9eem*	تطعيم
insect	*Hashara, Hasharaat*	حشرة
inside	*gowwa*	جوه
insist (v)	*yeSammim*	يصمم
insomnia	*araq*	أرق
installment	*dof9a, dof9aat*	دفعة
instead of	*badal*	بدل
instinct	*ghareeza, gharaayyiz*	غريزة
instrument	*aala, aalaat*	آلة
insult (n)	*ihaana, ihaanaat;*	إهانة
	sheteema, shataayim	شتيمة
insurance	*ta'meen*	تأمين
insurance policy	*boleeSit ta'meen*	بوليصة تأمين
intelligence (state)	*mukhabaraat*	مخابرات
intelligent	*zaki;*	ذكي
	nebeeh	نبيه
intend (v)	*yenwi*	ينوي
intensive care	*9inaaya murakkaza*	عناية مركزة
intention	*neyya, neyyaat*	نية
intermediary	*waseeT, wosaTaa'*	وسيط
international	*dawli*	دولي
interpreter	*torgoman, torgomanaat*	ترجمان
intestinal	*ma9awi*	معوي

intoxicated (adj)	sakraan, sakraneen	سكران
introduce (v)	ye'addim	يقدم
intruder	dakheel, dukhalaa'	دخيل
invitation	da9wa, da9waat	دعوة
invite (v)	ye9zim	يعزم
invoice	fatoora, fawateer	فاتورة
Iran	eeraan	إيران
Iranian	eeraani, eeraaniyeen	إيراني
Iraq	el 9iraaq	العراق
Iraqi	9iraa'i, 9iraa'iyyeen	عراقي
iron (n, metal)	Hadeed	حديد
iron (v, clothes, etc.)	yekwi	يكوي
ironing man	makwagi, makwageyya	مكوجي
ironsmith	Haddaad	حداد
Islamic	islaami	إسلامي
island	gezeera, guzur	جزيرة
Israel	isra'eel	إسرائيل
Israeli	isra'eeli	إسرائيلي
Istanbul	esTambool	اسطمبول
itching	Hakka	حكة
itemized list	kashf, koshoofaat	كشف
itself	zaat nafso	ذات نفسه
ivory	9aag	عاج

J

jack (car, etc.)	koreik	كريك
jail (n)	sign, sigoon	سجن
jam (n, jelly)	merabba, merabbaat	مربى
jar	barTamaan, barTamanaat	برطمان
jasmine	yasmeen	ياسمين
jaw	fakk	فك
jealousy	gheera	غيرة
jelly (n, jam)	merabba, merabbaat	مربى
jellyfish	andeel el baHr	قنديل البحر
Jerusalem	el ods	القدس
jet (military)	naffaasa, naffasaat	نفاثة
Jew(ish)	yahoodi, yahood	يهودي
jeweler	gawahergi	جواهرجي
job	shoghlaana, shoghlanaat;	شغلانة
	waDHeefa, waDHaayif	وظيفة
join (v, connect)	yeDumm	يضم
join (v, enroll)	yenDamm	ينضم
joke (n)	nokta, nokat	نكتة

joking	hezaar	هزار
Jordan	el urdunn	الأردن
Jordanian	urdoni, urdoniyeen	أردني
journalist	SaHafi, SaHafiyyeen	صحافي
journey	reHla, reHlaat	رحلة
joy and laughter	farfasha	فرفشة
judge	aaDi, qudaah	قاض
jug	shafsha', shafashi'	شفشق
juice (n)	9aSeer, 9asaayir	عصير
jump (v)	yenoTT	ينط
jumping	naTT	نط
junk	khorda; robabekya	خردة روبابيكيا
justice (n)	9adaala	عدالة
juvenile (adj)	9eyaali	عيالي

K

Kaaba (holy black stone in Mecca)	ek-ka9ba	الكعبة
kaftan	ofTaan, afaTeen	قفطان
keep (v, retain)	yekhalli	يخلّي
kennel (n, dog)	beit kalb, buyoot kilaab	بيت كلب
ketchup	ketshab	كتشب
kettle	ghallaayit el mayya	غلاية الماء
key	muftaaH, mafateeH	مفتاح
keyboard (computer, etc.)	keebord	كيبورد
keyhole	khorm el moftaaH	خرم المفتاح
khaki (color)	kaaki	كاكي
khamsin winds	riyaaH el khamaaseen	رياح الخماسين
khedive	khudaywee	خديوي
kidding	hezaar	هزار
kidnap (n)	khaTf	خطف
kidney	kela, kelaawi	كلية
kill (v)	ye'til	يقتل
kilogram	keelograam	كيلوجرام
kilometer	keelomitr	كيلومتر
kind (adj, good natured)	Tayyib	طيب
kindergarten	roDit aTfaal	روضة أطفال
kindness	9aTf	عطف
king	malik, muluuk	ملك
kingdom	mamlaka, mamaalik	مملكة
kiosk (news-papers, etc.)	kushk, ekshaak	كشك

kiss	bosa, bohs	بوسة
kitchen	maTbakh, maTaabikh	مطبخ
kite (bird)	Heddaaya, Heddayaat	حدأة
kleptomania	daa' es-ser'a	داء السرقة
knee	rukba, rukab	ركبة
kneel (v)	yerka9	يركع
knickknacks	karakeeb	كراكيب
knife (n)	sekkeena, sakakeen	سكين
knob (n, door handle, etc.)	ma'baD, ma'aabiD	مقبض
knock	khabTa	خبطة
knock (v, on door, etc.)	yekhabbaT	يخبط
knockout (n, in boxing)	Darba 'aaDya	ضربة قاضية
knot (n)	9o'da, 9o'ad	عقدة
know (v)	ye9raf	يعرف
knowledgeable	9aarif	عارف
kohl	koHl	كحل
Koran	el quraan	القرآن
Kurd	kurdi, akraad	كردي
Kuwait	ek-kuweit	الكويت

L

Labor Day	9eed el 9ummaal	عيد العمال
labor pains	aalaam el waD9	آلام الوضع
laboratory	ma9mal, ma9aamil	معمل
lace (n)	dantella	دنتلة
ladder	sillim, salaalim	سلم
ladies' (fashion, etc.)	Hareemi	حريمي
ladle	kabsha, kobash	كبشة
lady	sitt, sittaat	ستّ
lady (of stature)	haanim, hawaanim	هانم
lake	buHeira, buHeiraat	بحيرة
lamb (meat)	Daanee Soghayyar	ضاني صغير
land (n)	arD, araaDi	أرض
landmarks	ma9aalim	معالم
landscape (n)	manDHar, manaaDHir	منظر
landscape (adj, horizontal)	ufuqi	أفقي
lane	darb, doroob	درب
language	lugha, lughaat	لغة
lantern	fanoos, fawanees	فانوس
large	kebeer	كبير
laryngitis	iltihaab el Hangara	التهاب الحنجرة
last (most recent)	aakher	آخر

late	met'akh-khar	متأخّر
lather	raghwa	رغوة
lattice window (traditional)	mashrabeyya, mashrabeyyaat	مشربية
laugh (v)	yeDHak	يضحك
laughter	DiHk	ضحك
launch (n, motorboat)	lansh, lanshaat	لنش
laundry (n, clothes, etc.)	ghaseel	غسيل
laundry (n, facility)	maghsala	مغسلة
lavender (n, color)	banafsegi faateH	بنفسجي فاتح
law	qaanoon, qawaaneen	قانون
lawn grass	Hasheesh	حشيش
lawyer	moHaami, moHaamiyeen	محام
laxative	mulayyin, mulayyinaat	ملين
layer (n)	Taba'a, Taba'aat	طبقة
lazy	kaslaan, kaslaaneen	كسلان
lead (n, metal)	ruSaaS	رصاص
leader	za9eem, zo9ama; rayyis, royasa	زعيم رئيس
leaf	wara'it shagar, wara' shagar	ورقة شجر
leak (n)	tan'eeT	تنقيط
leaping	naTT	نط
learn (v)	yet9allim	يتعلّم
lease (v)	ye'aggar	يأجّر
least	a'ell	أقل
leather	geld, golood	جلد
leave (v, abandon)	yeseeb	يسيب
Lebanese	libnaani, libnaniyeen	لبناني
Lebanon	libnaan	لبنان
lecture (n)	muHaadra, muHadraat	محاضرة
left (opp. right)	shemaal	شمال
left-handed	ashwal	أشول
leg	rigl, reglein	رجل
legal	qanooni	قانوني
legend (myth)	usToora, asaaTeer	أسطورة
lemon (citrus fruit)	lamoon aDalia	ليمون أضاليا
lemonade	lamonata	ليمونادة
lend (v)	yesallif	يسلّف
length	Tool	طول
lens	9adasa, 9adasaat	عدسة
Lent	Siyaam el maseeHeyyeen	صيام المسيحيين
lentils	9ads	عدس

less (adj, fewer)	a'ell	أقل
lesson	dars, duroos	درس
lethal	mumeet	مميت
letter (alphabet)	Harf, Huroof	حرف
letter (mail)	gawaab, gawabaat	جواب
lettuce	khass	خس
Levant	el mashriq el 9arabi	المشرق العربي
level (n, standard, etc.)	mostawa, mostawayaat	مستوى
liar	kazzaab, kazzabeen	كذّاب
liberty	Horreyya, Horreyyaat	حرية
library	maktaba, maktabaat	مكتبة
Libya	lebia	ليبيا
Libyan	leebi, leebiyeen	ليبي
license	rokhSa, rokhaS	رخصة
licorice	9ir'soos	عرقسوس
life	Hayaah	حياة
lifeboat	aarib en-nagaah, awaarib en-nagaah	قارب النجاة
lifebuoy	Toh' en-nagaah, aTwaa' en-nagaah	طوق النجاة
lifetime	9omr, a9maar	عمر
light (adj, opp. heavy)	khafeef	خفيف
light (n, illumination)	noor, anwaar	نور
light (n, sunlight, etc.)	Doh', aDwaa'	ضوء
light blue (colloquial)	labani	لبني
lighter (n, for cigarettes, etc.)	walaa9a, wala9aat	ولاعة
lighthouse	fanaara, fanaraat	فنارة
lightning	bar'	برق
like (similar to)	zayy	زيّ
like (v)	yeHibb	يحب
like so	keda	كده
likeness	shabah	شبه
lime (citrus fruit)	lamoon banzaheer	ليمون بنزهير
limit	Hadd, Hudood	حدّ
limp (v)	ye9rog	يعرج
line (general)	khaTT, khuTooT	خط
line (on paper)	saTr, esTor	سطر
line (people, cars, etc.)	Saff, Sofoof	صف
linen (sheets, etc.)	bayaDaat	بياضات
lining (coats, etc.)	beTaana	بطانة
lion	sab9, sebo9a	سبع

lip	shiffa, shafaayef	شفاه
lipstick	aHmar shafaayef; rooj	أحمر شفايف؛ روج
liquid	saayil, sawaayil	سائل
liquor	khamra, khomoor	خمر
list (n)	ayma, awaayem	قائمة
listen (v)	yesma9	يسمع
liter	litr	لتر
literature	aadaab	آدب
litigation	igraa'aat qaDaa'eyya	إجراءات قضائية
litter (trash)	zibaala	زبالة
little	Soghayyar	صغير
live (adj, wire, etc.)	Hayy	حي
live (v, dwell)	yeskun	يسكن
liver (chicken, etc.)	kebda, kebadd	كبدة
liver (human)	kibd	كبد
lizard	siHliyya, saHaali	سحلية
load (n)	Himl, aHmaal	حمل
loaf (n, bread)	regheef, erghefa	رغيف
loan (n)	solfa, salafeyyaat	سلفة
lobster	estakohza	استاكوزا
local	maHalli	محلّي
lock (n)	ifl, i'faal	قفل
locksmith	betaa9 i'faal	بتاع أقفال
locust	garada, garaad	جرادة
lodging	es-sakan	السكن
logbook	daftar, dafaatir	دفتر
logic	manTiq	منطق
lonely	waHdaani	وحداني
long (adj)	Taweel	طويل
long for (v, miss)	yeHinn	يحن
loofah	loofa, leef	لوفة
look (v, see)	yeboSS	يبص
Look out!	khalli baalak!	خلّي بالك!
loose (adj, baggy)	waasi9	واسع
loose (adj, not packaged)	saayib	سايب
lorry	lori, lawaari	لوري
lose (v, misplace)	yeDayya9	يضيع
lose (v, opp. win)	yekhsar	يخسر
lose interest	yemill	يملّ
loss	khusaara	خسارة
lost (adj)	Daayi9, Day9een	ضايع
lotus	lootos	لوتس

loud	9aali eS-Soht	عالي الصوت
love (n)	Hubb;	حب
	maHabba	محبة
love (v)	yeHibb	يحب
low	waaTi, waTyeen	واطي؛
loyal (n)	wafy, awfeya	وفي
lozenge (pastille)	bastelya	بستيلية
lubrication	tazyeet	تزييت
luck	bakht;	بخت
	HaZZ	حظ
lucky (person)	maH-ZooZ,	محظوظ
	maH-ZooZeen	
lump (medical)	waram, awraam	ورم
lunar	amari	قمري
lunch	ghada	غداء
lung	ri'a, ri'aat	رئة
luxurious	fakhm	فخم

M

macaroni	makarohna	مكرونة
machine	makana, makann	ماكينة
mad (crazy)	magnoon, maganeen	مجنون
madness	genoon	جنون
magazine (periodical)	magalla, magallaat	مجلة
magician	saaHir, saHara	ساحر
mail (n, post)	bareed;	بريد
	bosTa	بوسطة
mail (v, letters, etc.)	yeb9at bil-bareed	يبعث بالبريد
main (adj)	ra'eesi	رئيسي
maintenance (servicing)	Siyaana	صيانة
maize	dura	ذرة
majority	aghlabeyya	أغلبية
make (v, do)	ye9mil	يعمل
make (v, manufacture)	yeSanna9	يصنع
make-up (n, lipstick, etc.)	mikyaaj	مكياج
malaria	malarya	ملاريا
male	dakar, dukora	ذكر
male nurse	tamargi, tamargeyya	تمرجي
mallet	shakoosh khashab	شاكوش خشب
malt	she9eer	شعير
man	raagil, reggaala	راجل
man-made	Sinaa9i	صناعي

management	*idaara*	إدارة
manager	*modeer, modeereen*	مدير
mandatory	*igbaari*	إجباري
mango	*mangaya, manga*	مانجو
mangy	*garbaan, garbaneen*	جربان
manhole	*bakabort, bakabortaat*	بكابورت
manicure	*manikeer*	مانيكير
manners	*zoh', azwaa'*	ذوق
mansion	*beit fakhm, buyoot fakhma*	بيت فخم
manual (adj, by hand)	*yadawi*	يدوي
manufacture (v)	*yeSanna9*	يصنع
many	*keteer*	كثير
map	*khareeTa, kharaayeT*	خريطة
marble (stone)	*rukhaam*	رخام
March	*maaris*	مارس
margin	*haamish, hawaamish*	هامش
marinate (v)	*yetabbil*	يتبل
marine (adj)	*baHari*	بحري
market (n)	*soo', aswaa'*	سوق
go to market	*yenzil es-soo'*	ينزل السوق
marketing	*taswee'*	تسويق
marmalade	*merabbit burtu'aan*	مربى البرتقال
marriage	*gawaaz*	جواز (زواج)
marrow	*nukhaa9*	نخاع
marry	*yetgawwiz*	يتزوج
Mars	*el marreekh*	المريخ
martyr	*shaheed, shohada*	شهيد
leyaah	**suolevram**	هائل
mascara	*maskaara*	مسكارا
mash (v)	*yehris*	يهرس
mask (n)	*qinaa9, aqni9a*	قناع
mass (church service)	*oddaas*	قدّاس
massage	*tadleek*	تدليك
massive	*Dakhm*	ضخم
master (head of school, train station, etc.)	*en-naaZir*	الناظر
master craftsman	*osTa, osTawaat*	أسطى
masterpiece	*tuHfa, tuHaf*	تحفة
Masters degree	*majesteir*	ماجستير
match-box	*9ilbit kabreet*	علبة كبريت
matches	*kabreet*	كبريت
material (fabric)	*omaash, a'misha*	قماش
materialistic (adj)	*maaddi*	مادّي

mathematics	riyaaDiyaat	رياضيات
mattress	martaba, maraatib	مرتبة
mausoleum	DareeH, aDreHa	ضريح
maximum	9alal aakher; aqSaa	على الآخر أقصى
maybe	yemkin	يمكن
mayor	9omda, 9omad	عمدة
meal	wagba, wagabaat	وجبة
meaning	ma9na, ma9aani	معنى
measles	el HaSba	الحصبة
measurement (size)	ma'aas	مقاس
meat	laHma	لحم
Mecca (Saudi Arabian city)	makka	مكة
Mecca's direction	ibla	قبلة
mechanic	mekaneeki	ميكانيكي
medal	neshaan, nayasheen; wisaam	نيشان وسام
medical	Tibbi	طبي
medicine; medication	dawa, adweya	دواء
medium (mid-)	mutawassiT	متوسط
meet (v)	ye'aabil	يقابل
melody	laHn, alHaan; nagham, anghaam	لحن نغم
melon	shammaama, shammaam	شمام
melt (v)	yedoob	يذوب
melted (adj)	saayeH	سايح
membership (n)	9oDweyya	عضوية
memento	tizkaar, tizkaraat	تذكار
memory (past image)	dhikra, dhikrayaat	ذكرى
mental disposition	mazaag, amzega	مزاج
mentality	9a'leyya, 9a'leyyaat	عقلية
menu	ayma, awaayem	قائمة
mercury	zeyba'	زيبق
mercy	raHma	رحمة
mess (n, chaos)	fawDa	فوضى
message	risaala, rasaayil	رسالة
metal (n)	ma9dan, ma9aadin	معدن
meter (electricity, taxi fare, etc.)	9addaad, 9addadaat	عداد
method	waseela, wasaayel	وسيلة
middle	wisT	وسط
midnight	noSS el-leil	منتصف الليل

migraine	Sodaa9 niSfi	صداع نصفي
military (adj)	9askari	عسكري
milk	Haleeb;	حليب
	laban	لبن
milk and cereal dish (traditional)	beleela	بليلة
minaret	madna, madaayin	مئذنة
mine (belonging to me)	betaa9i	بتاعي
mine (explosive)	lagham, alghaam	لغم
mine (coal, etc.)	mangam, manaagim	منجم
mineral water	mayya ma9daneyya	مياه معدنية
minimum charge	Hadd adnaa	حدّ أدنى
minister (government)	wazeer, wozara	وزير
mint (n, herb)	ni9naa9	نعناع
minute (n, time)	de'ee'a, da'aayi'	دقيقة
mirage	saraab	سراب
mirror	meraaya, merayaat	مرآة
miserable	ta9ees	تعيس
miserly (person)	bakheel, bokhala	بخيل
misery	nakad	نكد
missing (person)	maf'ood, maf'oodeen	مفقود
mist	shabboora	شبّورة
mistake (n)	ghalTa, ghalaTaat	غلطة
mistress	9ashee'a, 9ashee'aat	عشيقة
misunderstanding	soo' tafaahom	سوء تفاهم
mixture	khalTa	خلطة
mobile phone	mobaayel, mobaylaat	موبايل
moderate (adj)	mo9tadil, mo9tadileen	معتدل
modern	9aSri	عصري
molar tooth	Dirs, Diroos	ضرس
moment	laHza, laHazaat	لحظة
monastery	deir, adyera	دير
money	feloos	فلوس
monk	raahib, rohbaan	راهب
month	shahr, shuhoor	شهر
monthly	shahri	شهري
monuments	aathaar	آثار
moon	amar, a'maar	قمر
more (greater)	aktar	أكثر
more (extra)	zeyada	زيادة
morning	SobH; SabaaH	صبح؛ صباح
Moroccan (person)	maghrebi, magharba	مغربي
Morocco	el maghreb	المغرب

morsel (of bread)	lo'ma, lo'am	لقمة
mosque	masgid, masaagid	مسجد
mosquito	namoosa, namoos	ناموسة
most (greatest)	aktar	أكثر
mother (n)	umm, ummahaat	أم
mother-of-pearl	Sadaf	صدف
mountain	gabal, gebaal	جبل
mourning event	9aza	عزاء
mouse	faar, feraan	فأر
mouth	bo', eb'aa'	بق
mouthful	lo'ma, lo'am	لقمة
move (v, oneself)	yetHarrak	يتحرّك
move (v, something)	yeHarrak	يحرّك
movement	Haraka, Harakaat	حركة
movie	film, aflaam	فيلم
moving house	9izaal	عزال
mud	Teen	طين
muezzin	mo'adh-dhin, mo'adh-dhineen	مؤذّن
mufti	mufti	مفتي
mule	baghl, beghaal	بغل
mummy (Pharaonic, etc.)	momya, momyawaat	مومياء
murdered person	ateel, otala	قتيل
muscle	9aDala, 9aDalaat	عضلة
museum	matHaf, mataaHif	متحف
music	museeqa	موسيقى
mustache	shanab, shanabaat	شنب
mustard	mosTarda	مسطردة
mutton	Daanee	ضاني
My dear!	yaa 9azizi!	يا عزيزي!
mystery	loghz, alghaaz	لغز
myth	khuraafa, khurafaat	خرافة

N

nail (finger, toe)	Dofr, Dawaafir	ظفر
naivety	habal	هبل
name	ism, asaami	اسم
nap (n, snooze)	ta9seela	تعسيلة
narcissus	nargiss	نرجس
narrow	Dayya'	ضيق
nation	umma, umam	أمة
national	waTani, waTaniyeen	وطني

nationality	ginseyya, ginseyyaat	جنسية
natural	Tabee9i	طبيعي
naughtiness (esp. children)	sha'aawa	شقاوة
navigator	mallaaH, mallaaHeen	ملاح
navy blue	koHli	كحلي
near	orayyib	قريب
necessary (must)	laazim	لازم
necessities	Darooriyaat	ضروري
neck	re'aba, re'aab	رقبة
necklace	9o'd, e9-'aad	عقد
necktie	karavatta, karavattaat	كرافتة
need (v)	yeHtaag	يحتاج
needle	ibra, ibar	ابرة
neighbor	gaar, geraan	جار
neighborhood	Hayy, aHyaa'; Hitta, Hitat	حي حتة
nephew (son of brother)	ibn akh	ابن أخ
nephew (son of sister)	ibn okht	ابن أخت
nerve	9aSab, a9Saab	عصب
nervous breakdown	inhiyaar 9aSabi	انهيار عصبي
net (n)	shabaka, shabak	شبكة
never	abadan	أبدا
new	gedeed	جديد
news	khabar, akhbaar	خبر
news bulletin	en-nashra	النشرة
newspaper	gornaan, garaayed	جرنان
next	elli gaay	اللي جاي
next of kin	aqrab el aqribaa'	أقرب الأقرباء
nibbles (with drink)	mazza, mazzaat	مزّة
nice	Hilw	حلو
niece (daughter of brother)	bint akh	بنت أخ
niece (daughter of sister)	bint okht	بنت أخت
night	leil, leyaali	ليل
night guard	ghafeer, ghafar	غفير
night time	el-leil	الليل
nightmare	kaboos, kawabees	كابوس
nightstick	nabboot, nababeet	نبوت
Nile	en-neel	النيل
Nile boat (traditional sail)	felooka, falaayek	فلوكة
no	la'	لأ
noble	nabeel, nobalaa'	نبيل

nobody	walla waaHid	ولا واحد
noise	dawsha	دوشة
nomad(ic)	raHHaal	رحّال
north	shamaal	شمال
North African Maghreb	el maghreb el 9arabi	المغرب العربي
North facing	baHari	بحري
nose	manakheer	مناخير
not	mish	مش
not here	mish hena	مش هنا
not me	mish ana	مش أنا
not working	kharbaan	خربان
nothing	walla Haaga	ولا حاجة
novel (n, fiction)	rowaaya, rowayaat	رواية
novice	ghasheem, ghoshm	غشيم
now	delwa'ti	دلوقت
Nubia	en-nooba	النوبة
Nubian	noobi, noobiyeen	نوبي
nuisance (adj)	muz9ig	مزعج
number (figure)	nemra, nemar	نمرة
number (quantity)	9adad, a9daad	عدد
nurse (female)	momarriDa, momarriDaat	ممرضة
nut (as in nut and bolt)	Samoola, Sawameel	صامولة
nuts (n, walnuts, etc.)	mekassaraat	مكسرات

O

oasis	waaHa, waaHaat	واحة
obelisk	misalla, misallaat	مسلة
obituary	na9i	نعي
obligatory	igbaari	إجباري
obtain (v)	yegeeb	يجيب
obvious	waaDiH	واضح
occasion	munasba, munasbaat	مناسبة
ocean	muHeeT, muHeeTaat	محيط
odd (strange)	ghareeb	غريب
Of course!	Tab9an!	طبعاً!
offer (n)	9arD, 9urooD	عرض
offer (v)	ye9riD	يعرض
office	maktab, makaatib	مكتب
officer (military)	zaabiT, zubbaaT	ضابط
oil	zeit, zuyoot	زيت
Okay!	Tayyib!	طيب!

okra	bamya	بامية
old (object)	adeem	قديم
old (person)	9agooz, 9awageez	عجوز
olive (fruit)	zatoona, zatoon	زيتونة
olive-green color	akhDar zatooni	أخضر زيتوني
Oman	9omaan	عمان
Omani	9omaani, 9omaaniyyeen	عماني
on	9ala	على
once	marra	مرّة
onion	baSala, baSal	بصل
only	bass	بس
open (adj)	faateH; maftooH	فاتح مفتوح
opener (cans, bottles, etc.)	fattaaHa, fattaHaat	فتّاحة
opening (n)	fatHa, fatHaat	فتحة
operating theater	ghorfit el 9amaleyyaat	غرفة العمليات
operation	9amaleyya, 9amaleyyaat	عملية
operational	shagh-ghaal	شغّال
opportunity	furSa, furaS	فرصة
opposite	9aks	عكس
optician	naDDaraati	نظاراتي
optional	ikhtiyaari	اختياري
or	aw; walla	أو ولا
orange (adj, color)	burtu'aani	برتقالي
orange (n, fruit)	burtu'ana, burtu'aan	برتقان
orator	khaTeeb	خطيب
order (n, method)	niDHaam, anDHima	نظام
order (n, restaurant)	Talab, Talabaat	طلب
order (v, demand)	yo'mur	يأمر
ordinary	9aadi	عادي
organic	9oDwi; Hayawi	عضوي حيوي
organize (v)	yenazzam	ينظم
oriental	shar'i	شرقي
orientalist	mustashriq, mustashriqeen	مستشرق
original	aSli	أصلي
ornamental	zukhrufi	زخرفي
other	taani	تاني
oud (lute-like instrument)	9ood, e9waad	عود
ours	beta9na	بتاعنا
out of order	9aTlaan	عطلان

outside	*barra*	بره
oven	*furn, afraan*	فرن
overland	*barri*	بري
oversight	*sahw*	سهو
owl	*booma, boom*	بومة
own (v)	*yemlik*	يملك
owner (possessor)	*SaaHib, aS-Haab*	صاحب
owner (proprietor)	*maalik, mollaak*	مالك

P

pack (v) a bag	*yewaDDab esh-shanTa*	يوضّب الشنطة
package (n)	*Tard, Turood*	طرد
padlock (n)	*ifl, i'faal*	قفل
page (n)	*SafHa, SafaHaat*	صفحة
pain (n)	*waga9, awgaa9;*	وجع
	alam, aalaam	ألم
paint (n)	*booya, booyaat*	بوية
painter (artist)	*rassaam, rassameen*	رسّام
painter (decorator)	*na'-'aash, na'-'aasheen*	نقّاش
painting (n)	*tabloh, tablohaat*	تابلوه
pair	*gohz, egwaaz*	جوز
Pakistan	*bakistaan*	باكستان
Pakistani	*bakistaani, bakistaniyyeen*	باكستاني
palace	*aSr, oSoor;*	قصر
	saraaya, sarayaat	سراية
pale (adj)	*bahtaan*	بهتان
Palestine	*filisTeen*	فلسطين
Palestinian	*filisTeeni, filisTeeniyeen*	فلسطيني
palm (n, hand)	*kaff, kofoof*	كفّ
palm tree	*nakhla, nakhl*	نخلة
pancreas	*bankeryaas*	بنكرياس
panic	*dho9r*	ذعر
pants (trousers)	*banTalohn,*	بنطلون
	banTalonaat	
paper (n, document, etc.)	*wara'a, awraa'*	ورقة
papyrus	*wara' el bardi*	ورق البردي
paradise	*eg-ganna*	الجنّة
paralysis	*shalal*	شلل
parents	*ab wi-omm*	أبو وأم
park (v, cars, etc.)	*yerkin*	يركن
parliament	*barlamaan*	برلمان
parrot	*baghbaghaan,*	بغبغان
	baghbaghanaat	
parsley	*ba'doonis*	بقدونس

part (n, section)	guz', agzaa'	جزء
partner (n)	shereek, shuraka	شريك
party (n, ball)	Hafla, Hafalaat	حفلة
party (n, political)	Hizb, aHzaab	حزب
pass (v, by someone)	yefoot (9ala);	يفوت (على)
	yemurr (9ala)	يمر (على)
pass (n, permit)	taSreeH, taSareeH	تصريح
passenger	raakib, rukkaab	راكب
passport	gawaaz es-safar	جواز السفر
past (adj)	maaDi	ماضي
pasta	makarohna	مكرونة
paternal	abawi	أبوي
path	mamarr, mamarraat	ممر
patience (n)	Sabr	صبر
patient (sick person)	9ayyaan, 9ayyaneen	عيّان
patisserie	Halawaani, Halawaaneyya	حلواني
patriotic	waTani, waTaniyeen	وطني
paunch	kersh, koroosh	كرش
pay (v)	yedfa9	يدفع
pay rise	9ilaawa, 9ilawaat	علاوة
peace	salaam	سلام
peach	khokha, khohkh	خوخ
pear	kommetraaya, kommetra	كمثرى
pearl	loolaya, looli	لؤلؤة
peas	besella	بسلّة
pebble	HaSwa, HaSa;	حصوة
	zalaTa, zalaT	زلط
peel (n, fruit)	eshra	قشرة
peg (for tent, etc.)	watad, awtaad	وتد
pen	alam, a'laam	قلم
pencil	alam roSaaS	قلم رصاص
people	naas	ناس
pepper (n)	filfil	فلفل
perfect	kaamil	كامل
performance (show)	9arD, 9urooD	عرض
perfume	9iTr, 9oToor	عطر
period of time	fatra, fataraat	فترة
permission	ezn	إذن
permit (v)	yesmaH	يسمح
person	nafar, anfaar	نفر
person	shakhS, ash-khaaS	شخص
personality	shakhSeyya, shakhSeyyaat	شخصية
pertaining to	taba9	تبع

petrol(eum)	betrohl	بترول
petrol (gas for cars, etc.)	banzeen	بنزين
Pharaonic	fara9oni	فرعوني
pharmacy	agzakhaana, agzakhanaat; Saydaleyya, Saydaleyyaat	أجزخانة صيدلية
phenomenon	dhaahira, dhawaahir	ظاهرة
photographer	muSawwaraati, muSawwarateyya	مصور
pickles	Torshi	طرشي
picture (n, photo, etc.)	Soora, Siwar	صورة
pie	feTeera, feTeer	فطيرة
pie-maker	faTaTri	فطاطري
piece (of)	Hitta, Hitat	حتّة
pierce (v)	yokhrom	يخرم
pig	khanzeer, khanazeer	خنزير
pile (n)	kohm, ekwaam	كوم
pilgrim	Hagg, Huggaag	حاج
pilgrimage (to Mecca)	el Higg	الحج
pilgrimage (outside season)	9omra	عمرة
pill	orS, e'raaS	قرص
pillow case	kees makhadda, ekyaas makhaddaat	كيس مخذة
pilot (airline)	Tayyaar, Tayyareen	طيار
pin (n)	dabboos, dababees	دبوس
pincers	kammaasha, kammashaat	كماشة
pipe (water, etc.)	masoora, mawaseer	ماسورة
pistachio	fuzdo'	فستق
pistol	Tabanga, Tabangaat	طبنجة
place (n, location)	makaan, amaakin	مكان
plain (adj)	saada	سادة
plait	Defeera, Dafaayer	ضفيرة
plan (n)	kheTTa, kheTaT	خطة
planet	kawkab, kawaakib	كوكب
plant (n)	nabaat, nabataat	نبات
plant (v)	yezra9	يزرع
plate (n, gold)	eshra	قشرة
plate (n, dish)	saHn, SuHoon; Taba', eTbaa'	صحن طبق
platform (n, train, harbor, etc.)	raSeef, erSefa	رصيف
play (n)	masraHeyya, masraHeyyaat	مسرحية
play (v)	yel9ab	يلعب
please	min faDlak; lau samaHt	من فضلك لو سمحت

plenty	keteer	كثير
plug (electric, etc.)	feesha	فيشة
plug (stopper)	saddaada, saddadaat	سدادة
plumber	sabbaak, sabbakeen	سبّاك
pocket (n)	geib, goyoob	جيب
pocket knife	maTwa, maTaawi	مطوة
poetry	shi9r	شعر
point (n, dot)	nu'Ta, nu'aTT	نقطة
point (v, with finger)	yeshaawir	يشاور
poison	simm, sumoom	سمّ
police	el bolees	البوليس
police station	ism el bolees	قسم البوليس
polite (adj)	mo'addab, mo'addabeen	مؤدب
pomegranate	rummaana, rummaan	رمان
pool (n, pond, etc.)	birka, birak	بركة
poor (not rich)	fa'eer, fo'ara	فقير
poor (unfortunate)	ghalbaan, ghalaaba	غلبان
popcorn	feshaar	فشار
popular (of the people)	sha9bi	شعبي
porcelain	khazaf	خزف
port	meena, mawaani	ميناء
porter	shayyaal, shayyaleen	شيّال
portrait	tabloh, tablohaat	تابلوه
position	waD9	وضع
positive (attitude)	eegaabi	إيجابي
positive (electric)	moogab	موجب
possess (v)	yemlik	يملك
possibility	iHtimaal, iHtimalaat	احتمال
post office	maktab el bareed	مكتب البريد
postcard	kart bosTa	كارت بوسطة
potato	baTaTsaaya, baTaaTis	بطاطس
pottery	fukh-khaar	فخّار
powder	masHoo', masaHee'	مسحوق
powder (cosmetics, etc.)	bodra	بودرة
practical	9amali	عملي
prawns	gambareyyaya, gambari	جمبري
pray (v)	yeSalli	يصلّي
prayer	Salah	صلاة
prayer corner	zawya, zawaya	زاوية
precious	ghaali	غال
precious stone	Hagar kareem	حجر كريم
precisely	beZ-ZabT	بالظبط
predicament	warTa	ورطة

prefer (v)	yefaDDal	يفضّل
pregnant	Haamil;	حامل
	Hibla	حبلى
prescription	roshetta, roshettaat	روشتة
president	ra'ees	رئيس
press (n, newspapers, etc.)	garaayed	جرائد
press (printing)	maTba9a, maTaabi9	مطبعة
pressed date paste	9agwa	عجوة
pressure	DaghT, DoghooT	ضغط
pretext	Higga, Higag	حجة
prey	fareesa, faraayis	فريسة
price (n)	taman, atmaan;	ثمن
	si9r, as9aar	سعر
priest (Christian)	assees, osos	قسّيس
prime minister	ra'ees el wozara	رئيس الوزراء
prince	ameer, umara	أمير
princess	ameera, ameeraat	أميرة
printing	Tibaa9a	طباعة
prison	sign, sigoon	سجن
prisoner	sageen, masageen	سجين
private	khoSooSi	خصوصي
privatization	khaS-khaSa	خصخصة
problem	mushkila, mashaakil	مشكلة
product	muntag, muntagaat	منتج
professional	muHtarif, muHtarifeen	محترف
program	bernaamig, baraamig	برنامج
prohibited	mamnoo9	ممنوع
promise (n)	wa9d, wu9ood	وعد
promotion (work, etc.)	tar'eyya	ترقية
pronunciation	noT'	نطق
proof	burhaan, baraheen	برهان
prophet	nabee, anbeya;	نبي
	rasool, rosol	رسول
protruding	baariz	بارز
province (region, etc.)	iqleem, aqaleem	إقليم
provincial	baladi;	بلدي
	reefi	ريفي
public	9omoomi	عمومي
puff (n, cigarette, etc.)	nafas, anfaas	نفس
pull (v)	yesHab;	يسحب
	yeshidd	يشدّ
pulse (blood)	nabD	نبض
pump (n)	Toromba, Torombaat	طرمبة

puncture	khorm, ekhraam	خرم
puppet	aragohz, aragozaat	أراجوز
pure	Saafi;	صاف
	naqi	نقي
purple	banafsegi	بنفسجي
push (v)	yezo'	يزق
put (v)	yeHoTT	يحط
puzzle	fazzoora, fawazeer	فزورة
puzzled	Hayraan	حيران
pyramid	haram, ahraam	هرم

Q

Qatar	qaTar	قطر
Qatari	qaTari, qaTariyeen	قطري
quaint (amusing)	Zareef, Zoraaf	ظريف
quality	gooda	جودة
quantity	kimmeyya, kimmeyyaat	كمية
quarantine	Hagr SiHHi	حجر صحي
quarrel (v)	yetkhaani'	يتخانق
quarter (n)	rub9, erba9	ربع
queen	malika, malikaat	ملكة
question (n)	su'aal, as'ila	سؤال
quick	saree9	سريع
quiet (adj)	haadi	هادئ
quit (v)	yebaTTal	يبطّل

R

rabbi	Haakhaam	حاخام
rabbit	arnab, araanib	أرنب
race (n, running, etc.)	saba', siba'aat	سباق
racket (tennis, etc.)	maDrab, maDaarib	مضرب
raddish	figl	فجل
railroad	sikka Hadeed	سكة حديد
rain (n)	maTara	مطر
raisin	zebeeba, zebeeb	زبيب
Ramadan (month of fasting)	ramaDaan	رمضان
rat	faar kebeer, feraan kebeera	فار كبير
ravenous	fag9aan, fag9aaneen	فجعان
raw (not cooked)	nayy	نيء
raw (unprocessed)	khaam	خام
razor	moos, emwaas	موس
reach (v)	yewSal	يوصل
read (v)	ye'ra	يقرأ

reading	*eraaya*	قراءة
ready (adj)	*gaahiz, gahzeen*	جاهز
real	*Ha'ee'i*	حقيقي
realistic	*waaqe9i, waaqe9iyeen*	واقعي
reason (n, cause)	*sabab, asbaab*	سبب
reasonable	*ma9-'ool*	معقول
reasoning	*9a'l, 9o'ool*	عقل
receipt	*waSl, woSoolaat*	وصل
receive (v)	*yestelim*	يستلم
reception	*isti'baal*	استقبال
recipe	*waSfa, waSfaat*	وصفة
reckless	*Taayesh*	طائش
recommendation	*tawSeyya, tawSeyyaat*	توصية
reconciliation	*SolH*	صلح
record (music)	*osTowaana, osTowanaat*	اسطوانة
recover (from illness)	*yekheff*	يخف
rectangle	*mustaTeel, mustaTeelaat*	مستطيل
reduce (v)	*ye'allil*	يقلل
reef	*Sukhoor baHareyya*	صخور بحرية
referee	*Hakam, Hokkaam*	حكم
refrain from (v)	*yibaTTal*	يبطّل
refresh (v)	*yen9ish*	ينعش
refugee	*lagi', lagi'een*	لاجئ
refuse (v)	*yerfuD*	يرفض
regal	*melooki*	ملوكي
regional	*iqleemi*	إقليمي
register	*daftar, dafaatir*	دفتر
regret (v)	*yendam*	يندم
relationship	*9ilaa'a, 9ila'aat*	علاقة
relative (n, family)	*areeb, araayeb*	قريب
relax (v)	*yestagimm*	يستجم
relic	*athar, aathaar*	أثر
religion	*deen, adyaan*	دين
remain (v)	*yefDal*	يفضل
remaining	*faaDil*	فاضل
remedy (n)	*9ilaag*	علاج
remember (v)	*yeftekir*	يفتكر
remorse	*nadam*	ندم
remove (v)	*yesheel*	يشيل
renewal	*tagdeed, tagdeedaat*	تجديد
rent (v)	*ye'aggar*	يأجر
repair (n)	*taSleeH, taSleeHaat*	تصليح
repeat (v)	*yekarrar*	يكرر

repellent (n)	*Taarid*	طارد
reply (n)	*radd, rudood*	رد
reply (v)	*yerodd*	يردّ
reporter	*SaHafi, SaHafiyyeen*	صحافي
representative (n)	*mandoob, mandoobeen*	مندوب
republic	*gomhooreyya, gomhooreyyaat*	جمهورية
request (v)	*yeTlub*	يطلب
rescue (n)	*inqaadh*	إنقاذ
rescue (v)	*yenqiz*	ينقذ
reservation (n)	*Hagz, Huguzaat*	حجز
reserve (v)	*yeHgiz*	يحجز
reservoir	*khazzaan, khazzanaat*	خزان
residency	*iqaama*	إقامة
resident	*saakin, sokkaan*	ساكن
residential	*sakani*	سكني
resignation	*isti'aala, isti'alaat*	استقالة
resolve (a problem)	*yeHill (mushkila)*	يحلّ (مشكلة)
resort (n)	*muntaga9, muntaga9aat*	منتجع
respect (n)	*iHtiraam*	احترام
responsible	*mas'ool, mas'ooleen*	مسؤول
rest (v)	*yestarayyaH*	يستريح
restaurant	*maT9am, maTaa9im*	مطعم
restoration	*tagdeed, tagdeedaat*	تجديد
result (n)	*nateega, nataayeg*	نتيجة
retina	*shabakeyya*	شبكية
retirement (from work)	*taqaa'ud*	تقاعد
return (n)	*regoo9*	رجوع
return (v)	*yerga9*	يرجع
revenge	*enti'aam*	انتقام
revolution (uprising)	*thawra*	ثورة
revolutionaries	*thowwaar*	ثوار
reward (n)	*mokaf'a, mokaf'aat*	مكافأة
rhino	*kharteet, kharateet*	خرتيت
rib	*Dil9, Doloo9*	ضلع
rice	*rozz*	أرز
rid me (of)	*khallaSni (min)*	خلّصني (من)
riddle (n)	*loghz, alghaaz; fazzoora, fawazeer*	لغز فزورة
right (adj, correct)	*saHeeH*	صحيح
right (n, entitlement)	*Ha', Hu'oo'*	حق
right (opp. left)	*yemeen*	يمين
ring (jewelry)	*khaatim, khawaatim*	خاتم

risk (n)	mugazfa	مجازفة
ritual wash (Islamic)	weDoo'	وضوء
river bank	Daffa, Defaaf;	ضفة
	shaTT, sheTooT	شط
road	Taree', Turu'	طريق
road sweeper	kannaas, kannaseen	كناس
roadblock	kameen, kamaayin	كمين
rock	Sakhra, Sokhoor	صخرة
rocket	Sarookh, Sawareekh	صاروخ
romance	gharaam	غرام
roof	satH, estoH	سطح
room (hotel, etc.)	ghorfa, ghoraf;	غرفة
	ohDa, ohwaD	أوضة
rooster	deek, deyook	ديك
root (n)	gidr, godoor	جدر
rope	Habl, Hibaal	حبل
rosary	sibHa, sibaH	سبحة
rose	zahra, zuhoor	زهرة
rotten	baayeZ	بايظ
rough (not smooth)	kheshin	خشن
round (adj, spherical)	medawwar	مدوّر
round-trip	raayeH gayy	رايح جاي
route (n)	khaTT sair	خط سير
row (people, cars, soldiers, etc.)	Taboor, Tawabeer	طابور
royal	melooki	ملوكي
rubbish	zibaala	زبالة
ruby (n)	yaa'oot	ياقوت
rug	siggaada, sagageed	سجادة
ruin (financial, etc.)	kharaab	خراب
ruins (n)	aTlaal	أطلال
run (v, jog)	yegri	يجري
run (v, operate)	yedeer;	يدير
	yeshagh-ghal	يشغّل
rural	baladi;	بلدي
	qarawi	قروي
rush (v)	yesta'gil	يستعجل
Russia	rosia	روسيا
Russian	roosi, roos	روسي
rustic	reefi	ريفي

S

| sack (esp. jute) | shewaal, shewela | شوال |
| sacred | muqaddas | مقدّس |

sad	Hazeen; za9laan	حزين زعلان
saddle (n)	sarg, seroog	سرج
sadness	Hozn	حزن
safe (adj, not risky)	maDmoon	مضمون
safe (n, secure box)	khazna, khizann	خزنة
safety	salaama	سلامة
saffron	za9faraan	زعفران
sail (n)	shiraa9, shira9aat	شراع
sailor	baHHaar, baHHaara	بحّار
saint	qiddees, qiddeeseen	قديس
salad	salaTa, salaTaat	سلطة
salad dressing	tawaabil es-salaTa	توابل السلطة
salary	maheyya, maheyyaat	ماهيّة
sale (n, retail discount)	okazyon, okazyonaat	أوكازيون
sales representative	mandoob mabee9aat	مندوب مبيعات
salesman	bayyaa9, bayyaa9een	بياع
salt (n)	malH, amlaaH	ملح
salted fish (traditional)	feseekh	فسيخ
salty	Haadi'	حادق
same (adj)	dhaatuh	ذاته
sample (n, small example)	9ayyina, 9ayyinaat	عينة
sample (v, try)	yegarrab	يجرّب
sand (n)	raml	رمل
sanitary	SiHHi	صحّي
sarcophagus	taaboot Hagar	تابوت حجر
satellite	amar Senaa9i, a'maar Senaa9eyya	قمر صناعي
satisfaction	reDa	رضا
saucepan	kasarolla, kasarollaat	كسرولّة
Saudi Arabia	es-se9oodeyya	السعودية
Saudi Arabian	se9oodi, se9oodiyeen	سعودي
sausages	sogo'	سجق
savage	motawaHHish, motawaHHisheen	متوحّش
save (v, economize)	yewaffar	يوفّر
save (v, rescue)	yenqiz	ينقذ
say (v)	ye'ool	يقول
scalp (n)	farwit er-raas	فروة الرأس
scandal	feDeeHa, faDaayeH	فضيحة
scenery	manDHar, manaaDHir	منظر
school (n)	madrasa, madaaris	مدرسة

school of thought	mazhab, mazhaahib	مذهب
scientific	9elmi	علمي
scissors	ma'aSS, ma'aSSaat	مقص
scorpion	9a'raba, 9a'aarib	عقربة
scratch	kharboosh, kharabeesh	خربوش
scream (v)	yesarrakh	يصرخ
scribble (n)	shakhbooT, shakhabeeT	شخبوط
scuba diver	ghaTTaas, ghaTTaaseen	غطّاس
scuba diving (n)	ghaTs	غطس
sea	baHr	بحر
search (v)	yedawwar	يدوّر
seashore	shaTT el baHr	شطّ البحر
season (of year)	faSl, fuSool	فصل
season (of something)	moosim, mawaasim	موسم
season (v, add spices)	yetabbil	يتبّل
seat (n)	korsi, karaasi	كرسي
second (after first)	taani	ثان
second (n, time)	sanya, sawaani	ثانية
secret (adj)	sirri	سري
secret (n)	sirr, asraar	سر
secret policeman	mokhber, mokhbereen	مخبر
sect	mazhab, mazhaahib	مذهب
security (n)	amn	أمن
sedative	musakkin, musakkinaat	مسكّن
see (v)	yeshoof	يشوف
seed	bezra, bezr	بذرة
seizure (n, fit)	nohba, nohbaat	نوبة
select (v)	yekhtaar	يختار
selected (carefully)	na'aawa	نقاوة
sell (v)	yebee9	يبيع
selling	bey9	بيع
send	yeb9at	يبعث
sensibility	9a'l, 9o'ool	عقل
sensitive	Hassaas	حسّاس
sentence (court)	Hokm, aHkaam	حكم
sentence (grammar)	gomal, gomal	جملة
separately	koll waaHid lewaHdo	كل واحد لوحده
serial killer	saffaaH, saffaaHeen	سفّاح
serious	gadd	جدّ
service (n, favor)	khidma, khadamaat	خدمة
sesame paste	TeHeena	طحينة
session (in court, boardroom, clinic, etc.)	galsa, galasaat	جلسة

set (n, specific group)	*Ta'm, oT'um*	طقم
set (v, adjust)	*yezbuT*	يضبط
sex (gender)	*gins*	جنس
shade (n, from sun)	*Dill*	ظل
shadow	*khayaal*	خيال
shake (n)	*hazza, hazzaat*	هزّة
shame	*9eib, 9eyoob*	عيب
shape (n)	*shakl, ashkaal*	شكل
share (n, allocation, lot)	*naSeeb*	نصيب
shark	*(samakit) el 'ersh*	(سمكة) القرش
shave (v)	*yeHlaq*	يحلق
shaved head	*zalabaTTa*	زلبطة
sheep (flock)	*ghanam*	غنم
sheet (linen, etc.)	*milaaya, milayaat*	ملاءة
sheik	*sheikh, shuyookh*	شيخ
shelf	*raff, rofoof*	رف
sherbet	*sharbaat*	شربات
ship (n)	*safeena, sufun*	سفينة
shipment (n)	*shuHna, shuHnaat*	شحنة
shirt	*ameeS, omSaan*	قميص
shiver (n)	*ra9sha*	رعشة
shock (n)	*Sadma, Sadamaat*	صدمة
shoe	*gazma, gizam*	جزمة
shoelace	*robaaT eg-gazma*	رباط الجزمة
shop (n)	*maHall, maHallaat;*	محل
	dokkaan, dakakeen	دكّان
shopping mall	*mohl, mohlaat*	مول
short (opp. long/tall)	*oSayyar*	قصير
short (of something)	*naa'iS*	ناقص
shortfall	*9agz*	عجز
shot (from gun, etc.)	*Tal'a, Tala'aat*	طلقة
shoulder (n)	*kitf, ketaaf*	كتف
show (n)	*9arD, 9urooD*	عرض
show (v)	*yewarri;*	يورّي
	ye9riD	يعرض
shower (n)	*dush, edshaash*	دش
showing (visible)	*zhaahir*	ظاهر
shrimp	*gambareyyaya, gambari*	جمبري
shrine	*DareeH, aDreHa*	ضريح
shut (v)	*ye'fil*	يقفل
sick (person)	*9ayyaan, 9ayyaneen*	عيّان
side (n)	*naaHya, nawaaHi*	ناحية
sidewalk	*raSeef, erSefa*	رصيف

sign (n, display board)	yafTa, yofaT	يافطة
sign (n, mark)	9alaama, 9alamaat	علامة
signature	tawqee9, tawqee9aat	توقيع
Silence!	sekoot!	سكوت!
silk (n, adj)	Hareer	حرير
silliness	habal	هبل
silly	sakheef	سخيف
silver (adj)	faDDi	فضي
silver (n)	faDDa	فضة
similarity	tashaabuh	تشابه
simple	baseeT	بسيط
sing (v)	yeghanni	يغني
singer	moghanni, moghanniyeen	مغني
sink (n)	HowD, eHwaaD	حوض
sister	okht, ekhwaat	أخت
sit (v)	yo'-9od	يقعد
size (n, magnitude)	Hagm, aHgaam	حجم
size (S, M, L, etc.)	ma'aas	مقاس
skeleton	haikal 9azmi	هيكل عظمي
skewer	seekh, asyaakh	سيخ
skilled technician	fanni, fanniyeen	فني
skillful (adj)	Harreef, Harreefa	حريف
skimmed milk	laban khaali d-dassam	لبن خالي الدسم
skin (n)	geld, golood	جلد
skin rash	TafH geldi	طفح جلدي
skirt (n)	gunella, gunellaat;	جونلة
	jeeba, jeebaat	جيبة
skull	gomgoma, gamaagim	جمجمة
skullcap (traditional)	Ta'eyya, Tawaa'i	طاقية
sky	sama, samawaat	سماء
slacks (trousers)	banTalohn, banTalonaat	بنطلون
sleep (v)	yenaam	ينام
sleepy (adj)	na9saan, na9saneen	نعسان
sleeve (n)	komm, komaam	كم
slice (n)	teransh, teranshaat	ترنش
slip (v, lose footing)	yetzaH-la'	يتزحلق
slippers	shibshib, shabaashib	شبشب
slow (adj)	baTee'	بطيء
small	Soghayyar	صغير
smart (intelligent)	nebeeh, nobaha	نبيه
smartness (appearance)	wagaaha	وجاهة
smell (n, scent)	reeHa, rawaayeH	رائحة
smell (n, sense)	shamm	شم

smell (v)	*yeshimm*	يشم
smile (n)	*ibtisaama, ibtisaamaat*	ابتسامة
smoke (n)	*dokh-khaan*	دخان
smoke (v)	*yedakh-khan*	يدخّن
smooth (adj)	*naa9im*	ناعم
snake	*ti9baan, ta9abeen*	ثعبان
snare (n)	*fakh, fekhaakh*	فخّ
snooze (n)	*ta9seela*	تعسيلة
snoring	*shekheer*	شخير
snorkel (n)	*unboobit et-tanaffus*	أنبوبة التنفس
soap (n)	*Saboon*	صابون
soccer	*ek-kohra*	كرة القدم
socket (electric)	*kobs, ekbaas*	كبس
socks	*sharaab, sharabaat*	شراب
soda pop	*kazooza*	كازوزة
sofa	*kanaba, kanab*	كنبة
soft	*Tari*	طري
soldier	*9askari, 9asaakir*	عسكري
solution (n, answer)	*Hall, Hulool*	حل
solution (n, liquid)	*maHlool*	محلول
some	*shewayyit*	شوية
someone	*Hadd*	حد (أحد)
something	*Haaga, Hagaat*	حاجة
son	*ibn, welaad*	ابن
song	*ughneyya, aghaani*	أغنية
soon	*orayyib*	قريب
soot	*hibaab*	هباب
sore (adj)	*multahib*	ملتهب
sorrow	*Hasra*	حسرة
Sorry!	*aasif!*	آسف!
sound (n)	*Soht, aSwaat*	صوت
soup	*shorba*	شوربة
south	*ganoob*	جنوب
southern Egypt	*ibli*	قبلي
Spain	*asbania*	أسبانيا
spare parts	*qeTa9 gheyaar*	قطع غيار
sparrow	*9aSfoor, 9aSafeer*	عصفور
speak (v)	*yetkallim*	يتكلّم
speech (address)	*khoTba, khoTab*	خطبة
speed (n)	*sur9a, sur9aat*	سرعة
spices	*bohaaraat*	بهارات
spider	*9ankaboot, 9anaakib*	عنكبوت
spinach	*sabaanikh*	سبانخ

spirit (soul)	rohH, arwaaH	روح
sponge	safenga, safeng	سفنجة
spoon (n)	ma9la'a, ma9aali'	ملقة
sport (n)	riyaaDa	رياضة
spot (n, stain)	bu'9a, bu'a9	بقعة
spot (v, see)	yelmaH	يلمح
spring (season)	er-rabee9	الربيع
spring (in watch, etc.)	zambalik	زمبلك
spy (n)	gasoos, gawasees	جاسوس
square (geometric)	murabba9, murabba9aat	مربّع
square (in town)	meedaan, mayadeen	ميدان
stables	esTabl, esTablaat	اسطبل
stairs	sillim, salaalim	سلم
stake (e.g. wooden)	watad, awtaad	وتد
stamp (n, postage)	Taabi9 bosta, Tawaabi9 bosta	طابع بوسطة
stampede (n)	hohga, hohgaat	هوجة
stand (v, opp. sit)	yo'af	يقف
stand (n, stadium)	modarrag, modarragaat	مدرّج
standing	waa'if	واقف
star (n)	nigm, nugoom	نجم
start (v, begin)	yebtedi	يبتدي
start (v, motor, etc.)	yedawwar	يدوّر
state (n, country)	dawla, duwal	دولة
state (n, region)	wilaaya, wilaayaat	ولاية
static	saabit	ثابت
station (n, radio, train, etc.)	maHaTTa, maHaTTaat	محطّة
statue	timsaal, tamaseel	تمثال
status	waD9	وضع
stay (v)	yefDal	يفضل
steam	bokhaar	بخار
step (n)	khaTwa, khaTawaat	خطوة
steward(ess)	moDeef(a)	مضيفة
stitch	ghorza, ghoraz	غرزة
stock exchange	borSa	بورصة
stomach	baTn, boToon; me9da	بطن معدة
stone (n, fruit)	bezra, bezr	بذرة
stone (n, rock)	Hagar, Higaara	حجر
Stop!	bass!	بس١
store (n, shop)	maHall, maHallaat; dokkaan, dakakeen	محل دكّان

storm (n)	9aaSifa, 9awaaSif	عاصفة
story (n, tale)	qiSSa, qiSaS;	قصة
	Hekaaya, Hekayaat	حكاية
story (n, level in building)	dohr, edwaar	دور
straight ahead	doghri	دوغري
strange	ghareeb	غريب
stranger	ghareeb, ghoraba	غريب
straw	ash-sh	قش
strawberry	farawlaaya, farawla	فراولة
street	shaari9, shawaari9	شارع
street corner	naSya, nawaSee	ناصية
streetwise	naaSiH, nas-Heen	ناصح
strength	ewwa	قوة
stretcher	na'-'aala	نقّالة
string (cord)	khaiT, khuyooT	خيط
strong	shedeed;	شديد
	awi	قوي
stubborn	9inadi, 9inadeyyeen	عندي
student (n)	Taalib, Talaba	طالب
study (v, for a test)	yezaakir	يذاكر
(v, a subject)	yedris	يدرس
stupid	9abeeT, 9obT	عبيط
subject to	Hasab	حسب
submarine	ghawwaaSa, ghawwaaSaat	غواصة
suburb	DaHya, DawaaHi	ضاحية
succeed (v, opp. fail)	yengaH	ينجح
successful (passed exam)	naagiH, nagHeen	ناجح
Sudan	es-soodaan	السودان
Sudanese	soodaani, soodaaniyeen	سوداني
suddenly	fag'a	فجأة
sugar (n)	sukkar	سكر
suggestion	iqtiraaH, iqtiraaHaat	اقتراح
suicide	entiHaar	انتحار
suit (n, clothing)	badla, bidal	بدلة
suitable	munaasib	مناسب
suitcase	shanTa, shonaT	شنطة
sultan	sulTaan, salaTeen	سلطان
sum total	el-magmoo9	المجموع
summer	eS-Seif	الصيف
sun (n)	shams	شمس
sunburn (n)	Huroo' esh-shams	حروق الشمس
sunrise	esh-shoroo'	الشروق
sunset	el ghoroob	الغروب

sunstroke	*Darbit shams*	ضربة شمس
suppression	*kabt*	كبت
sure (of himself)	*waathiq (min nafso)*	واثق (من نفسه)
surface (area)	*mesaaHa, mesaaHaaat*	مساحة
surgery (n, operation)	*giraaHa*	جراحة
surprise (n)	*mofag'a, mofag'aat*	مفاجأة
swallow (v)	*yebla9*	يبلع
sweat	*9ara'*	عرق
sweet	*Hilw*	حلو
sweet potato	*baTaTaaya, baTaaTa*	بطاطا
swelling	*entifaakh; iltihaab*	انتفاخ التهاب
swim (v)	*ye9oom*	يعوم
swindler	*naSSaab, naSSaabeen*	نصاب
swing (n, children's, etc.)	*morgeiHa, marageeH*	مرجيحة
swollen	*multahib*	ملتهب
Syrian	*shaami*	شامي
Syrian people	*shawaam*	شوام
syringe (n)	*Huqna, Huqan*	حقنة
system	*niDHaam, anDHima*	نظام

T

T-shirt	*fanella, fanellaat*	فانلّة
table	*tarabeyza, tarabeyzaat*	ترابيزة
tablet (pill)	*orS, e'raaS*	قرص
tailor (n)	*tarzi, tarzeyya*	ترزي
take (v)	*yaakhud*	يأخذ
talk (v)	*yetkallim*	يتكلّم
tall	*Taweel*	طويل
tank (reservoir)	*khazzaan, khazzanaat*	خزان
tank (military)	*dabbaaba, dabbabaat*	دبّابة
tar	*zift*	زفت
taste (n, sense)	*estiT9aam*	استطعام
taste (style)	*zoh', azwaa'*	ذوق
tasty	*lazeez*	لذيذ
tattoo	*washm*	وشم
tax (n)	*Dareeba, Daraayeb*	ضريبة
tea (n)	*shaay*	شاي
teach (v)	*ye9allim*	يعلم
teacher	*modarris, modarriseen; ostaaz, asatza*	مدرّس أستاذ
team	*fer'a, fera'*	فرقة

tear (v, cut)	ye'aTTa'	يقطّع
tear (n, from eye)	dam9a, dumoo9	دمعة
teenager	muraahiq, murahqeen	مراهق
tell (v)	ye'ool	يقول
teller	Sarraaf, Sarrafeen	صرّاف
temperature	daraget el Haraara	درجة الحرارة
temple	ma9bad, ma9aabid	معبد
temporary	moowa'-'at	مؤقت
tenant (n)	musta'gir, musta'gireen	مستأجر
tent	kheima, kheyam	خيمة
terrace (balcony)	balakohna, balakohnaat	بلكونة
terrible	faDHee9	فظيع
terrific	haayel	هايل
test (n)	ikhtibaar, ikhtibaraat	اختبار
testimony	shahaada, shahadaat	شهادة
textile	naseeg	نسيج
thankful (adj)	shaakir, shakreen	شاكر
that (masc./fem.)	dah/dee	ده/دي
theater (plays, etc.)	masraH, masaariH	مسرح
theft	ser'a, ser'aat	سرقة
theoretical	nazari	نظري
therapy	9ilaag	علاج
there	hinaak	هناك
thermometer	termometr	ترمومتر
these	dool	دول
thick	sameek	سميك
thief	Haraami, Harameyya	حرامي
thigh	fakhd, fekhaad;	فخذ
	wirk, weraak	ورك
thin	rofayya9	رفيع
thing	Haaga, Hagaat	حاجة
think (v, consider)	yefakkar	يفكّر
think (v, assume)	yeftekir	يفتكر
thirsty	9atshaan	عطشان
this (masc./fem.)	dah/di	ده/دي
thorns (rose, etc.)	shohk	شوك
thoroughbred	aSeel	أصيل
those	dool	دول
thread (n)	fatla, fitall	فتلة
throat	zohr	زور
throne	9arsh, 9oroosh	عرش
throw	yermi	يرمي
throw out (v)	yeTrud	يطرد

thunder	ra9d	رعد
thyme	za9tar	زعتر
ticket (n)	tazkara, tazaakir	تذكرة
tidy (adj, organized)	metsaawi	متساو
tie (n, neck)	karavatta, karavattaat	كرافتة
tie (v)	yerbuT	يربط
tiger	nimr, nomoor	نمر
tight (narrow)	Dayya'	ضيق
tights	kolohn, kolohnaat	كولونات
tile	balaaTa, balaaT	بلاطة
tiller (of the soil)	fellaaH, fellaHeen	فلاح
time (of day)	wa't, aw'aat	وقت
time (era, etc.)	zaman	زمن
a long time ago	(min) zamaan	(من) زمان
tip (n, gratuity)	ikrameyya, ikrameyyaat	إكرامية
tire (v)	yet9ab	يتعب
tire (n, vehicle)	fardit kawitch	فردة كاوتش
tired (adj)	ta9baan	تعبان
today	ennaharda	النهاردة
toe	Sobaa9 rigl, Sawaabi9 rigl	صباع رجل
together (adj)	ma9a ba9D	مع بعض
tomato	TamaaTim; ooTa	طماطم؛ أوطة
tomato sauce	SalSit TamaaTim	صلصة طماطم
tomb	maqbara, maqaabir	مقبرة
tomorrow	bokra	بكرة
tongue	lisaan, lesena	لسان
tonight	el-leila	الليلة
tools	9idda	عدّة
tooth	sinna, senaan	سنة
topic (n, subject)	mawDoo9, mawaDee9	موضوع
torpedo (n)	Torbeed, Tarabeed	طوربيد
torture (n)	9azaab	عذاب
touch (n)	lams	لمس
touch (v)	yelmis	يلمس
tough	shedeed	شديد
tour (n)	gawla, gawlaat	جولة
tour (v, visit)	yaakhod gawla	ياخد جولة
tourist (n)	saayiH, suyyaaH	سائح
tow (v)	yegorr	يجرّ
towards	naHyit	ناحية
towel	fooTa, fowaT	فوطة
tower	burg, ebraag	برج

toy	le9ba, le9ab	لعبة
track (lane)	darb, doroob	درب
track suit	treng, trengaat	ترنج
tractor	garraar, garraaraat	جرّار
trader	taagir, tuggaar	تاجر
traditional (adj)	taqleedi	تقليدي
traditions (customs)	taqaaleed	تقاليد
traffic (n, cars, etc.)	muroor	مرور
train (n)	aTr, oTora	قطار
train (v)	yetmarran	يتمرّن
traitor	khaayin, khayneen	خاين
transfer (n, money, etc.)	taHweel, taHweelaat	تحويل
transfer (v, money, etc.)	yeHawwil	يحوّل
transform	yeHawwil	يحوّل
translation	targama	ترجمة
translator	torgoman, torgomanaat	ترجمان
transparent	shaffaaf	شفّاف
transportation (goods, etc.)	en-na'l	النقل
trap (n)	fakh, fekhaakh	فخّ
trash (n)	zibaala	زبالة
trash can	SafeeHit zibaala	صفيحة زبالة
trash dump	mazbala, mazaabil	مزبلة
trashy	9ifish	عفش
travel (n)	safar	سفر
travel (v)	yesaafir	يسافر
travelers' checks	sheekaat seyaaHeyya	شيكات سياحية
tray	Seneyya, Sawaani	صينية
treacherous	ghaddaar	غدّار
treasure	kenz, konooz	كنز
treat (v, behave towards)	ye9aamil	يعامل
tree	shagara, shagar	شجرة
tremor	hazza, hazzaat	هزّة
trend	dhaahira, dhawaahir	ظاهرة
triangle	muthallath, muthallathaat	مثلّث
tribe	qabeela, qabaayel	قبيلة
trill	zaghrooTa, zaghareeT	زغرودة
trip (n, journey)	reHla, reHlaat	رحلة
trip (v, stumble)	yetshankil	يتشنكل
tripe	kersha	كرشة
trotters (cow, sheep, etc.)	kawaari9	كوارع
troubles (n)	mataa9ib	متاعب
trousers	banTalohn, banTalonaat	بنطلون

truck	lori, lawaari	لوري
true	Ha'ee'i	حقيقي
truncheon	nabboot, nababeet	نبّوت
trunk (box)	Sandoo', Sanadee'	صندوق
trust (v)	yathiq	يثق
try (v, sample)	yegarrab	يجرّب
try (v, make effort)	yeHaawil	يحاول
tube (n)	masoora, mawaseer	ماسورة
tumor	waram, awraam	ورم
tune	laHn, alHaan;	لحن
	nagham, anghaam	نغم
Tunis(ia)	toonis	تونس
Tunisian	tonsi, tawansa	تونسي
tunnel (n)	nafa', anfaa'	نفق
turkey	deek roomi, deyook roomi	ديك رومي
Turkey	torkeya	تركيا
turn (n, have a go)	dohr, edwaar	دور
turn (v, go around)	yedoor;	يدور
	yeliff	يلفّ
turn (v, transform)	yeHawwil	يحوّل
twins	taw'am, tawaa'im	توأم
type (n, variant)	now9, anwaa9;	نوع
	Sanf, aSnaaf	صنف

U

U.S.	amreeka	أمريكا
ulcer	qurHa	قرحة
ultimate (adj)	aakher	آخر
umbrella	shamseyya, shamaasi	شمسية
unable	mish 'aadir	مش قادر
unbearable	laa yuTaaq	لا يطاق
unbelievable	mish ma9ool	مش معقول
uncertain	mish akeed	مش أكيد
uncle (maternal)	khaal, khilaan	خال
uncle (paternal)	9amm, 9imaam	عمّ
unclothed	9iryaan, 9iryaneen	عريان
uncomfortable	mish mureeH	مش مريح
uncommon	gheir 9aadi	غير عادي
unconscious	moghma 9aleih	مغمى عليه
uncover (v)	yekshif	يكشف
undecided	mela'la'	ملألأ
under (prep)	taHt	تحت
undergraduate	Taalib gam9a	طالب جامعة

understand (v)	*yefham*	يفهم
undertaker	*Hanuti, Hanuteyya*	حانوتي
unemployed	*9aaTil, 9aTleen*	عاطل
unemployment (n)	*biTaala*	بطالة
unexpected (adj)	*mofaagi'*	مفاجئ
unfortunate	*ghalbaan, ghalaaba*	غلبان
unhappy	*za9laan*	زعلان
unhealthy	*mish SiHHi*	مش صحّي
uniform (women and children)	*maryala, maraayil*	مريلة
unintelligent	*ghabi*	غبي
United Nations	*el umam el muttaHida*	الأمم المتحدة
United States	*el wilaayaat el muttaHida*	الولايات المتحدة
university	*gam9a, gam9aat*	جامعة
university degree	*shahaada gaame9eyya*	شهادة جامعية
unknown (adj)	*mag-hool*	مجهول
unlucky (adj)	*9aleel el bakht*	قليل البخت
unofficial	*mish rasmi*	مش رسمي
unreal	*wahmi*	وهمي
unreasonable	*mish ma9ool*	مش معقول
unstable (wobbly)	*melakh-lakh*	ملخلخ
unsuitable	*mish munaasib*	مش مناسب
unsupervised	*bedoon riqaaba*	بدون رقابة
until (prep)	*leghaayet*	لغاية
up	*foh'*	فوق
upfront payment	*mo'addam*	مقدّم
Upper Egypt	*eS-Se9eed*	الصعيد
Upper Egyptian	*Se9eedi, Sa9ayda*	صعيدي
uprising	*intifaaDa*	انتفاضة
upset	*za9laan*	زعلان
urban (adj)	*madani*	مدني
urine	*bohl*	بول
use (v)	*yesta9mil*	يستعمل
use-by date	*eS-SalaaHeyya*	الصلاحية
useful	*mufeed*	مفيد

V

vacancies (in hotel)	*ghoraf khaalya*	غرف خالية
vacate (v)	*yekhlee*	يخلي
vacation	*agaza, agazaat*	أجازة
vaccination	*taT9eem*	تطعيم
vain	*maghroor*	مغرور

validity	SalaaHeyya	صلاحية
valley	waadi, widyaan	واد
value	eema	قيمة
vanish (v)	yekhtefi	يختفي
varnish	warneesh	ورنيش
veal	(laHma) betello	(لحم) بتللو
vegetables	khuDaar	خضار
vegetarian	nabaati, nabaatiyeen	نباتي
veil (n, full face)	niqaab	نقاب
veil (n, headscarf)	Higaab	حجاب
vein (anatomy)	wareed, awrida;	وريد
	9ir', 9oroo'	عرق
velvet	aTeefa	قطيفة
ventilation	tahweya	تهوية
verbal	shafawi	شفوي
vermicelli (pasta)	shi9reyya	شعرية
vertical	9amoodi;	عامودي
	ra'si	رأسي
very (big)	(kebeer) khaaliS	(كبير) خالص
very much	awi	قوي
vest	fanella, fanellaat	فانلة
veterinary	beTari	بيطري
vibration	zabzaba, zabzabaat	ذبذبة
view (n, opinion)	ra'yy, aaraa'	رأي
vigilant	meSaH-SaH	مصحصح
vigor	9afia	عافية
village	qarya, quraa	قرية
villager	qarawi, qarawiyeen	قروي
vinegar	khall	خل
violent	9aneef	عنيف
violin	kamanga, kamangaat	كمنجة
virtuous	SaaliH, SaliHeen;	صالح
	faaDil, afaaDil	فاضل
visa	ta'sheera, ta'sheeraat	تأشيرة
visible	baayin	باين
visit (n, trip)	zeyaara, zeyaraat	زيارة
visit (v)	yezoor	يزور
voice (n)	Soht, aSwaat	صوت
void (adj, invalid)	baaTil	باطل
voluntary	tatawwu9i	تطوعي
volunteer (n)	met-Tawwa9, met-Tawwa9een	متطوع
vomit (v)	yestafragh	يستفرغ
voyage	reHla, reHlaat	رحلة

W

wages (payment)	*maheyya, maheyyaat*	ماهية
waist	*wisT*	وسط
wait (v)	*yestanna*	يستنى
waiter (restaurant)	*garsoon, garsonaat*	جرسون
waiter (in the home)	*sofragi, sofrageyya*	سفرجي
wake up (v)	*yesHa*	يصحى
walk (v)	*yemshi*	يمشي
walk behind	*yemshi wara*	يمشي وراء
walk towards	*yemshi naHyit*	يمشي ناحية
walking	*mashyy*	مشي
walking stick	*9okkaaz, 9okkazaat*	عكاز
wall	*HeiTa, HeTaan*	حيطة
wall socket	*bareeza, barayyiz*	بريزة
wallet	*maHfaza, maHaafiz*	محفظة
want (v)	*ye9ooz*	يعوز
war	*Harb, Horoob*	حرب
(go to) war against	*yeHaarib*	يحارب
ward (hospital)	*9anbar, 9anaabir*	عنبر
warm (adj)	*daafi*	دافئ
warmth (kindness)	*Hanaan*	حنان
warning (n, caution)	*inzhaar, inzharaat*	تحذير
warranty	*Damaan*	ضمان
wash (v)	*yeghsil*	يغسل
washing dishes	*tashTeeb SoHoon*	تشطيب صحون
washing line	*Habl ghaseel*	حبل غسيل
washing machine	*ghassaalit hodoom*	غسالة هدوم
watch (n, wrist)	*saa9it yad*	ساعة
watch (v, observe)	*yeraa'ib*	يراقب
watchman	*ghafeer, ghafar*	غفير
water	*mayya*	مياه
water buffalo	*gamoosa, gawamees*	جاموسة
water pipe	*sheesha, sheyash*	شيشة
water spring	*9ein, 9uyoon*	عين
waterfall	*shallaal, shallalaat*	شلال
watermelon	*baTTeekha, baTTeekh*	بطيخ
wave (n, in sea, fashion, etc.)	*moga, mowg*	موجة
wave (v, with hand)	*yeshaawir*	يشاور
wax (n)	*sham9*	شمع
way (n, method)	*Taree'a, Turu'*	طريقة
WC	*dort el mayyah*	دورة المياه
weak	*Da9eef*	ضعيف

wealthy	*ghani*	غني
weapon	*silaaH, asliHa*	سلاح
wear (v)	*yelbis*	يلبس
weather (n)	*gaww*	جو
wedding party	*faraH, afraaH*	فرح
wedding procession	*zaffa*	زفة
wedding ring	*dibla, dibal*	دبلة
week	*osboo9, asaabee9*	أسبوع
weekly	*osboo9i*	أسبوعي
weeping	*9yaaT*	عياط
weight (n)	*wazn, awzaan*	وزن
welcome (n)	*tarHeeb*	ترحيب
You're welcome!	*9afwan!*	عفوا!
well (health, etc.)	*kewaiyis, kewaiyiseen*	كويس
well (n, water, oil)	*beer, aabaar*	بئر
Well done!	*biraavo 9aleik!*	برافو عليك!
well-done (cooking)	*mestewi*	مستوي
well-dressed	*sheek*	شيك
wellbeing	*9afia*	عافية
west	*gharb*	غرب
wet (adj)	*mablool*	مبلول
whale	*Hoot, Hitaan*	حوت
what?	*eih?*	إيه؟
wheat	*amH*	قمح
wheel	*9agala, 9agal*	عجلة
when?	*emta?*	امتى؟
where?	*fein?*	فين؟
which?	*anhi?*	أنهي؟
whisked (in blender)	*maDroob bil-khallaaT*	مضروب بالخلاط
whispering (n)	*hams*	همس
whistle (n)	*Soffaara, Safafeer*	صفارة
white	*abyaD*	أبيض
who?	*meen?*	مين؟
whole	*kaamil*	كامل
wholesale	*gumla*	جملة
wholesale price	*si9r eg-gomla*	سعر الجملة
whooping cough (n)	*so9aal deeki*	سعال ديكي
why?	*leih?*	ليه؟
wide	*9areeD;*	عريض
	waasi9	واسع
widow	*armala, araamil*	أرملة
widower	*armal, araamil*	أرمل
wife	*meraat, merataat*	(زوجة) مرات

wild (adj, savage)	*mutawaHHish*	متوحش
will (auxiliary verb)	*Ha...*	ح ...
will (n, inheritance)	*weSeyya, waSaaya*	وصية
win (v)	*yeksab*	يكسب
winch (n)	*winsh, ewnaash*	ونش
wind (n)	*reeH, reeyaaH*	ريح
wind instrument	*zommaara, zamameer*	زمّارة
windmill	*TaaHoona, TawaHeen*	طاحونة
window	*shibbaak, shababeek*	شبّاك
windscreen	*ezaaz oddamaani*	إزاز قدّاماني
wine	*nebeet*	نبيذ
wing (n)	*ginaaH, gineHa*	جناح
winter	*esh-sheta*	الشتاء
wipe (v)	*yemsaH*	يمسح
wire	*silk, aslaak*	سلك
wireless	*laselki*	لاسلكي
wish (n)	*umniya, amaani*	أمنية
with	*bi...;*	ب ...؛
	ma9	مع
withdraw (v, cash, etc.)	*yesHab*	يسحب
within (prep)	*khilaal*	خلال
witness	*shaahid, shohood*	شاهد
woman	*sitt, sittaat*	ست
womb	*raHim, arHaam*	رحم
won't...	*mish Ha...*	مش ح ...
wonderful	*9ageeb*	عجيب
wood (n, timber)	*khashab, akh-shaab*	خشب
wooden bench	*dikka, dikak*	دكّة
wool	*Soof, aSwaaf*	صوف
word	*kelma, kalaam*	كلمة
work (n, job)	*9amal*	عمل
working (operational)	*shagh-ghaal*	شغّال
workshop	*warsha, wirash*	ورشة
world	*donia;*	دنيا
	9aalam	عالم
worm	*dooda, dood*	دودة
worry (n)	*hamm*	همّ
worse; worst	*awHash*	أوحش
worth (n)	*eema*	قيمة
wound (n)	*garH, gorooH*	جرح
wrap (v)	*yeliff*	يلفّ
wrapped parcel	*laffa, lifaf*	لفّة
wreckage	*HuTaam*	حطام

wristwatch	saa9it yad	ساعة يد
write (v)	yektib	يكتب
writer	kaatib, kottaab	كاتب
wrong (adj)	ghalaT	غلط

X/Y/Z

x-ray	ashe99it eks	أشعة اكس
yacht	yakht, yukhoot	يخت
yarn (n, thread)	ghazl	غزل
year	sana, seneen	سنة
yearly	sanawi	سنوي
yeast	khameera	خميرة
yelling (in anger)	shakhT	شخط
Yemen	el yaman	اليمن
Yemeni	yamani, yamaniyeen	يمني
yes	aywah	أيوه
yes (I will)	HaaDir	حاضر
yesterday	embaariH	إمبارح
yogurt	zabaadi	زبادي
young (adj)	Soghayyar fis-sinn	صغير في السن
young man	gada9, gid9aan	جدع
youth hostel	beit esh-shabaab	بيت الشباب
youths; youthfulness	shabaab	شباب
zebra	Homaar waHshi, Himeer waHsheyya	حمار وحشي
zero	Sifr, eSfaar	صفر
zipper	sosta, sosat	سوستة
zoo	geneinet el Hayawaanaat	جنينة الحيوانات
zucchini	kohsaaya, kohsa	كوسة

Arabic-English Dictionary

This Arabic-English dictionary is arranged in alphabetical order according to the *Egyptian pronunciation*. This is to enable you to look up a word that you hear and find its English meaning. The pronunciation reflects what you will actually hear to make it easier for you to find a particular word.

Notes for using the dictionary:

- Emphatic and non-emphatic letters (see page 8) are alphabetized together to make it easier for you to identify words. For example, **d** (د) and **D** (ض).

- Words beginning with **9ein** (ع, see page 8) appear in a separate section at the end of the dictionary.

- Words beginning with **kh** (خ) appear under **k**; words beginning with **gh** (غ) appear under **g**.

- The plural is shown after the singular, e.g.

    beit, beyoot   *house*

- Verbs are listed in the present tense, third person masculine singular ("he" form), e.g.

    yezoor   *visit (v)*

- The Arabic script is included to improve your reading skills, or to confirm the word with a native speaker.

- The definite article **el** (*the*) is ignored for the purposes of alphabetization.

A

a'ell	less (fewer); least	أقل
a9la	higher	أعلى
a9maa, 9imyaan	blind (adj, sightless)	أعمى
aadaab	literature	آداب
aaDi, qudaah	judge (n)	قاض
aakher	end (n); last (adj); most recent	آخر
aala, aalaat	instrument	آلة
aalaam el waD9	labor pains	آلام الوضع
aarib en-nagaah, awaarib en-nagaah	lifeboat	قارب النجاة
aasif!	Sorry!	آسف!
aathaar	monuments	آثار
ab	father	أب
ab wi-omm	parents	أب وأم
abadan	never; ever (adv)	أبدا
abawi	paternal	أبوي
abl	before	قبل
abreel	April	أبريل
abu	father of	أبو
abyaD	white	أبيض
adaan	call for prayer	آذان
adab	politeness	أدب
adam, a'daam	foot	قدم
adeem	old (object)	قديم
aDeyya, aDaaya	case (n, court)	قضية
afaS, e'faaS	cage; wicker basket	قفص
affaaq, affaaqeen	imposter	أفاق
afghaani, afghaan	Afghan (adj)	أفغاني
afghaanistaan	Afghanistan	أفغانستان
agaza, agazaat	vacation; holiday	أجازة
aghlabeyya	majority	أغلبية
agnabi, agaanib	foreigner	أجنبي
agzakhaana, agzakhanaat	pharmacy	أجزخانة
aHmar shafaayef	lipstick	أحمر شفايف
aHsan	better; best	أحسن
ahwa	coffee (beverage)	قهوة
akbar	bigger; elder	أكبر
akeed	certainly	أكيد
akh, ekhwaat	brother	أخ
akhDar zatooni	olive-green color	أخضر زيتوني
akl	food	أكل

aktar	more; most	أكثر
al9a	castle; citadel; fortress	قلعة
ala'	concern; anxiety	قلق
alam, a'laam	pen	قلم
alam roSaaS	pencil	قلم رصاص
alam, aalaam	pain; ache (n)	ألم
alb, oloob	heart	قلب
allaah	God	الله
almaaz, almaazaat	diamonds	الماس
amar, a'maar	moon	قمر
amar Senaa9i, a'maar Senaa9eyya	satellite	قمر صناعي
amari	lunar	قمري
ameer, umara	emir; prince	أمير
ameera, ameeraat	princess	أميرة
ameeS, omSaan	shirt	قميص
amH	wheat	قمح
amn	security (n)	أمن
amraaD nisa	gynecology	أمراض نسا
amreeka	U.S.A.; America	أمريكا
amreekaani	American	أمريكاني
andeel el baHr	jellyfish	قنديل البحر
anhi?	which?	أنهي ؟
anteeka	antique	أنتيكا
aqrab el aqribaa'	next of kin	أقرب الأقرباء
aqSaa	maximum	أقصى
aragohz, aragozaat	puppet	أراجوز
araq	insomnia	أرق
arD, araaDi	land (n)	أرض
arDeyya, arDeyyaat	floor (n)	أرضية
areeb, araayeb	relative (n, family)	قريب
armal, araamil	widower	أرمل
armala, araamil	widow	أرملة
armann	Armenians	أرمن
arn, oroon	horn (bull, etc.)	قرن
arnab, araanib	rabbit	أرنب
arnabeeT	cauliflower	قرنبيط
asaas, asasaat	base (n, foundation)	أساس
asaasi	essential; basic	أساسي
asanseyr, asanseyraat	elevator	أسانسير
asbania	Spain	أسبانيا
aSd	intention; aim	قصد
aSeel	thoroughbred	أصيل

ash-sh	straw; hay	قش
ash'ar	blonde (adj)	أشقر
ashe99it eks	x-ray	أشعة اكس
ashwal	left-handed	أشول
aSla9	bald	أصلع
aSli	original; authentic	أصلي
asmant	cement	أسمنت
aSr, oSoor	palace	قصر
assees, osos	priest (Christian)	قسّيس
aTeefa	velvet	قطيفة
athar, aathaar	relic	أثر
aTlaal	ruins (n)	أطلال
aTr, oTora	train (n)	قطار
aTrash	deaf	أطرش
aw	or	أو
awHash	worse; worst	أوحش
awi	strong; very much	قوي
awwil	first	أول
ayma, awaayem	menu; list (n)	قائمة
ayqoona, ayqoonaat	icon	أيقونة
ayy	any	أي
aywah	yes	أيوه
ayy Haaga	anything	أي حاجة
ayy Hadd	anybody	أي حد
ayy Hetta	anywhere	أي حتة
azma, azamaat	crisis	أزمة
azra'	blue	أزرق
azra' samaawi	azure (sky blue)	أزرق سماوي

B

b ...	with ...	ب...
ba'-'aal, ba'-'aleen	grocer	بقّال
ba'ara, ba'ar	cow	بقرة
ba'doonis	parsley	بقدونس
ba9d	after (prep)	بعد
ba9d eD-Duhr	afternoon (n)	بعد الظهر
baab, bebaan	door	باب
baarid	cold (adj)	بارد
baariz	embossed; protruding	بارز
baaTil	void (adj, invalidated)	باطل
baayeZ	rotten; broken down (not working)	بايظ
baayin	visible; apparent	باين

badal	instead of	بدل
badawi	bedouin	بدوي
badla, bidal	suit (n, clothing)	بدلة
badr	full moon	بدر
badri	early	بدري
baghbaghaan, baghbaghanaat	parrot	بغبغان
baghdaad	Baghdad	بغداد
baghl, beghaal	mule	بغل
baHari	marine (adj); North facing	بحري
baHHaar, baHHaara	sailor	بحّار
baHr	sea	بحر
el baHreyn	Bahrain	البحرين
baHreyni	Bahraini	بحريني
bahtaan	pale (adj)	بهتان
bakabort, bakabortaat	manhole	بكابورت
bakh-khaakha, bakh-khakhaat	spray nozzle	بخاخة
bakheel, bokhala	miserly; miser	بخيل
bakht	luck	بخت
bakistaan	Pakistan	باكستان
bakistaani, bakistaniyyeen	Pakistani	باكستاني
balaaTa, balaaT	tile	بلاطة
baladi	provincial; rural	بلدي
balaHa, balaH	date (fruit)	بلحة
balakohna, balakohnaat	balcony; terrace	بلكونة
ballaa9a, balla9aat	drain	بلاعة
ballohna, ballohnaat	balloon	بالونة
balTa, bolaT	axe	بلطة
balTo, balaaTi	coat (clothing)	بالطو
balwa, balaawi	calamity	بلوة
bamya	okra	بامية
banafsegi	purple	بنفسجي
banafsegi faateH	lavender (n, color)	بنفسجي فاتح
bangar	beetroot	بنجر
bankeryaas	pancreas	بنكرياس
banTalohn, banTalonaat	pants; trousers	بنطلون
banzeen	gas; petrol (cars, etc.)	بنزين
bar'	lightning	برق
baraka, barakaat	blessing	بركة
bard	cold (weather or illness)	برد

baree'	innocent (adj, not guilty)	بريء
bareed	mail (n, post)	بريد
bareed gawwi	airmail (n)	بريد جوي
bareeza, barayyiz	wall socket	بريزة
barghoot, baragheet	flea	برغوث
barlamaan	parliament	برلمان
barmeel, barameel	barrel	برميل
barra	outside	بره
barraani	exterior	براني
barri	overland	بري
barTamaan, barTamanaat	jar	برطمان
baSala, baSal	onion	بصل
baseeT	simple	بسيط
baskohta, baskoht	biscuit	بسكوت
bass	but; only	بس
bass!	Stop!; Enough!	بس!
bastelya	lozenge (pastille)	بستيلية
baTal, abTaal	hero	بطل
baTaTaaya, baTaaTa	sweet potato	بطاطا
baTaTsaaya, baTaaTis	potato	بطاطس
baTee'	slow (adj)	بطيء
baTn, boToon	stomach; abdomen	بطن
baTTa, baTT	duck (n)	بطة
baTTaneyya, baTaTeen	blanket	بطانية
baTTareyya, baTTareyyaat	battery	بطارية
baTTeekha, baTTeekh	watermelon	بطيخ
bawwaaba, bawwabaat	gate	بوابة
bayaan mufaSSal	detailed statement	بيان مفصل
bayaDaat	linen (sheets, etc.)	بياضات
bayyaa9, bayyaa9een	salesman	بياع
be'aala, be'alaat	grocery	بقالة
be9eed	far	بعيد
bebalaash	complimentary; free (adj, gratis)	ببلاش
bedoon riqaaba	unsupervised	بدون رقابة
bee'a, bee'aat	environment; habitat	بيئة
beer, aabaar	well (n, water, oil)	بئر
beera	beer	بيرة
beeroqraTeyya	bureaucracy	بيروقراطية
beiDa, beiD	egg	بيضة

bein	between	بين
beit esh-shabaab	youth hostel	بيت الشباب
beit fakhm, buyoot fakhma	mansion	بيت فخم
beit kalb, buyoot kilaab	kennel (n, dog)	بيت كلب
beit laHm	Bethlehem	بيت لحم
beit, beyoot	house; home	بيت
beiti	homemade	بيتي
bel-9afia	by force	بالعافية
belaaj, belajaat	beach	بلاج
beleela	milk and cereal dish (traditional)	بليلة
bernaamig, baraamig	program	برنامج
besella	peas	بسلة
beskeletta, beskelettaat	bicycle	بسكيتة
betaa9i	mine (belonging to me)	بتاعي
beta9na	ours	بتاعنا
betaa9 i'faal	locksmith	بتاع أقفال
betaa9 el kheil	equestrian (adj)	بتاع الخيل
beTaana	lining (coats, etc.)	بطانة
beTari	veterinary	بيطري
betingaan	eggplant	بتنجان
betrohl	petrol	بترول
bey9	selling	بيع
beZ-ZabT	precisely	بالظبط
bezra, bezr	seed; stone (fruit)	بذرة
bi-lughatein	bilingual	بلغتين
bil-9arD	across (sideways)	بالعرض
bilooza, biloozaat	blouse	بلوزة
bint, banaat	girl; daughter	بنت
bint akh	niece (daughter of brother)	بنت أخ
bint okht	niece (daughter of sister)	بنت أخت
biraavo 9aleik!	Well done!	برافو عليك!
biriTaani, biriTaaneyyeen	British (adj)	بريطاني
biriTaanya	Britain	بريطانيا
birka, birak	pool (n, pond, etc.)	بركة
biTaala	unemployment (n)	بطالة
biZ-Zabt	exactly	بالضبط
bo', eb'aa'	mouth	بق
bodra	powder	بودرة

bofteik	beef steak	بفتيك
boharaat	spices	بهارات
bohl	urine	بول
bokhaar	steam	بخار
bokra	tomorrow	بكرة
el bolees	the police	البوليس
boleeSit shaHn	bill of lading	بوليصة شحن
boleeSit ta'meen	insurance policy	بوليصة تأمين
boltTi	a Nile fish	بلطي
bonboni	candy	بنبوني
bonni	brown	بنّي
booma, boom	owl	بومة
booSa, booS	bamboo cane	بوصة
booSa, booSaat	inch	بوصة
booya, booyaat	paint	بوية
borneiTa, baraneeT	hat	برنيطة
borS, ebraaS	gecko	برص
borSa	stock exchange	بورصة
bosa, bohs	kiss	بوسة
bosTa	mail (n, post)	بوسطة
bu'9a, bu'a9	spot (n, stain)	بقعة
buHeira, buHeiraat	lake	بحيرة
bukhoor	incense (aromatic products)	بخور
bunn	coffee (beans)	بنّ
burg, ebraag	tower	برج
burhaan, baraheen	proof	برهان
burtu'aani	orange (adj, color)	برتقالي
burtu'ana, burtu'aan	orange (n, fruit)	برتقال

D

da'n, do'oon	chin; beard	ذقن
Da9eef	weak	ضعيف
da9wa, da9waat	invitation; calling	دعوة
daa' es-ser'a	kleptomania	داء السرقة
daafi	warm (adj)	دافئ
Daanee Soghayyar	lamb (meat)	ضاني صغير
ed-daar el beyDa	Casablanca	الدار البيضاء
Daayi9, Day9een	lost (adj)	ضائع
Dab9, Debo9a	hyena	ضبع
Dabaab	fog	ضباب
dabbaaba, dabbabaat	tank (military)	دبابة
dabboor, dababeer	hornet	دبور

dabboos, dababees	*pin (n)*	دبوس
Daffa, Defaaf	*river bank*	ضفّة
daffaaya, daffayaat	*heater (domestic)*	دفاية
daftar, dafaatir	*register; logbook*	دفتر
daggaal, daggaleen	*impostor*	دجال
DaghT, DoghooT	*pressure*	ضغط
dah	*this/that (masc.)*	ده
dahab	*gold (n)*	ذهب
Dahr, Duhoor	*back (n)*	ظهر
dahya, dawaahi	*calamity*	داهية
DaHya, DawaaHi	*suburb*	ضاحية
dakar, dukora	*male*	ذكر
dakheel, dukhalaa'	*intruder*	دخيل
dakhl	*income*	دخل
Dakhm	*massive*	ضخم
daleel siyaaHee	*guidebook (travel)*	دليل سياحي
dalma	*dark (unlit); darkness*	ظلمة
dam9a, dumoo9	*tear (n, from eye)*	دمعة
Damaan	*warranty*	ضمان
Dameer, Damaayer	*conscience*	ضمير
damm	*blood (n)*	دم
dantella	*lace (n)*	دنتلة
darabokka	*drum (traditional)*	دربكة
darabzeen, darabzeenaat	*banister*	درابزين
daraga, daragaat	*degree; extent*	درجة
daraget el Haraara	*temperature*	درجة الحرارة
Darar	*harm (n)*	ضرر
darb, doroob	*track; lane*	درب
Darba qaaDeyya	*knockout (n, in boxing)*	ضربة قاضية
darbaka	*chaos; kerfuffle*	دربكة
Darbit shams	*sunstroke*	ضربة شمس
dardasha	*chit-chat*	دردشة
Dareeba, Daraayeb	*tax (n)*	ضريبة
DareeH, aDreHa	*mausoleum; shrine*	ضريح
darfeel, darafeel	*dolphin*	درفيل
Darooriyaat	*necessities*	ضروريات
dars, duroos	*lesson*	درس
darweesh, daraweesh	*dervish*	درويش
dasta, desat	*dozen*	دستة
dawa, adweya	*medicine; medication; drug*	دواء

dawaraan	*curve; circle*	دوران
dawla, duwal	*state (n, country)*	دولة
dawli	*international*	دولي
dawsha	*noise*	دوشة
dayem	*constant*	دائم
dayman	*always*	دائماً
dayra, dawaayer	*circle (n)*	دائرة
Dayya'	*tight; narrow*	ضيق
de'ee'	*flour*	دقيق
de'ee'a, da'aayi'	*minute (n, time)*	دقيقة
debbaana, debbaan	*fly (n, insect)*	ذبابة
deblomaaseyya	*diplomacy*	دبلوماسية
deblomaasi, deblomaasiyeen	*diplomatic; diplomat*	دبلوماسي
dee	*this/that (fem.)*	دي
deek, deyook	*rooster; cock*	ديك
deek roomi, deyook roomi	*turkey*	ديك رومي
deen, adyaan	*religion*	دين
defaa9	*defense*	دفاع
Defeera, Dafaayer	*plait*	ضفيرة
Deif, Duyoof	*guest (n)*	ضيف
dein, deyoon	*debt*	دين
deir, adyera	*monastery, abbey*	دير
delwa'ti	*now*	دلوقت
demaagh, demegha	*head (anatomy)*	دماغ
deraa9, dera9aat	*arm (n, anatomy)*	ذراع
dhaahira, dhawaahir	*trend; phenomenon*	ظاهرة
dhaatuh	*same (adj)*	ذاته
dharra, dharraat	*atom*	ذرة
dhikra, dhikrayaat	*memory (past image)*	ذكرى
dho9r	*panic*	ذعر
dibla, dibal	*wedding ring*	دبلة
Didd	*against*	ضد
DiHk	*laughter*	ضحك
dihn, dohoon	*fat (n)*	دهن
dikka, dikak	*wooden bench*	دكّة
Dil9, Doloo9	*rib*	ضلع
Dill	*shade (n, from sun)*	ظل
dimesh'	*Damascus*	دمشق
Dirs, Diroos	*molar tooth*	ضرس
doctohr sinaan	*dentist*	دكتور أسنان
dof9a	*low-ranking soldier; conscript*	دفعة

dof9a, dof9aat	*installment*	دفعة
Dofr, Dawaafir	*nail (finger, toe)*	ظفر
doghri	*straight ahead*	دوغري
Doh', aDwaa'	*light (n, sunlight, etc.)*	ضوء
Doh' 9aali	*headlights*	ضوء عال
dohkha	*dizziness*	دوخة
dohr, edwaar	*turn (n, having a go); story (of building)*	دور
dohra', dawaari'	*carafe*	دورق
dokh-khaan	*smoke (n)*	دخان
dokkaan, dakakeen	*store; shop*	دكّان
doktohr, dakatra	*doctor*	دكتور
donia	*world*	دنيا
dooda, dood	*worm*	دودة
dool	*these/those*	دول
dorg, edraag	*drawer*	درج
Dorra	*other current wife*	ضرّة
dort el mayya	*WC; bathroom*	دورة المياه
dulaab, dawaleeb	*closet (cupboard)*	دولاب
dura	*maize*	ذرة
dush, edshaash	*shower (n)*	دش

E

eblees, abalsa	*devil*	ابليس
ebTi, a'baaT	*Copt (n)*	قبطي
eed, edein	*hand (n, anatomy)*	يد
eegaabi	*positive (attitude)*	إيجابي
eema	*worth (n); value*	قيمة
eeman	*faith; belief*	إيمان
eeqaa9	*beat (n, tempo, music)*	إيقاع
eeraan	*Iran*	إيران
eeraani, eeraaniyeen	*Iranian*	إيراني
eg-gom9a	*Friday*	الجمعة
eih?	*what!*	إيه؟
el ekhwaan	*The (Muslim) Brotherhood*	الإخوان
illa	*except*	إلا
elli gaay	*next*	اللي جاي
embaariH	*yesterday*	إمبارح
emta?	*when!*	امتى؟
ena	*I*	أنا
enfigaar, enfigaraat	*explosion*	انفجار
en-nagda!	*Help!*	النجدة!
ennaharda	*today*	النهاردة

ensaneyya	humanity; gentleness	انسانية
ensigaam	harmony	انسجام
enti'aam	revenge	انتقام
entifaakh	swelling	انتفاخ
entiHaar	suicide	انتحار
eraaya	reading	قراءة
ersh	shark	قرش
eshra	peel (n, fruit); plate (n, gold)	قشرة
eshTa	cream (n, dairy)	قشطة
esTabl, esTablaat	stables	اسطبل
estakohza	lobster	استاكوزا
esTambool	Istanbul	اسطمبول
estiT9aam	taste (n, sense)	استطعام
eswid	black (color)	أسود
ewwa	strength	قوة
eyaas	fitting (trying on)	قياس
ezaaz	glass (n, window, etc.)	إزاز (زجاج)
ezaaz oddamaani	windscreen	إزاز قدّاماني
ezaaza, azaayez	bottle (n)	إزازة
ezn	permission	إذن
ezzay?	how!	ازاي؟

F

fa'eer, fo'ara	poor (person)	فقير
fa9-9aal	effective	فعّال
faa'i9	garishly bright	فاقع
faaDi	empty; not busy	فاضي
faaDil	remaining; virtuous	فاضل
faar, feraan	mouse	فأر
faar kebeer, feraan kebeera	rat	فار كبير
faasid	corrupt	فاسد
faaSil	divider; TV ad break	فاصل
faateH	open (adj)	فاتح
faDDa	silver (n)	فضّة
faDDi	silver (adj)	فضّي
faDHee9	terrible	فظيع
fag'a	suddenly	فجأة
fag9aan, fag9aaneen	gluttonous; ravenous	فجعان
fagr	dawn (n)	فجر
faHm	coal; charcoal	فحم
faHS, fuHooSaat	examination (n, medical)	فحص

fak-ha, fawaakih	*fruit*	فاكهة
fakh, fekhaakh	*trap; snare (n)*	فخ
fakhd, fekhaad	*thigh*	فخذ
fakhm	*luxurious*	فخم
fakk	*jaw*	فك
fakka	*change (n, coins)*	فكّة
falaki	*astronomical*	فلكي
falSo	*fake*	فالصو
fanaara, fanaraat	*lighthouse*	فنارة
fanella, fanellaat	*T-shirt; vest*	فانلّة
fangari, fangareyya	*big spender*	فنجري
fann, fonoon	*art*	فن
fann el khaTT	*calligraphy*	فن الخط
fannaan, fannaneen	*artist*	فنان
fanni, fanniyeen	*skilled technician*	فني
fanoos, fawanees	*lantern*	فانوس
far', furoo'aat	*difference*	فرق
far'a9ah, far'a9aat	*explosion; loud bang*	فرقعة
far9, furoo9	*branch*	فرع
fara9oni	*Pharaonic*	فرعوني
faraasha, faraash	*butterfly*	فراشة
faraH, afraaH	*wedding party; happiness*	فرح
farawlaaya, farawla	*strawberry*	فراولة
fardit kawitch	*tire (n, vehicle)*	فردة كاوتش
fareesa, faraayis	*prey*	فريسة
farfasha	*joy and laughter*	فرفشة
farkha, feraakH	*chicken; hen*	فرخة
farmala, faraamil	*brakes (n, vehicle)*	فرامل
farraash, farraasheen	*coffee boy (in office)*	فرّاش
farwit er-raas	*scalp (n)*	فروة الرأس
fas'eyya, fas'eyyaat	*fountain*	فسقية
fasaad	*corruption*	فساد
faSeelet ed-damm	*blood group*	فصيلة الدم
fash-shaar, fash-shaareen	*fabricator (of heroics about himself)*	فشّار
fashal	*failure (n)*	فشل
faSl, fuSool	*classroom; season (of year)*	فصل
faSla, faSlaat	*comma*	فاصلة
faSolya khaDra	*beans (French/green)*	فاصوليا خضراء
fatafeet	*crumbs*	فتافيت
faTaTri	*pie-maker*	فطاطري

fatHa, fatHaat	aperture, opening (n)	فتحة
fatla, fitall	thread (n); cotton wool	فتلة
fatoora, fawateer	invoice; check (n, bill)	فاتورة
fatra, fataraat	period of time; a while	فترة
fattaaHa, fattaHaat	opener (cans, etc.)	فتّاحة
fatwa, fataawi	formal opinion/ advice	فتوى
fawaatiH esh-shaheyya	appetizers	فواتح الشهية
fawDa	mess (n, chaos)	فوضى
fawri	immediate	فوري
fayaDaan, fayaDanaat	flood (river)	فيضان
fayda, fawaayid	benefit (n); bank interest	فائدة
fazzoora, fawazeer	puzzle; riddle (n)	فزّورة
feDeeHa, faDaayeH	scandal	فضيحة
fee	in	في
feel, feyela	elephant	فيل
feesha	plug (electric, etc.)	فيشة
fein?	where?	فين ؟
fellaaH, fellaHeen	tiller (of the soil)	فلاح
felooka, falaayek	Nile boat (traditional)	فلوكة
feloos	money	فلوس
fer'a, fera'	team; band	فرقة
feraakh	chicken	فراخ
feroseyya	horsemanship	فروسية
feSaal	haggling	فصال
feseekh	salted fish (traditional)	فسيخ
feshaar	popcorn	فشار
feTaar	breakfast	فطار
feTeera, feTeer	pie	فطيرة
fi9l faaDiH	indecent act	فعل فاضح
figl	raddish	فجل
fikra, afkaar	idea	فكرة
filfil	pepper (n)	فلفل
filisTeen	Palestine	فلسطين
filisTeeni, filisTeeniyeen	Palestinian	فلسطيني
fill	cork	فل
film, aflaam	movie	فيلم
fingaan, fanageen	cup (n, for drinks)	فنجان
fogr	immorality; debauchery	فجر
foh'	above; up	فوق
folaan el folaani	Joe Public on the street; Mr. Anybody	فلان الفلاني
foll	Arabian Jasmine	فل

fool	*fava beans*	فول
fooTa, fowaT	*towel*	فوطة
fukh-khaar	*pottery*	فخّار
fundu', fanaadi'	*hotel*	فندق
el furaat	*Euphrates*	الفرات
furn, afraan	*oven; bakery*	فرن
furSa, furaS	*opportunity*	فرصة
fustaan, fasateen	*dress (n, clothes)*	فستان
fuzdo'	*pistachio*	فستق

G

gaahil, gahala	*ignorant (adj)*	جاهل
gaahiz, gahzeen	*ready (adj)*	جاهز
gaar, geraan	*neighbor*	جار
gabaan, gobana	*coward*	جبان
gabal, gebaal	*mountain*	جبل
gabr	*algebra*	جبر
gada9, gid9aan	*young man*	جدع
gadd	*serious*	جدّ
gahl	*ignorance*	جهل
gaHsh, goHosha	*young donkey*	جحش
galabeyya, galale	*galabeyya (traditional robe)*	جلابية
galoon	*gallon*	جالون
galsa, galasaat	*session (in court, boardroom, clinic, etc.)*	جلسة
gam9a, gam9aat	*university*	جامعة
gam9eyya, gam9eyyaat	*co-operative organization*	جمعية
gamal, gimaal	*camel*	جمل
gambareyyaya, gambari	*shrimp; prawns*	جمبري
gamee9	*entire*	جميع
gameel	*beautiful*	جميل
gamoosa, gawamees	*water buffalo*	جاموسة
ganaaza, ganazaat	*funeral*	جنازة
ganb	*beside*	جنب
eg-ganna	*paradise*	الجنّة
ganoob	*south*	جنوب
ganzabeel	*ginger (n, herb)*	جنزبيل
garaayed	*press (n, newspapers, etc.)*	جرائد
garada, garaad	*locust*	جرادة
garas el baab	*doorbell*	جرس الباب
garbaan, garbaneen	*mangy*	جربان

gardal, garaadel	bucket	جردل
garee'	brave	جريء
gareema, garaayem	crime	جريمة
gargeer	watercress; rocket-like leaf	جرجير
garH, gorooH	wound (n)	جرح
garraar, garraaraat	tractor	جزّار
garrab	try (v)	جرب
garsoon, garsonaat	waiter (n)	جرسون
garthooma, garatheem	germ	جرثومة
gasoos, gawasees	spy (n)	جاسوس
gawaab, gawabaat	letter (mail)	جواب
gawaaz	marriage	جواز (زواج)
gawaaz es-safar	passport	جواز السفر
gawafaya, gawaafa	guava	جوافة
gawahergi	jeweler	جواهرجي
gawhara, gawaahir	gem	جوهرة
gawla, gawlaat	excursion; tour (n)	جولة
gawla baHareyya	cruise (n)	جولة بحرية
gaww	weather (n)	جو
gayza, gawaayiz	award (n)	جائزة
eg-gazaayir	Algeria	الجزائر
gazaa'iri, gazaa'ireyyeen	Algerian	جزائري
gazara, gazar	carrot	جزر
gazma, gizam	shoe	جزمة
gazzaab	attractive	جذّاب
gazzaar, gazzaareen	butcher (n)	جزار
gedeed	new	جديد
geel, agyaal	generation	جيل
geib, goyoob	pocket (n)	جيب
geish, goyoosh	army	جيش
geld, golood	skin (n); leather	جلد
genaaya, genayaat	criminal offence	جناية
geneina, ganaayin	garden	جنينة
geneinet el Hayawaanaat	zoo	جنينة الحيوانات
genn	genie	جنّ
genoon	madness	جنون
gewanti	gloves	جوانتي
gezeera, guzur	island	جزيرة
ghaaDbaan	angry	غضبان
ghaali	expensive; precious	غال
ghaamiD	vague (adj)	غامض
ghaara	air raid	غارة

ghaayib	*absent*	غائب
ghabi	*unintelligent*	غبي
ghada	*lunch*	غداء
ghaddaar	*treacherous*	غدّار
ghaDroof, ghaDareef	*cartilage*	غضروف
ghafeer, ghafar	*watchman;* *night guard*	غفير
ghalabaawi	*chatterbox*	غلباوي
ghalaT	*wrong (adj), incorrect*	غلط
ghalayaan	*boiling*	غليان
ghalbaan, ghalaaba	*poor; unfortunate*	غلبان
ghallaayit el mayya	*kettle*	غلاية الماء
ghalTa, ghalaTaat	*mistake (n); error*	غلطة
ghanam	*sheep (flock)*	غنم
ghani	*wealthy*	غني
ghara'	*drowning*	غرق
gharaam	*romance*	غرام
gharaama, gharamaat	*fine (n)*	غرامة
gharb	*west*	غرب
ghareeb	*odd (adj); stranger*	غريب
ghareeza, gharaayyiz	*instinct*	غريزة
ghaseel	*laundry (n, clothes, etc.)*	غسيل
ghasheem, ghoshm	*novice*	غشيم
ghassaalit eTbaa'	*dishwasher*	غسالة أطباق
ghassaalit hodoom	*washing machine*	غسالة هدوم
ghaTa, ghoTyaan	*cover (n, lid)*	غطاء
ghaTs	*scuba diving (n)*	غطس
ghaTTaas, ghaTTaseen	*scuba diver*	غطّاس
ghaweeT	*deep (adj)*	غويط
ghawwaaSa, ghawwaaSaat	*submarine*	غوّاصة
ghazaala, ghizlaan	*deer; gazelle*	غزالة
ghazl	*yarn (n, thread)*	غزل
gheera	*jealousy*	غيرة
gheir 9aadi	*uncommon*	غير عادي
gheweisha, ghawaayish	*bracelet*	غويشة
ghish	*cheating*	غش
ghiyaar	*replacement item*	غيار
gholaaf, aghlefa	*cover (book,* *magazine, etc.)*	غلاف
ghoraab, gherbaan	*crow*	غراب
ghorfa, ghoraf	*room (hotel, etc.)*	غرفة
el ghoroob	*sunset*	الغروب
ghoraf khaalya	*vacancies (in hotel)*	غرف خالية

ghorfit el 9amaleyyaat	operating theater	غرفة العمليات
ghorfit nawm	bedroom	غرفة نوم
ghorza, ghoraz	stitch	غرزة
ghudda, ghuddad	gland	غدة
gibna, giban	cheese	جبنة
gidd, godood	grandfather	جدّ
gidr, godoor	root (n)	جدر
gihaaz, aghiza	appliance	جهاز
ginaaH, gineHa	wing (n); suite (hotel, etc.)	جناح
gins	sex (gender)	جنس
ginseyya, ginseyyaat	nationality	جنسية
giraaHa	surgery (n, operation)	جراحة
gism, agsaam	body	جسم
goghrafia	geography	جغرافيا
gohz (zohg), egwaaz	husband; pair; couple	جوز (زوج)
gohz el hind	coconut	جوز الهند
gombaaz	gymnastics	جمباز
gomgoma, gamaagim	skull	جمجمة
gomhoor, gamaheer	audience	جمهور
gomhooreyya, gomhooreyyaat	republic	جمهورية
gomrok, gamaarik	customs (n, import duties)	جمارك
gonHa, gonaH	misdemeanor	جنحة
goo9	hunger (n)	جوع
gooda	quality (n)	جودة
gornaan, garaayed	newspaper	جرنان
gowwa	inside	جوه
gowwaani	inner	جوّاني
guhd, guhood	effort	جهد
gumla	wholesale	جملة
gumla, gumal	sentence (grammar)	جملة
gunella, gunellaat	skirt	جونلة
gur9a, gur9aat	dosage	جرعة
guz', agzaa'	part (n, section)	جزء

H

Ha...	will (auxiliary verb)	ح ...
Ha', Hu'oo'	right (n, entitlement)	حق
Ha'ee'a, Haqaa'iq	fact	حقيقة
Ha'ee'i	real; true	حقيقي
haadi	quiet (adj)	هادئ
Haadi'	salty	حادق

HaaDir	yes (I will); certainly	حاضر
Haafir, Hawaafir	hoof	حافر
Haaga, Hagaat	thing; something	حاجة
Haaga sa'-9a	cold refreshments	حاجة ساقعة
Haagib, Hawaagib	eyebrow	حاجب
Haakhaam	rabbi	حاخام
Haala, Haalaat	case; state (n)	حالة
Haamil	pregnant	حامل
haamish, hawaamish	margin	هامش
haanim, hawaanim	lady (of stature)	هانم
Haaris, Haras	guard (n); doorman	حارس
haat!	bring (me)!; give (me)!	هات!
haayel	marvelous; terrific	هائل
habal	silliness; naivety	هبل
Habbahaan	cardamom	حبّ الهال
Habl, Hibaal	rope	حبل
Habl ghaseel	washing line	حبل غسيل
HaDaara, HaDaaraat	civilization	حضارة
Hadd	someone; anyone	حدّ (أحد)
Hadd, Hudood	edge; limit	حدّ
Hadd adnaa	minimum charge	حدّ أدنى
Haddaad	ironsmith; blacksmith	حدّاد
Haddoota, Hawadeet	children's tale	حدوتة
Hadeed	iron (n, metal)	حديد
Hadsa, Hawaadis	accident (road, etc.)	حادثة
Hafeed, aHfaad	grandchild	حفيد
HaffaaDa, HaffaDaat	diaper	حفاضة
Hafla, Hafalaat	party (n, ball)	حفلة
Hafla museeqeyya	concert (n)	حفلة موسيقية
Hagar, Higaara	stone (n)	حجر
Hagar el asaas	foundation stone	حجر الأساس
Hagar kareem	precious stone	حجر كريم
Hagg, Huggaag	pilgrim	حاج
el Higg	pilgrimage (to Mecca)	الحج
Hagm, aHgaam	size (n)	حجم
Hagr SiHHi	quarantine	حجر صحّي
Hagz, Huguzaat	reservation (n)	حجز
haikal 9azmi	skeleton	هيكل عظمي
Hakam, Hokkaam	referee	حكم
Hakka	itching	حكّة
Hala'a (agnabeyya)	TV serial (foreign)	حلقة (أجنبية)
Halawaani, Halawaaneyya	patisserie	حلواني

Haleeb	milk	حليب
halkaan	exhausted	هلكان
Hall, Hulool	solution (n, answer)	حل
Hall wasaT	compromise (n)	حل وسط
Halla, Hilal	cooking pot	حلة
Hallaa', Halla'een	barber	حلاق
halwasa	hallucination	هلوسة
Hama	father-in-law	حم
Hamla, Hamlaat	campaign	حملة
hamm	anxiety; worry (n)	هم
Hammaam, Hammamaat	bathroom	حمام
hams	whispering (n)	همس
Hanaan	warmth (kindness)	حنان
Hanafeyya, Hanafeyyaat	faucet	حنفية
handasa	engineering; architecture	هندسة
Hanuti, Hanuteyya	undertaker	حانوتي
hanyyaalak!	Good for you!	هنيئا لك!
Haqeer	despicable	حقير
Haraam	forbidden (religion)	حرام
Haraami, Harameyya	burglar; thief	حرامي
Haraara	dialing tone	حرارة (تليفون)
Harag	embarrassment	حرج
Haraka, Harakaat	movement	حركة
haram, ahraam	pyramid	هرم
Haras el Hodood	border guards	حرس الحدود
Harb, Horoob	war	حرب
harbaan, harbaneen	fugitive	هربان
Haree'a, Harayi'	fire, (uncontrolled)	حريق
Hareemi	ladies' (fashion, etc.)	حريمي
Hareer	silk (n, adj)	حرير
Harf, Huroof	letter (alphabet)	حرف
Harr	hot (weather)	حر
Harreef, Harreefa	skillful (adj)	حريف
Hasab	according to; subject to	حسب
Hasad	envy	حسد
HaSal	(it) happened	حصل
Hasana, Hasanaat	charity, good deed	حسنة
el HaSba	measles	الحصبة
Hashara, Hasharaat	insect	حشرة
Hasheesh	lawn grass; cannabis	حشيش
Hasra	sorrow; grief	حسرة
Hassaas	sensitive; allergic	حساس
HaSwa, HaSa	pebble	حصوة

Hatta	even (e.g. even you!!)	حتّى
hawa	air (n)	هواء
Hawalein	around	حوالين
Hayaah	life	حياة
hayagaan	excitement	هيجان
Hayawaan, Hayawanaat	animal	حيوان
Hayawi	organic	حيوي
Hayraan	puzzled	حيران
Hayy	alive; live (wire, etc.)	حي
Hayy, aHyaa'	neighborhood	حي
Hayy tigaari	commercial district	حي تجاري
Hazeen	sad	حزين
HaZZ	luck	حظ
hazza, hazzaat	tremor; shake (n)	هزّة
Heddaaya, Heddayaat	kite (bird)	حدأة
hedeyya, hadaaya	gift	هدية
hedoom	clothes	هدوم
heeroghleefee	hieroglyphic	هيروغليفي
hegoom	attack	هجوم
HeiTa, HeTaan	wall	حيطة
Hekaaya, Hekayaat	story	حكاية
Henna	henna	حنة
Herbaaya, Herbayaat	chameleon	حرباء
Hewaar	dialogue	حوار
hezaar	kidding; joking	هزار
hibaab	soot	هباب
Hibla	pregnant	حبلى
Hibr, aHbaar	ink	حبر
Higaab	veil (n, headscarf)	حجاب
Higga, Higag	pretext; excuse	حجة
higra	emigration	هجرة
hilaal	crescent	هلال
Hilm, aHlaam	dream (n)	حلم
Hilw	sweet; nice	حلو
el Hilw	dessert	الحلو
Himl, aHmaal	load (n)	حمل
hina	here	هنا
hinaak	there	هناك
Hirfa, Hiraf	craft	حرفة
Hisaab, Hisabaat	account (n, bank)	حساب
el Hisaab	the check (restaurant, etc.)	الحساب
Hisaab gaari	current account	حساب جار
Hitta, Hitat	piece (of); neighborhood	حتّة

Hizaam, Hizema	belt	حزام
Hizb, aHzaab	party (n, political)	حزب
HoDn, aHDaan	hug	حفن
Hodood	borders	حدود
hohga, hohgaat	stampede; mad rush	هوجة
Hokm, aHkaam	governance; sentence (from court)	حكم
Hokuma, Hokumaat	government	حكومة
Homaar, Himeer	donkey	حمار
Homaar waHshi, Himeer waHsheyya	zebra	حمار وحشي
Hoot, Hitaan	whale	حوت
Horreyya, Horreyyaat	liberty	حرية
Horr, aHraar	free; at large	حر
HoSaan, HeSena	horse	حصان
HowD, eHwaaD	sink (n)	حوض
Hozn	sadness	حزن
Hu'na, Hu'an	syringe (n); jab	حقنة
Hubb	love (n)	حب
Huboob el fiTaar	breakfast cereal	حبوب الفطار
Humma, Hummyyaat	fever	حمى
HummuS	chickpeas	حمص
HumooDa	acidity	حموضة
Huroo' esh-shams	sunburn (n)	حروق الشمس
HuTaam	wreckage	حطام
huwaaya, huwayaat	hobby	هواية

I

i9laan, i9lanaat	advertising (n)	إعلان
ibla	Mecca's direction	قبلة
ibli	southern Egypt	قبلي
ibn, welaad	son	ابن
ibn akh	nephew (son of brother)	ابن أخ
ibn okht	nephew (son of sister)	ابن أخت
ibra, ibar	needle	ابرة
el ibtikaar	creativity	الابتكار
ibtisaama, ibtisaamaat	smile (n)	ابتسامة
idaara	administration; management	إدارة
ifl, i'faal	lock (n); padlock (n)	قفل
igbaari	obligatory; mandatory	إجباري
igraa'aat qaDaa'eyya	litigation	إجراءات قضائية
ihaana, ihaanaat	insult (n)	إهانة
iHtifaal, iHtifalaat	celebration	احتفال

iHtimaal, iHtimalaat	possibility	احتمال
iHtiraam	respect (n)	احترام
iHtiraas	caution (n, prudence)	احتراس
ikhtibaar, ikhtibaraat	test (n)	اختبار
ikhtiyaar, ikhtiyaraat	choice	اختيار
ikhtiyaari	optional	اختياري
ikrameyya, ikrameyyaat	tip (n, gratuity)	إكرامية
ilghaa'	cancellation	إلغاء
iltihaab, iltihabaat	swelling	التهاب
iltihaab el Hangara	laryngitis	التهاب الحنجرة
imaam, a'imma	imam (Islamic religious leader)	إمام
el imaaraat	Emirates, the UAE	الإمارات
imsaak	constipation	إمساك
imtiHaan, imtiHaanaat	examination (n, school, etc.)	امتحان
imtinaan	gratitude (adj)	امتنان
imtiyaaz	excellence	امتياز
in	if	إن
ingeel	bible	انجيل
ingeleezi, ingeleez	English (person); English language	انجليزي
ingeltera	England	انجلترا
inhiyaar 9aSabi	nervous breakdown	انهيار عصبي
inqaadh	rescue (n)	إنقاذ
intifaaDa	uprising	انتفاضة
inzhaar, inzharaat	warning (n, caution)	إنذار
iqaama	accommodation; residency	إقامة
iqleem, aqaleem	region (province, etc.)	إقليم
iqleemi	regional	إقليمي
iqtiraaH, iqtiraaHaat	suggestion	اقتراح
iqtiSaadi	economic; budget	اقتصادي
irtibaaT, irtibaTaat	commitment; engagement (appointment, etc.)	ارتباط
irtifaa9, irtifa9aat	altitude	ارتفاع
irtigaag	concussion	ارتجاج
is-haal	diarrhea	إسهال
el is9aaf	ambulance	الإسعاف
iSaaba, iSabaat	injury	إصابة
islaami	Islamic	إسلامي
ism, asaami	name	اسم

ism, e'saam	department	قسم
ism el bolees	police station	قسم البوليس
isra'eel	Israel	إسرائيل
isra'eeli	Israeli	إسرائيلي
isti'aala, isti'alaat	resignation	استقالة
isti'baal	reception	استقبال
istiraaHa	break (n, interval)	استراحة
istishaari, istishaariyeen	consultant	استشاري

J

jeeba, jeebaat	skirt (n)	جيبة
jeelaati	ice cream	جيلاتي

K

ka'an	as if it were	كأن
ka9b, ko9oob	heel (foot, shoe)	كعب
ek-ka9ba	Kaaba (holy black stone in Mecca)	الكعبة
kaaki	khaki (n, color)	كاكي
kaamil	full; perfect; whole	كامل
kaas, kasaat	cup (n, trophy); drink (n)	كأس
kaatib, kottaab	writer; author; clerk	كاتب
kabaab	grilled lamb dish	كباب
kabboot	hood (car)	كبوت
kabeena, kabaayen	cabin (n)	كابينة
kaboos, kawabees	nightmare	كابوس
kaboria	crab	كابوريا
kabreet	matches; sulfur	كبريت
kabsha, kobash	ladle	كبشة
kabt	frustration; suppression	كبت
kafaala	bail	كفالة
kaff, kofoof	palm (n, hand)	كف
kahf, kuhoof	cave (n)	كهف
kahraba	electricity	كهرباء
kahramaan	amber	كهرمان
kalabshaat	handcuffs	كلابشات
kalaks, kalaksaat	horn; hoot (of a vehicle)	كلاكس
kalb, kilaab	dog	كلب
kamanga, kamangaat	violin	كمنجة
kameen, kamaayin	roadblock; ambush	كمين
kammaasha, kammashaat	pincers	كماشة

kammoon	cumin	كمّون
kanaba, kanab	sofa; couch	كنبة
kanaka, kanak	brass coffee pot (traditional)	كنكة
kannaas, kannaseen	road sweeper	كنّاس
karafs	celery	كرفس
karakeeb	junk; knickknacks	كراكيب
karam eD-Diyaafa	hospitality	كرم الضيافة
karavatta, karavattaat	necktie	كرافتة
kareem	generous	كريم
karmasha, karameesh	crease (in clothes)	كرمشة
kart, koroot	card	كارت
kart bosTal	postcard	كارت بوسطة
kart el bank	charge card	كارت البنك
kasarolla, kasarollaat	saucepan	كسرولة
kash-shaaf, kash-shafaat	headlights; searchlights	كشّاف
ek-kash-shaafa	the boy scouts	الكشّافة
kashf, koshoofaat	check up (at doctor); itemized list	كشف
kaslaan, kaslaaneen	lazy	كسلان
kasr, kosoor	fracture (n)	كسر
kawaari9	trotters (cow, etc.)	كوارع
kawkab, kawaakib	planet	كوكب
kazooza	soda pop	كازوزة
kazzaab, kazzabeen	liar	كذّاب
kebda, kebadd	liver (chicken, etc.)	كبدة
kebeer	big; large	كبير
keda	like so	كده
keebord	keyboard (computer, etc.)	كيبورد
keelograam	kilogram	كيلوجرام
keelomitr	kilometer	كيلومتر
kees makhadda, ekyaas makhaddaat	pillow case	كيس مخدّة
kefaaya	enough	كفاية
kela, kalaawi	kidney	كلية
kelma, kalaam	word	كلمة
kemya	chemistry	كيمياء
keneesa, kanaayis	church	كنيسة
kenz, konooz	treasure	كنز
kereim, keremaat	cream (cosmetics, etc.)	كريم
kereiza, kereiz	cherries	كرز
kersh, koroosh	beer belly; paunch	كرش

kersha	tripe	كرشة
keteer	many; plenty	كثير
ketshab	ketchup	كتشب
kewafeer, kewafeeraat	hairdresser (women)	كوافير
kewaiyis, kewaiyiseen	good; well (health, etc.)	كويس
khaal, khilaan	uncle (maternal)	خال
khaala, khalaat	aunt (maternal)	خالة
(kebeer) khaaliS	very (big)	(كبير) خالص
(mafeesh) khaaliS	(none) at all	(ما فيش) خالص
khaam	raw (unprocessed)	خام
khaatim, khawaatim	ring (jewelry)	خاتم
khaayef, khayfeen	afraid	خايف
khaayin, khayneen	traitor	خاين
khabar, akhbaar	news	خبر
khabbaaz, khabbazeen	baker	خباز
khabeer, khobara	expert	خبير
khabTa	knock	خبطة
khafeef	light (adj, opp. heavy); mild	خفيف
khaish	canvas	خيش
khaiT, khuyooT	string (cord)	خيط
khal9	extraction (tooth, etc.)	خلع
khalaaS	finished	خلاص
khaleefa, kholafaa'	caliph	خليفة
khaleeg	gulf	خليج
khalal	fault (n)	خلل
khaleyya, khalaaya	cell (tissue)	خلية
khall	vinegar	خل
khallaaT, khallaTaat	blender	خلاط
khallaSni (min)	rid me (of)	خلّصني (من)
khalli baalak!	Look out!	خلّي بالك!
khalTa	blend; mixture	خلطة
khameera	yeast	خميرة
khamra, khomoor	alcoholic drinks; liquor	خمرة
khangar, khanaagir	dagger	خنجر
khanzeer, khanazeer	pig	خنزير
kharaab	ruin (financial, etc.)	خراب
kharToom, kharaTeem	hose	خرطوم
kharazaan	bamboo (n)	خرزان
kharbaan	not working	خربان

kharboosh, kharabeesh	scratch	خربوش
el khareef	fall (n, season); autumn	الخريف
khareeTa, kharaayeT	map	خريطة
kharshoof	artichoke	خرشوف
kharteet, kharateet	rhino	خرتيت
khaS-khaSa	privatization	خصخصة
khashab, akh-shaab	wood (n, timber)	خشب
khashab ez-zaan	beech (wood)	خشب الزان
khaSm, khuSumaat	discount (n)	خصم
khass	lettuce	خس
khaTar, akhTaar	hazard	خطر
khaTeeb	fiancé (male); orator	خطيب
khaTeeba	fiancée (female)	خطيبة
khaTeer	dangerous (adj)	خطير
khaTf	kidnap (n)	خطف
khaTT, khuTooT	line; handwriting	خط
khaTT sair	route (n)	خط سير
khaTTaaT, khaTTaTeen	calligrapher	خطاط
khaTwa, khaTawaat	step (n)	خطوة
khawaaga, khawagaat	foreigner	خواجة
khayaal	shadow; imagination	خيال
khazaf	porcelain	خزف
khazna, khizann	safe (n, secure box)	خزنة
khazzaan, khazzanaat	tank; reservoir	خزان
kheiba	failure; flop	خيبة
kheibit amal	disappointment	خيبة أمل
kheil	horses	خيل
kheima, kheyam	tent	خيمة
kheir	blessings; riches	خير
kheshin	rough (adj, not smooth)	خشن
kheTTa, kheTaT	plan (n)	خطة
khibra, khibraat	experience (n)	خبرة
khidma, khadamaat	service (n, favor)	خدمة
khidmit el 9umalaa	service (n, favor)	خدمة العملاء
khilaal	within; during (prep)	خلال
khirreeg, khirreegeen	graduate (adj/n)	خريج
khiyaara, khiyaar	cucumber	خيار
khohf	fear (n)	خوف
khokha, khohkh	peach	خوخ
kholkhaal, khalakheel	anklet (bangle)	خلخال
khonfessa, khanaafis	beetle	خنفسة
khorda	junk	خردة
khordawaat	knickknacks	خردوات

khorm, ekhraam	*hole; puncture*	خرم
khorm el moftaaH	*keyhole*	خرم المفتاح
khoSooSi	*private*	خصوصي
khoTba, khoTab	*speech (address to an audience)*	خطبة
khuDaar	*vegetables*	خضار
khudaywee	*khedive*	خديوي
khuraafa, khurafaat	*myth*	خرافة
khusaara	*loss*	خسارة
khuTooba	*engagement (n, to be married)*	خطوبة
kibd	*liver (human)*	كبد
kimmeyya, kimmeyyaat	*quantity*	كمية
kitaab, kutub	*book (n)*	كتاب
kitf, ketaaf	*shoulder (n)*	كتف
kobbaaya, kobbayaat	*glass (n, tumbler, etc.)*	كبابة
kobri, kabaari	*bridge (n)*	كوبري
kobs, ekbaas	*socket (electric)*	كبس
kofta	*prepared minced meat (traditional)*	كفتة
koHHa	*cough*	كحة
koHl	*kohl*	كحل
koHli	*navy blue*	كحلي
kohm, ekwaam	*pile (n); heap (n)*	كوم
kohra, kowar	*ball*	كرة
ek-kohra	*soccer*	كرة القدم
ek-kohra l-arDeyya	*Earth (planet)*	الكرة الأرضية
kohsaaya, kohsa	*zucchini; courgette*	كوسة
koll	*all; each; every*	كل
koll waaHid lewaHdo	*separately*	كل واحد لوحده
kolleyya, kulleyyaat	*college*	كلية
kolohn, kolohnaat	*tights*	كولونات
komm, komaam	*sleeve (n)*	كم
kommetraaya, kommetra	*pear*	كمثرى
koo9, ke9aan	*elbow*	كوع
koreik	*jack (car, etc.)*	كريك
koromb	*cabbage*	كرنب
korsi, karaasi	*chair; seat (n)*	كرسي
kostaleita	*cutlet; chop (lamb, veal, etc.)*	كستليتة
kozbara	*cilantro; coriander*	كزبرة
el kuHool	*alcohol*	الكحول
kurdi, akraad	*Kurd*	كردي

kushk, ekshaak	*kiosk (newspapers, etc.)*	كشك
kutayyib, kutayyibaat	*booklet*	كتيب
ek-kuweit	*Kuwait*	الكويت

L

la'	*no*	لأ
la'an	*because*	لأن
la'eem, lo'ama	*cunning*	لئيم
la9na, la9naat	*curse (n, evil spell)*	لعنة
laa yuTaaq	*unbearable*	لا يطاق
laakin	*but*	لكن
laazim	*necessary; a must*	لازم
laban	*milk*	لبن
laban khaali d-dassam	*skimmed milk*	لبن خالي الدسم
labani	*light blue (colloquial)*	لبني
laffa, laffaat	*tour (in car, etc.)*	لفة
laffa, lifaf	*wrapped parcel*	لفة
lagham, alghaam	*mine (explosive)*	لغم
lagi', lagi'een	*refugee*	لاجئ
lagna, legaan	*committee*	لجنة
lahga, lahgaat	*dialect; accent (n, speech)*	لهجة
laHma	*meat*	لحم
laHma betello	*veal*	لحم بتللو
laHma kandooz	*beef*	لحم كندوز
laHn, alHaan	*melody; tune*	لحن
laHza, laHazaat	*moment*	لحظة
lamba, lomuD	*bulb (light)*	لمبة
lamonata	*lemonade*	ليمونادة
lamoon aDalia	*lemon (citrus fruit)*	ليمون أضاليا
lamoon banzaheer	*lime (citrus fruit)*	ليمون بنزهير
lams	*touch*	لمس
lansh, lanshaat	*launch (n, motorboat)*	لنش
laselki	*wireless*	لاسلكي
laTeef, loTaaf	*amusing; amiable*	لطيف
lau	*if*	لو
lau samaHt	*please; excuse me*	لو سمحت
lazeez	*tasty*	لذيذ
le9ba, le9ab	*toy; game*	لعبة
lebana, lebaan	*chewing gum*	لبان
lebia	*Libya*	ليبيا
leebi, leebiyeen	*Libyan*	ليبي
leghaayet	*until (prep)*	لغاية
leih?	*why!*	ليه ؟

leil, leiyaali	*night*	ليل
el-leil	*night time*	الليل
el-leila	*tonight*	الليلة
letaHt	*downwards*	لتحت
lewaHdo	*alone*	لوحده
libnaan	*Lebanon*	لبنان
libnaani, libnaniyeen	*Lebanese*	لبناني
lisaan, lesena	*tongue*	لسان
litr	*liter*	لتر
lo'ma, lo'am	*morsel (of bread); mouthful*	لقمة
lo'Ta, lo'aT	*bargain (n, adj)*	لقطة
loghz, alghaaz	*riddle; mystery*	لغز
lohn, alwaan	*color (n)*	لون
lohza, lohz	*almonds*	لوز
loofa, leef	*loofah*	لوفة
loolaya, looli	*pearl*	لؤلؤة
lootos	*lotus*	لوتس
lori, lawaari	*truck; lorry*	لوري
lugha, lughaat	*language*	لغة

M

ma'aas	*measurement; size (S, M, L, XL, etc.)*	مقاس
ma'aSS, ma'aSSaat	*scissors*	مقص
ma'baD, ma'aabiD	*knob (door handle, etc.)*	مقبض
ma'fool	*closed*	مقفول
ma9	*with (prep)*	مع
ma9 at-tayyar	*down river (with the current)*	مع التيار
ma9-'ool	*reasonable*	معقول
ma9a ba9D	*together*	مع بعض
ma9aada	*except*	ما عدا
ma9aalim	*landmarks*	معالم
ma9awi	*gastric; intestinal*	معوي
ma9bad, ma9abid	*temple*	معبد
ma9dan, ma9aadin	*metal (n)*	معدن
ma9fi	*exempt*	معفي
ma9la'a, ma9aali'	*spoon (n)*	ملعقة
ma9loomaat	*information*	معلومات
ma9mal, ma9aamil	*laboratory*	معمل
ma9na, ma9aani	*meaning*	معنى
ma9raD, ma9aariD	*gallery; exhibition*	معرض
maaddi	*materialistic*	مادّي

maaDi	past (adj)	ماضي
maalik, mollaak	owner (proprietor)	مالك
maaris	March	مارس
mablool	wet (adj)	مبلول
mabna, mabaani	building	مبنى
mabnal maTaar	airport terminal	مبنى المطار
madani	urban (adj); civilian (not military)	مدني
madkhal, madaakhil	entrance	مدخل
maDmoon	guaranteed; safe (adj)	مضمون
madna, madaayin	minaret	مئذنة
maDrab, maDaarib	racket; bat (n)	مضرب
madrasa, madaaris	school (n)	مدرسة
maDroob bil-khallaaT	whisked	مضروب بالخلاط
madyoon, madyooneen	indebted	مديون
maf'ood, maf'oodeen	missing (person)	مفقود
mafeesh Haaga	there's nothing	مفيش حاجة
mafeesh Hadd	there's nobody	مفيش حد
maftooH	open (adj)	مفتوح
mag-hool	unknown (adj)	مجهول
magalla, magallaat	magazine (periodical)	مجلّة
maggaani	complimentary; free (adj, gratis)	مجاني
el maghreb	Morocco	المغرب
el maghreb el 9arabi	North African Maghreb	المغرب العربي
maghrebi, magharba	Moroccan (person)	مغربي
maghroor	conceited, vain	مغرور
maghsala	laundry (n, facility)	مغسلة
magmoo9a, magmoo9aat	group (n); collection	مجموعة
el magmoo9	sum total; exam score	المجموع
magnoon, maganeen	mad (crazy)	مجنون
maHabba	love (n)	محبّة
maHall, maHallaat	store (n); shop (n)	محل
maHall ward	florist	محل ورد
maHalli	local	محلّي
maHaTTa, maHaTTaat	station (n, radio, train, etc.)	محطّة
maheyya, maheyyaat	salary; wages	ماهية
maHfaza, maHaafiz	wallet	محفظة
maHlool	solution (n, liquid); unhinged	محلول
mahr	bridal dowry	مهر

mahragaan, mahraganaat	*festival*	مهرجان
maHZooZ, maHZooZeen	*lucky (person)*	محظوظ
majesteir	*Masters Degree*	ماجستير
makaan, amaakin	*place (n, location)*	مكان
makana, makann	*machine*	ماكينة
makarohna	*macaroni; pasta*	مكرونة
makhbaz, makhaabiz	*bakery*	مخبز
makhbool, makhabeel	*crazy*	مخبول
makhrag, makhaarig	*exit (n)*	مخرج
makka	*Mecca (Saudi Arabian city)*	مكة
maktab, makaatib	*office; desk*	مكتب
maktab el bareed	*post office*	مكتب البريد
maktaba, maktabaat	*bookshop; library*	مكتبة
makwagi, makwageyya	*ironing man*	مكوجي
malarya	*malaria*	ملاريا
malH, amlaaH	*salt (n)*	ملح
malik, muluuk	*king*	ملك
malika, malikaat	*queen*	ملكة
mallaaH, mallaaHeen	*navigator*	ملاح
malyaan	*full*	مليان
mamarr, mamarraat	*path; corridor*	ممر
mamlaka, mamaalik	*kingdom*	مملكة
mamnoo9	*forbidden; prohibited*	ممنوع
man'oosh	*embellished (adj)*	منقوش
manakheer	*nose*	مناخير
mandeel, manadeel	*handkerchief*	منديل
mangam, manaagim	*mine (coal, etc.)*	منجم
manDHar, manaaDHir	*landscape; scenery*	منظر
mandoob, mandoobeen	*representative (n)*	مندوب
mandoob mabee9aat	*sales representative*	مندوب مبيعات
mangaya, manga	*mango*	مانجو
manikeer	*manicure*	مانيكير
manTiq	*logic*	منطق
ma'bara, ma'aabir	*tomb; graveyard*	مقبرة
maraD, amraaD	*disease; illness*	مرض
maraD es-sukkar	*diabetes*	مرض السكر
marka, markaat	*brand (n)*	ماركة
markazi	*central (adj, main)*	مركزي
markib, maraakib	*boat*	مركب
marra	*once; one (turn, go, etc.)*	مرة

el marreekh	Mars	مَرّيخ (ال)
martaba, maraatib	mattress	مرتبة
marwaHa, maraawiH	fan (n, cooling)	مروحة
maryala, maraayil	uniform (women and children)	مريلة
mas'ool, mas'ooleen	(person) responsible	مسئول
masaafa, masafaat	distance (n)	مسافة
maSareef	expenses	مصاريف
masdood	blocked	مسدود
el maseeHeyya	Christianity	المسيحية
masgid, masaagid	mosque	مسجد
mash-ghool	busy (adj)	مشغول
mash-hoor	famous	مشهور
masHoo', masaaHee'	powder	مسحوق
mashrabeyya, mashrabeyyaat	lattice window (traditional)	مشربية
el mashriq el 9arabi	the Levant	المشرق العربي
mashroob, mashroobaat	drink (n)	مشروب
mashyy	on foot; walking	مشيّ
maskaara	mascara	مسكارا
maSna9, maSaani9	factory	مصنع
masoora, mawaseer	pipe; tube (n)	ماسورة
maSr	Egypt	مصر
masraH, masaariH	theater (plays, etc.)	مسرح
masraHeyya, masraHeyyaat	play (n)	مسرحية
maSri, maSriyeen	Egyptian	مصري
maT9am, maTaa9im	restaurant	مطعم
mataa9ib	troubles (n)	متاعب
maTaar, maTaraat	airport	مطار
maTara	rain (n)	مطر
maTba9a, maTaabi9	(printing) press	مطبعة
maTbakh, maTaabikh	kitchen	مطبخ
mathaana	bladder	مثانة
matHaf, mataaHif	museum	متحف
maTwa, maTaawi	pocket knife	مطواة
maw'af el otobees	bus stop	موقف الأوتوبيس
mawDoo9, mawaDee9	topic; subject	موضوع
mawTin	habitat	موطن
mayya	water	مياه
mayya ma9daneyya	mineral water	مياه معدنية
mazaad, mazadaat	auction (n)	مزاد
mazaag, amzega	mental disposition	مزاج
mazbala, mazaabil	trash dump	مزبلة

mazbooT	*exact*	مضبوط
mazhab, mazhaahib	*sect; school of thought*	مذهب
mazza, mazzaat	*nibbles (with drinks, etc.)*	مزّة
me9aad, mawa9eed	*appointment*	موعد
me9addeyya, me9addeyyaat	*ferry (n)*	معدّية
me9da	*stomach (n)*	معدة
me9za, me9eez	*goat*	معزة
medawwar	*round (adj, spherical)*	مدوّر
meedaan, mayadeen	*square (in town, etc.)*	ميدان
meen?	*who?*	مين؟
meena, mawaani	*harbor; port*	ميناء
mefalTTaH	*flat (adj, opp. bumpy)*	مفلطح
mekaneeki	*mechanic*	ميكانيكي
mekassaraat	*nuts (n, walnuts, etc.)*	مكسرات
mela'la'	*undecided; hesitant*	ملألأ
melakh-lakh	*unstable (wobbly)*	ملخلخ
melooki	*royal, regal*	ملوكي
meraat, merataat	*wife*	مرات (زوجة)
meraaya, merayaat	*mirror*	مرآة
merabba, merabbaat	*jelly; jam*	مربى
merabbit burtu'aan	*marmalade*	مربى البرتقال
mesa	*evening*	مساء
mesaaHa, mesaaHaaat	*surface area*	مساحة
meSaH-SaH	*vigilant*	مصحصح
meseeHi, meseeHiyeen	*Christian*	مسيحي
mestewi	*well-done (cooking)*	مستوي
met-Tawwa9, met-Tawwa9een	*volunteer (n)*	متطوّع
met'addim, met'addimeen	*advanced (adj)*	متقدّم
met'akh-khar	*late*	متأخّر
meTarraz	*embroidered*	مطرّز
metsaawi	*even (adj, level); tidy*	متساو
mezaan, mawazeen	*balance (n, scales)*	ميزان
mezaneyya, mezaneyyaat	*budget (n, fiscal framework)*	ميزانية
mikyaaj	*make-up (lipstick, etc.)*	مكياج
milaaya, milayaat	*sheet (linen, etc.)*	ملاءة
min Dimn	*included (in); part (of)*	من ضمن
min faDlak	*please*	من فضلك
misalla, misallaat	*obelisk*	مسلة
mish	*not; won't; don't*	مش

mish 'aadir	unable	مش قادر
mish 9aarif	don't know	مش عارف
mish akeed	uncertain	مش أكيد
mish ana	not me	مش أنا
mish aSli	imitation (adj, copied)	مش أصلي
mish faahim	don't understand	مش فاهم
mish Ha'ool	won't say	مش حاقول
mish HarooH	won't go	مش حاروح
mish hena	not here	مش هنا
mish ma9ool	unbelievable; unreasonable	مش معقول
mish munaasib	unsuitable	مش مناسب
mish mureeH	uncomfortable	مش مريح
mish qaanooni	illegal	مش قانوني
mish rasmi	unofficial	مش رسمي
mish SiHHi	unhealthy	مش صحّي
mishmishaya, mishmish	apricot	مشمش
mishmishi	apricot-colored	مشمشي
mishT, emshaaT	comb	مشط
mithaal, amthila	example	مثال
el mithli, mithliyeen	homosexual	المثلي
mo'addab, mo'addabeen	polite (adj)	مؤدب
mo'addam	upfront payment	مقدّم
mo'adh-dhin, mo'adh-dhineen	muezzin	مؤذّن
mo'allif, mo'allifeen	author (n)	مؤلّف
mo9aaq, mo9aqeen	disabled (n)	معاق
mo9addal	altered (to improve)	معدّل
mo9di	infectious; contagious	معد
mo9tadil, mo9tadileen	moderate (adj)	معتدل
mobaashir	direct (adj, non-stop)	مباشر
mobaayel, mobaylaat	cellphone; mobile	موبايل
mobadla	exchange (n)	مبادلة
mobilia, mobiliaat	furniture	موبيليا
moDa	fashion	موضة
modarrag, modarragaat	stand (n, stadium)	مدرّج
modarrib, modarribeen	coach (n, trainer)	مدرّب
modarris, modarriseen	teacher	مدرّس
moDeef/moDeefa	flight attendant (m/f)	مضيف/مضيفة
modeer, modeereen	director, manager (n, senior executive)	مدير
mofaagi'	unexpected (adj)	مفاجئ
mofag'a, mofag'aat	surprise (n)	مفاجأة

moga, mohwg	wave (n, in sea, fashion, art, etc.)	موجة
mogammad	frozen (adj)	مجمد
moghanni, moghanniyeen	singer	مغني
moghma 9aleih	unconscious	مغمى عليه
moHaami, moHaamiyeen	attorney; lawyer	محام
moHaasib, moHasbeen	accountant	محاسب
mohandis, mohandiseen	engineer	مهندس
mohandis mi9maari	architect	مهندس معماري
moharrig, moharrigeen	clown	مهرج
mohl, mohlaat	shopping mall	مول
mohza, mohz	banana	موزة
mokaf'a, mokaf'aat	reward (n)	مكافأة
mokhber, mokhbereen	secret policeman; informer	مخبر
mokhrig, mokhrigeen	director (movies, etc.)	مخرج
momarriDa, momarriDaat	nurse (f)	ممرضة
momya, momyawaat	mummy (Pharaonic, etc.)	مومياء
moogab	positive (electric)	موجب
moos, emwaas	razor	موس
moosim, mawaasim	season (of something)	موسم
moowa'-'at	temporary	مؤقت
morgeiHa, marageeH	swing (children's, etc.)	مرجيحة
morr	bitter (taste)	مرّ
mosTarda	mustard	مسطردة
mostawa, mostawayaat	level (n, standard, etc.)	مستوى
motaaH	available	متاح
motohr, mawateer	engine	موتور
moTraan, maTarna	archbishop	مطران
muD-Hik	funny (humorous)	مضحك
mufeed	useful	مفيد
muftaaH, mafateeH	key	مفتاح
mufti	mufti; Islamic scholar	مفتي
mugazfa	risk (n)	مجازفة
mughamra, mughamaraat	adventure	مغامرة
mugrim, mugrimeen	criminal (n)	مجرم
muHaadra, muHadraat	lecture (n)	محاضرة
muHeeT, muHeeTaat	ocean	محيط
muhimm	important	مهم

muHtarif, muHtarifeen	*professional*	محترف
mukalma, mukalmaat	*call (n, phone)*	مكالمة
mukawwinaat	*ingredients*	مكونات
mukh, emkhaakh	*brain*	مخ
mukhabaraat	*intelligence (state)*	مخابرات
mukhaddaraat	*drugs (narcotics)*	مخدرات
mulayyin, mulayyinaat	*laxative*	ملين
multahib	*sore (adj); swollen*	ملتهب
mumeet	*fatal; deadly*	مميت
mumill	*boring; tedious*	ممل
munaasib	*convenient; suitable*	مناسب
munaDH-DHama khaireyya	*charitable organization*	منظمة خيرية
munaDH-DHif, munaDH-DHifaat	*detergent*	منظف
munasba, munasbaat	*occasion*	مناسبة
muntag, muntagaat	*product*	منتج
muntaga9, muntaga9aat	*resort (n)*	منتجع
muntagaat el albaan	*dairy products*	منتجات الألبان
muqaddas	*holy; sacred*	مقدس
muraahiq, murahqeen	*adolescent; teenager*	مراهق
murabba9, murabba9aat	*square (n, geometric)*	مربع
murabba9aat	*checked (adj, pattern)*	مربعات
mureeH	*comfortable*	مريح
muroor	*traffic (n, cars, etc.)*	مرور
musaa9da	*help (n)*	مساعدة
musakkin, musakkinaat	*sedative*	مسكّن
musawi	*equal (adj)*	مساو
muSawwaraati, muSawwarateyya	*photographer*	مصور
museeqa	*music*	موسيقى
mushkila, mashaakil	*problem*	مشكلة
musta'bal	*future (n)*	مستقبل
musta'gir, musta'gireen	*tenant (n)*	مستأجر
mustaHeel	*impossible*	مستحيل
mustaqill	*independent*	مستقل
mustashfa, mustashfayaat	*hospital*	مستشفى
mustashriq, mustashriqeen	*orientalist*	مستشرق
mustaTeel, mustaTeelaat	*rectangle*	مستطيل

mustawrad	imported (adj)	مستورد
muTahhir	antiseptic; disinfectant	مطهر
mutanaaqiD	contradictory	متناقض
mutawaHHish, mutawaHHisheen	savage, wild	متوحش
mutawassiT	average; medium (mid-)	متوسط
muthallath, muthallathaat	triangle	مثلّث
muthaqqaf, muthaqqafeen	cultured; erudite	مثقّف
muwaDH-DHaf, muwaDH-DHafeen	employee	موظّف
muz9ig	nuisance (adj)	مزعج
muzayyaf	fake (adj)	مزيّف
muzmin	chronic	مزمن

N

na'-'aala	stretcher	نقّالة
na'-'aash, na'-'aasheen	painter (decorator)	نقّاش
na'aawa	choicest; selected	نقاوة
na'dee	cash payment	نقدي
na'l damm	blood transfusion	نقل دم
en-na'l	transportation	النقل
na9i	obituary	نعي
na9saan, na9saneen	sleepy (adj)	نعسان
naa'iS	incomplete; short (of something)	ناقص
naa9im	smooth (adj)	ناعم
naadi, nawaadi	club (sporting, etc.)	نادي
naagiH, nagHeen	successful; passed an exam	ناجح
naaHya, nawaaHi	side (n)	ناحية
naar	fire (n, flame)	نار
naas	people	ناس
naashif	dry (adj)	ناشف
naaSiH, nas-Heen	astute; streetwise	ناصح
naay	bamboo flute (traditional)	ناي
naayim	asleep	نايم
en-naaZir	master (head of school, train station)	الناظر
nabaat, nabataat	plant (n)	نبات
nabaati, nabaatiyeen	vegetarian	نباتي
nabboot, nababeet	nightstick; truncheon	نبّوت

nabD	pulse (blood)	نبض
nabee, anbeya	prophet	نبي
nabeel, nobalaa'	noble	نبيل
nada	dew	ندى
nadam	remorse	ندم
naDDaara	glasses (eye)	نظارة
naDDaraati	optician	نظاراتي
nafa', anfaa'	tunnel (n)	نفق
nafa'a	alimony	نفقة
nafar, anfaar	person	نفر
nafas, anfaas	breath; puff	نفس
naffaasa, naffasaat	jet (military)	نفاثة
nafoora, nafooraat	fountain	نافورة
nagafa, nagaf	chandelier	نجفة
naggaar, naggareen	carpenter	نجار
nagham, anghaam	tune; melody	نغم
naHaas aHmar	copper	نحاس أحمر
naHaas aSfar	brass	نحاس أصفر
naHla, naHl	bee	نحلة
naHs	bad luck	نحس
naHyit	towards	ناحية
nakad	misery	نكد
nakhla, nakhl	palm tree	نخلة
namla, naml	ant	نمل
namoosa, namoos	mosquito	ناموسة
naqi	pure	نقي
nargiss	narcissus	نرجس
naSeeb	share (allocation, lot)	نصيب
naseeg	textile	نسيج
naSeeHa, naSaayeH	advice (n)	نصيحة
nashaaT, anshiTa	activity	نشاط
nasheed, anasheed	anthem	نشيد
nasheeT	active, energetic	نشيط
en-nashra	news bulletin	النشرة
naSSaab, naSSaabeen	crook; swindler	نصاب
naSya, nawaSee	street corner	ناصية
nateega, nataayeg	result (n); calendar	نتيجة
naTT	leaping; jumping	نط
nayy	raw	نيء
naZar	eyesight	نظر
nazeef	hemorrhage	نزيف
nebeeh, nobaha	smart; intelligent	نبيه
nebeet	wine	نبيذ

neDeef	clean (adj)	نظيف
neefa	goat meat	نيفة
en-neel	the Nile	النيل
nefaaq	hypocrisy	نفاق
nemra, nemar	number	نمرة
neshaan, nayasheen	medal	نيشان
nesma, neseem	breeze	نسيم
neyya, neyyaat	intention	نية
ni9ma, ni9am	blessing (from God)	نعمة
ni9naa9	mint (n, herb)	نعناع
niDHaam, anDHima	system; order (n)	نظام
nigm, nugoom	star (n)	نجم
nihaa'i	final	نهائي
nimr, nomoor	tiger	نمر
niqaab	veil (n, full face)	نقاب
nisr, nisoor	eagle	نسر
nohba, nohbaat	seizure (n, fit)	نوبة
nokta, nokat	joke (n)	نكتة
en-nooba	Nubia	النوبة
noobi, noobiyeen	Nubian	نوبي
noor, anwaar	light (n, illumination)	نور
noskha, nosakh	copy (n, duplicate)	نسخة
noSS, enSaaS	half	نص
noSS el-leil	midnight	نص الليل
noT'	pronunciation	نطق
now9, anwaa9	type (n)	نوع
nu'Ta, nu'aTT	point (n, dot)	نقطة
nukhaa9	marrow	نخاع

O

obba, obab	dome	قبة
obTaan, abaTna	captain (in a ship)	قبطان
oddaas	mass (church service)	قداس
oddamaani	front (adj)	قدماني
odra, odraat	ability	قدرة
el-ods	Jerusalem	القدس
ofTaan, afaTeen	kaftan	قفطان
ogra	charge (fee); fare	أجرة
ohDa, ohwaD	room (hotel, etc.)	أوضة
okazyon, okazyonaat	sale (n, retail discount)	أوكازيون
okht, ekhwaat	sister	أخت
olayyil	few (adj)	قليل

omaar	gambling	قمار
omaash, a'misha	fabric; material	قماش
onSuleyya, onSuleyyaat	consulate	قنصلية
ooTa	tomato	أوطة
oozi	lamb (whole young sheep)	أوزي
orayyib	near; soon	قريب
orobba	Europe	أوروبا
orobbi, orobbiyyeen	European	أوروبي
oronfil	clove	قرنفل
orS, e'raaS	tablet; pill	قرص
orTaas	cone-shaped paper bag	قرطاس
oSayyar	short (adj, opp. long/tall)	قصير
osboo9, asaabee9	week	أسبوع
osboo9i	weekly	أسبوعي
osTa, osTawaat	master craftsman	أسطى
ostaaz, asatza	teacher, lecturer	أستاذ
osTowaana, osTowanaat	cylinder; record (music)	اسطوانة
oteel, otelaat	hotel	أوتيل
otobees, otobeesaat	coach (n, bus)	أوتوبيس
oTTa, oTaT	cat	قطة

Q

el qaahira	Cairo	القاهرة
qaamoos, qawaamees	dictionary	قاموس
qaanoon, qawaaneen	law	قانون
qabeela, qabaayel	tribe	قبيلة
qadhir	dirty (adj)	قذر
qanaah, qanawaat	canal (n, channel)	قناة
qanooni	legal	قانوني
qaraar, qararaat	decision (official)	قرار
qarawi, qarawiyeen	rural; villager	قروي
qarya, quraa	village	قرية
qaTar	Qatar	قطر
qaTari, qaTariyeen	Qatari	قطري
qawloon	colon	قولون
qaySareyya	Caesarean (delivery)	قيصرية (ولادة)
qeTaa9 9aam	public sector	قطاع عام
qeTa9 gheyaar	spare parts	قطع غيار
qiddees, qiddeeseen	saint	قدّيس
qinaa9, aqni9a	mask (n)	قناع
qiSSa, qiSaS	story (n, novel)	قصة
qonbela, qanaabil	bomb (n)	قنبلة

el quraan	the Koran	القرآن
qurHa	ulcer	قرحة
quTn	cotton (n)	قطن

R

ra'-'aaSa, ra'-'aaSaat	dancer (f)	راقصة
ra'ee'	fragile; delicate	رقيق
ra'ees	president	رئيس
ra'ees el wozara	prime minister	رئيس الوزراء
ra'eesi	main (adj); head	رئيسي
ra'S	dancing	رقص
ra'si	vertical	رأسي
ra'yy, aaraa'	opinion	رأي
ra9d	thunder	رعد
raagil, reggaala	man	راجل
raahib, rohbaan	monk	راهب
raakib, rukkaab	passenger	راكب
raas, roos	head (n, anatomy)	رأس
raashid, rashdeen	adult	راشد
raaya, rayaat	flag	راية
raayeH gayy	round-trip	رايح جاي
er-rabee9	spring (n, season)	الربيع
rabu	asthma	ربو
radd, rodood	answer (n); reply (n)	رد
raff, rofoof	shelf	رف
raghwa	lather	رغوة
rahaan, rahanaat	bet (n)	رهان
raHeel	departure	رحيل
raHHaal	nomad(ic)	رحّال
raHim, arHaam	womb	رحم
raHma	mercy	رحمة
ramaDaan	Ramadan (month of fasting)	رمضان
raml	sand (n)	رمل
raSeef, erSefa	platform (n, train, harbor, etc.); sidewalk	رصيف
rashaaqa	grace (n, elegance)	رشاقة
rasheed	Rosetta	رشيد
rasm ed-dokhool	entry fee	رسم الدخول
rasm, rosoom	fee	رسم
rasm, rosumaat	drawing (n)	رسم
rasmi	formal (adj)	رسمي
rasool, rosol	prophet; messenger	رسول
rassaam, rassameen	painter (art)	رستام

rayyis, royasa	leader (n, chief)	ريّس
re'aba, re'aab	neck	رقبة
reDa	satisfaction	رضا
reef	countryside	ريف
reefi	provincial; rustic	ريفي
reeH, reeyaaH	wind (n)	ريح
reeHa, rawaayeH	smell (n, scent)	رائحة
reeHaan	basil	ريحان
refee', refaa'	companion	رفيق
regheef, erghefa	loaf (n, bread)	رغيف
regoo9	return (n)	رجوع
reHla, reHlaat	trip; journey; voyage	رحلة
reHlit Tayaraan	flight (n, air journey)	رحلة طيران
rejeem	diet	ريجيم
rekheeS	inexpensive; cheap	رخيص
ri'a, ri'aat	lung	رئة
rigl, reglein	leg	رجل
rimsh, rumoosh	eyelash	رمش
risaala, rasaayil	message	رسالة
riyaaDa	sport (n)	رياضة
riyaaDi	athletic	رياضي
riyaaDiyaat	mathematics	رياضيات
riyaaH el khamaaseen	khamsin winds	رياح الخماسين
ro9b	horror	رعب
robaaT eg-gazma	shoelace	رباط الجزمة
robabekya	old junk	روبابيكيا
roDit aTfaal	kindergarten	روضة أطفال
rofayya9	thin	رفيع
rohH, arwaaH	spirit; soul	روح
rokhSa, rokhaS	license	رخصة
rooj	lipstick	روج
roosi, roos	Russian	روسي
roSaaSa, roSaaS	bullet	رصاصة
roSaaSi	dark gray	رصاصي
roshetta, roshettaat	prescription	روشتة
rosia	Russia	روسيا
rowaaya, rowayaat	novel (n, fiction)	رواية
rozz	rice	أرز
rub9, erba9	quarter (n)	ربع
rukba, rukab	knee	ركبة
rukhaam	marble (stone)	رخام
rukn, erkaan	corner (n)	ركن
rukoob el khail	horseback riding (n)	ركوب الخيل

rukoob el 9agal	cycling	ركوب العجل
rummaana, rummaan	pomegranate	رمان
ruSaaS	lead (n, metal)	رصاص
ruTooba	humidity	رطوبة

S

Sa'r, Su'oor	falcon; hawk	صقر
Sa9b	difficult	صعب
sa9eed	happy	سعيد
saa9a, saa9aat	hour; clock	ساعة
saa9it yad	wristwatch	ساعة يد
saabit	constant; firm; static	ثابت
saada	plain (adj)	سادة
Saafi	clear (adj, unclouded); pure	صاف
SaaHib, aS-Haab	friend; owner (of)	صاحب
saaHil, sawaaHil	coast (n, shore)	ساحل
saaHir, saHara	magician	ساحر
saakin, sokkaan	resident	ساكن
Saala, Salaat	hall	صالة
SaaliH, SaliHeen	virtuous	صالح
saayeH	melted (adj)	سايح
saayib	loose (adj, not packaged)	سايب
Saayigh, Soyyaagh	goldsmith	صائغ
saayiH, suyyaaH	tourist (n)	سائح
saayil, sawaayil	liquid	سائل
sab9, sebo9a	lion	سبع
saba', siba'aat	race (n, running, etc.)	سباق
SabaaH	morning	صباح
sabaanikh	spinach	سبانخ
sabab, asbaab	reason (n, cause)	سبب
sabat, sebeta	basket	سبت
sabbaak, sabbakeen	plumber	سباك
Sabbaar	cactus	صبار
sabboora	blackboard	سبورة
sabeel	free public faucet	سبيل
Sabgha, Sabghaat	dye	صبغة
Saboon	soap (n)	صابون
Sabr	patience (n)	صبر
Sada'a, Sada'aat	charity (n, donation)	صدقة
Sadaf	mother-of-pearl	صدف
sadd, sudood	dam	سد
saddaada, saddadaat	plug (n)	سدادة
Sadeeq, aSdiqaa'	friend	صديق

Sadma, Sadamaat	shock (n)	صدمة
safar	travel	سفر
SafeeHit zibaala	trash can	صفيحة زبالة
safeena, sufun	ship (n)	سفينة
safeer, sufara	ambassador	سفير
safenga, safeng	sponge	سفنجة
Saff, Sofoof	line (people, cars, etc.)	صف
saffaaH, saffaaHeen	serial killer	سفاح
SafHa, SafaHaat	page (n)	صفحة
eS-Safra	hepatitis	الصفراء
sageen, masageen	prisoner	سجين
saHaaba, saHaab	cloud	سحابة
SaHafi, SaHafiyyeen	journalist; reporter	صحافي
saHeeH	right (correct)	صحيح
sahl	easy	سهل
saHn, SuHoon	plate (n, dish)	صحن
SaHra	desert (n)	صحراء
sahra, sahraat	evening event	سهرة
sahw	oversight	سهو
sakan	lodging	سكن
sakani	residential	سكني
sakheef	silly, annoying	سخيف
Sakhra, Sokhoor	rock	صخرة
sakraan, sakraneen	drunk, intoxicated	سكران
sakta	heart failure	سكتة
Sal9a	bald patch	صلعة
eS-SalaaHeyya	validity; use-by date	الصلاحية
salaam	peace	سلام
salaam, salamaat	greeting	سلام
salaama	safety	سلامة
salaf	borrowing; ancestry	سلف
Salah, Salawaat	prayer	صلاة
Salat eg-gom9a	Friday prayer	صلاة الجمعة
salaTa, salaTaat	salad	سلطة
Saleeb, Solbaan	cross (n, crucifix)	صليب
Saloon Helaa'a	barber shop	صالون حلاقة
SalSit TamaaTim	tomato sauce	صلصة طماطم
sama, samawaat	sky	سماء
samaka, samak	fish (n)	سمك
samakit el 'ersh	shark	سمكة القرش
sameek	thick	سميك
Samgh	glue	صمغ
samna	ghee	سمنة

Samoola, Sawameel	nut (nut and bolt)	صامولة
sana, seneen	year	سنة
Sanai9i, Sanai9eyya	craftsman	صنايعي
sanama	hump (n, camel's back)	سنام
sanawi	yearly	سنوي
Sandoo', Sanadee'	trunk; box	صندوق
Sanf, aSnaaf	type (variant)	صنف
sanya, sawaani	second (n, time)	ثانية
saqf, es'of	ceiling	سقف
Sara9	epilepsy (n)	صرع
saraab	mirage	سراب
saraaya, sarayaat	palace	سراية
saree9	fast; quick	سريع
SareeH, SoraHa	frank (honest)	صريح
sarg, seroog	saddle (n)	سرج
Sarookh, Sawareekh	rocket	صاروخ
Sarraaf, Sarrafeen	cashier; teller	صرّاف
satH, estoH	roof	سطح
saTr, esTor	line (on paper)	سطر
sawwaa', sawwa'een	driver	سائق
Saydaleyya, Saydaleyyaat	pharmacy	صيدلية
eS-Se9eed	Upper Egypt (South)	الصعيد
Se9eedi, Sa9ayda	Upper Egyptian	صعيدي
es-se9oodeyya	Saudi Arabia	السعودية
se9oodi, se9oodiyeen	Saudi Arabian	سعودي
seekh, asyaakh	skewer	سيخ
eS-Seen	China	الصين
sefon, sefonaat	flush (n)	سيفون
segaara, sagaayer	cigarette	سيجارة
Seid	hunting	صيد
Seid es-samak	fishing	صيد السمك
eS-Seif	summer	الصيف
seil, seyool	flood	سيل
sekkeena, sakakeen	knife (n)	سكين
sekoot!	Silence!	سكوت١
Seneyya, Sawaani	tray	صينية
ser'a, ser'aat	theft	سرقة
sereer, saraayir	bed	سرير
setara, sataayer	curtain	ستارة
sha''a, shu'a'	apartment	شقة
sha'aawa	naughtiness (esp. children)	شقاوة
sha9bi	popular; folkloric	شعبي

sha9r	*hair*	شعر
shaahid, shohood	*witness*	شاهد
shaakir, shakreen	*thankful (adj)*	شاكر
shaami	*Syrian*	شامي
shaari9, shawaari9	*street*	شارع
shaari9 sadd	*cul-de-sac*	شارع سدّ
shaaTir	*clever; astute*	شاطر
shaay	*tea (n)*	شاي
shab9aan, shab9aaneen	*full (not hungry)*	شبعان
shabaab	*youths; youthfulness*	شباب
shabah	*likeness*	شبه
shabaH, ashbaaH	*ghost*	شبح
shabaka, shabak	*net (n)*	شبكة
shabakeyya	*retina*	شبكية
shabat	*dill*	شبت
shabboora	*mist*	شبورة
shabka	*pre-wedding jewelry gift (traditional)*	شبكة
shafawi	*verbal*	شفوي
shaffaaf	*transparent*	شفّاف
shafsha', shafashi'	*jug*	شفشق
shagara, shagar	*tree*	شجرة
shagee9	*brave (person); hero (in movie)*	شجع
shagh-ghaal	*working; operational*	شغّال
shahaada, shahadaat	*certificate; testimony*	شهادة
shahaada gaame9eyya	*university degree*	شهادة جامعية
shaheed, shohada	*martyr*	شهيد
shaHHaat, shaHHateen	*beggar*	شحّات
shahm	*gallant*	شهم
shaHm, shoHoom	*grease (n)*	شحم
shahr, shuhoor	*month*	شهر
shahri	*monthly*	شهري
shakhbooT, shakhabeeT	*scribble (n)*	شخبوط
shakhS, ash-khaaS	*person*	شخص
shakhSeyya, shakhSeyyaat	*personality; character*	شخصية
shakhT	*yelling (in anger)*	شخط
shakk, shokook	*doubt (n)*	شك
shakl, ashkaal	*shape (n)*	شكل
shakoosh khashab	*mallet*	شاكوش خشب
shakoosh, shawakeesh	*hammer*	شاكوش

shakwa, shakaawi	complaint	شكوى
shalal	paralysis	شلل
shallaal, shallalaat	waterfall	شلال
sham9	wax (n)	شمع
sham9a, sham9	candle	شمعة
shamaal	north	شمال
shamm	smell (n, sense)	شم
shammaama, shammaam	melon	شمام
shams	sun (n)	شمس
shamseyya, shamaasi	umbrella	شمسية
shanab, shanabaat	mustache	شنب
shanTa, shonaT	bag; suitcase	شنطة
shanTit eed	handbag	شنطة إيد
shar'	east (n)	شرق
shar'i	eastern; oriental	شرقي
sharaab, sharabaat	socks	شراب
sharaf	honor	شرف
sharbaat	sherbet	شربات
sharH	explanation	شرح
sharm	bay	شرم
sharT, shurooT	condition; stipulation	شرط
shaTT, sheTooT	river bank; seashore	شط
shaTaara	cleverness	شطارة
shaTarang	chess	شطرنج
shaTTa	hot chili	شطة
shawaam	Syrian people	شوام
shawwaaya, shawwayaat	grill (n)	شواية
shayyaal, shayyaleen	porter	شيال
she9eer	barley; malt	شعير
shedeed	tough; strong	شديد
sheek	elegant; well-dressed	شيك
sheek, sheekaat	check (cheque)	شيك
sheek 9ala bayaaD	blank check	شيك على بياض
sheekaat seyaaHeyya	travelers' checks	شيكات سياحية
sheesha, sheyash	water pipe; hookah	شيشة
sheikh, shuyookh	sheik	شيخ
shekheer	snoring	شخير
shemaal	left (opp. right)	شمال
shereek, shuraka	partner (n)	شريك
sherka, sherikaat	company (n, business)	شركة
esh-sheta	winter	الشتاء
sheTaan, shayaTeen	devil	شيطان

sheTaani	wild; uncultivated	شيطاني
sheteema, shataayim	insult (n)	شتيمة
shewaal, shewela	sack (esp. jute)	شوال
shewayyit	some	شوية
shezooz	deviance	شذوذ
shi9r	poetry	شعر
shi9reyya	vermicelli (pasta)	شعرية
shibbaak, shababeek	window	شبّاك
shibr, eshbaar	hand span (measure)	شبر
shibshib, shabaashib	slippers	شبشب
shidda, shadaayed	adversity	شدّة (وقت)
shiffa, shafaayef	lip	شفّة
shilla, shelal	group of friends	شلة
shiraa9, shira9aat	sail (n)	شراع
sho9aab morganeyya	coral	شعاب مرجانية
shoghl, ashghaal	work; occupation	شغل
shoghlaana, shoghlanaat	job	شغلانة
shohka, shuwak	fork	شوكة
shohk	thorns (rose, etc.)	شوك
shohk samak	fish bones	شوك سمك
shonaT	baggage (n)	شنط
shorba	soup	شوربة
shoroo'	sunrise	شروق
shoryaan, sharayeen	artery	شريان
shuHna, shuHnaat	shipment (n)	شحنة
si9r, as9aar	price (n)	سعر
si9r eg-gomla	wholesale price	سعر الجملة
sibHa, sibaaH	rosary	سبحة
Sidr, Sudoor	breast	صدر
sifaara, sifaaraat	embassy	سفارة
Sifr, eSfaar	zero	صفر
siggaada, sagageed	carpet (n); rug	سجادة
sign, sigoon	jail (n); prison	سجن
SiHHa	health	صحة
SiHHi	sanitary	صحّي
siHliyya, saHaali	lizard	سحلية
sikka Hadeed	railroad	سكة حديد
silaaH, asliHa	weapon	سلاح
silk, aslaak	wire; cable (n)	سلك
sillim, salaalim	ladder; stairs	سلم
simm, sumoom	poison	سمّ
simsaar, samasra	broker	سمسار
Sinaa9a, Sinaa9aat	industry	صناعة

Sinaa9i	man-made; artificial	صناعي
sinn	age (n)	سن
sinna, senaan	tooth	سنة
sinnaara, sananeer	fishing rod/hook	سنارة
Siraafa	currency exchange	صرافة
sirdaab, saradeeb	catacomb	سرداب
sirr, asraar	secret; mystery	سر
sirri	confidential	سري
sitt, sittaat	woman	ست
Siyaam	fasting (n)	صيام
Siyaam el maseeHeyyeen	Lent	صيام المسيحيين
Siyaana	maintenance; servicing	صيانة
so9aal deeki	whooping cough (n)	سعال ديكي
Sobaa9, Sawaabi9	finger	صبع
Sobaa9 rigl, Sawaabi9 rigl	toe	صبع رجل
SobH	morning	صبح
Sodaa9	headache	صداع
Sodaa9 niSfi	migraine	صداع نصفي
Soffaara, Safafeer	whistle (n)	صفارة
sofra: oDit sofra, owaD sofra;	dining room	أوضة سفرة
tarabeizit sofra, tarabeizaat sofra	dining table	ترابيزة سفرة
sofragi, sofrageyya	waiter (in the home)	سفرجي
Soghayyar	little; small	صغير
Soghayyar fis-sinn	young (adj)	صغير في السن
sogo'	sausages	سجق
solfa, salafeyyaat	loan (n)	سلفة
SolH	reconciliation	صلح
soo' tafaahom	misunderstanding	سوء تفاهم
soo', aswaa'	market (n)	سوق
soodaan: es-soodaan	Sudan	السودان
soodaani, soodaaniyeen	Sudanese	سوداني
Soof, aSwaaf	wool	صوف
soor, aswaar	fence (enclosure)	سور
Soora, Siwar	picture (n, photo, etc.)	صورة
Sorsaar, SaraSeer	cockroach	صرصار
sosta, sosat	fly (n); zipper	سوستة
sotyaan, sotyanaat	brassiere	سوتيان
Soht, aSwaat	sound (n); voice (n)	صوت
su'aal, as'ila	question (n)	سؤال
Sudfa, Sudaf	coincidence; chance	صدفة

sukhoneyya	heat (n)	سخونة
Sukhoor baHareyya	reef	صخور بحرية
sukkar	sugar (n)	سكر
sulaala, sulalaat	breed (n)	سلالة
sulTaan, salaTeen	sultan	سلطان
sur9a, sur9aat	speed (n)	سرعة

T

ta'deer	estimate (n)	تقدير
Ta'eyya, Tawaa'i	skullcap (traditional)	طاقية
ta'leed	imitation (adj, copied)	تقليد
Ta'm senaan	dentures	طقم أسنان
Ta'm, oT'um	set (n, specific group)	طقم
ta'meen	insurance	تأمين
ta'reeban	almost, nearly	تقريبا
ta'sheera, ta'sheeraat	visa	تأشيرة
Ta'Too'a, Ta'aTee'	ashtray	طقطوقة
ta9baan	tired (adj)	تعبان
ta9beer, ta9beeraat	expression (phrase)	تعبير
ta9ees	miserable	تعيس
ta9lab, ta9aalib	fox	ثعلب
ta9leem	education	تعليم
Ta9m	flavor	طعم
Ta9meyya	falafel	طعمية
ta9seela	snooze (n); nap (n)	تعسيلة
ta9weeD	compensation	تعويض
Taabi9 bosta, Tawaabi9 bosta	stamp (n, postage)	طابع بوسطة
taaboot Hagar	sarcophagus	تابوت حجر
taagir, tuggaar	trader	تاجر
TaaHoona, TawaHeen	windmill	طاحونة
Taalib, Talaba	student (n)	طالب
Taalib gam9a	undergraduate	طالب جامعة
taani	other; another; second (after first); again (adv)	تاني
Taarid	repellent (n)	طارد
Taasa, Tasaat	frying pan	طاسة
Taayesh	reckless	طائش
Taaza	fresh	طازه
Tab9an!	Of course!	طبعا!
Taba', eTbaa'	plate; dish (n)	طبق
Taba'a, Taba'aat	layer (n); class (society)	طبقة

taba9	belonging to; pertaining to	تبع
Tabanga, Tabangaat	pistol	طبنجة
Tabbaakh, Tabbaakheen	cook (n, chef)	طباخ
Tabee9i	natural	طبيعي
Tabeekh	cooked food	طبيخ
Tabla, Tobal	drum	طبلة
tabloh, tablohaat	painting (n); portrait	تابلوه
Taboor, Tawabeer	row (people, cars, soldiers, etc.)	طابور
tadleek	massage	تدليك
tafaaSeel	details	تفاصيل
TafH geldi	skin rash (n)	طفح جلدي
tagdeed, tagdeedaat	renewal; restoration	تجديد
taghyeer, taghyeeraat	change (n); alteration	تغيير
tagweef, tagweefaat	cavity	تجويف
taHeyya, taHeyyaat	greeting (n)	تحية
taHleel	analysis	تحليل
taHleel damm	blood test	تحليل دم
taHneeT	embalming (n)	تحنيط
taHt	below; under (prep)	تحت
taHweel, taHweelaat	transfer (money, etc)	تحويل
tahweya	ventilation	تهوية
taHzeer, taHzeeraat	caution (n, warning)	تحذير
takeef (el hawa)	air conditioning	تكييف (الهواء)
takhareef	hallucinations	تخاريف
takhyeem	camping (n)	تخييم
taksi, takaasi	cab (n)	تاكسي
tal, tilaal	hill	تل
Tal'a, Tala'aat	shot (from gun, etc.)	طلقة
Talaa'	divorce (n)	طلاق
Talab, Talabaat	request (n); order (restaurant, etc.)	طلب
talaf, talafeyyaat	damage (n)	تلف
talg	ice	ثلج
tallaaga, tallagaat	fridge	ثلاجة
Tama9	greed	طمع
TamaaTim	tomato	طماطم
taman, atmaan	cost (n); price	ثمن
tamargi, tamargeyya	male nurse	تمرجي
Tammaa9, Tammaa9een	greedy	طماع
tamreen, tamreenaat	exercise (n); training	تمرين
tan'eeT	leak, drip (n)	تنقيط

tanqeeb	excavation	تنقيب
taqaa'ud	retirement (from work)	تقاعد
taqaaleed	customs; traditions	تقاليد
taqleedi	traditional (adj)	تقليدي
tar'eyya	promotion (n, work, etc.)	ترقية
taraaDi	consent (n)	تراض
tarabeyza, tarabeyzaat	table	ترابيزة
Tarboosh	fez	طربوش
Tard, Turood	package (n, postal)	طرد
Taree', Turu'	road; route	طريق
Taree'a, Turu'	way (n, method)	طريقة
tareekh, tawareekh	date (n, calendar)	تاريخ
et-tareekh	history	التاريخ
Tarf, aTraaf	edge (outer tip)	طرف
targama	translation	ترجمة
tarHeeb	welcome (n)	ترحيب
Tari	soft	طري
TarToor, TaraTeer	cone-shaped cap; a nonentity	طرطور
tarzi, tarzeyya	tailor (n)	ترزي
taSaadum	crash (n, car, etc.)	تصادم
tash-kheeS	diagnosis	تشخيص
tashaabuh	similarity	تشابه
tashkeela	assortment	تشكيلة
tashTeeb SoHoon	washing dishes	تشطيب صحون
tashTeebat	finishing touches (buildings, etc.)	تشطيبات
taSleeH, taSleeHaat	repair (n)	تصليح
tasliya, tasaali	entertainment	تسلية
taSreeH, taSareeH	pass (n, permit)	تصريح
taSreeH, taSreeHaat	official statement	تصريح
taswee'	marketing	تسويق
taT9eem	inoculation; vaccination	تطعيم
tatawwu9i	voluntary	تطوعي
taw'am, tawaa'im	twins	توأم
tawaabil	spices; herbs	توابل
tawaabil es-salaTa	salad dressing	توابل السلطة
Tawaari'	emergency (n)	طوارئ
Taweel	long (adj); tall	طويل
Tawla	backgammon	طاولة
tawqee9, tawqee9aat	signature	توقيع
tawSeyya, tawSeyyaat	recommendation	توصية
Tayaraan 9aariD	charter flights	طيران عارض

tayyaar ek-kahraba	*current (electric)*	تيار الكهرباء
tayyaar el mayya	*current (water)*	تيار المياه
Tayyaar, Tayyareen	*pilot (airline)*	طيّار
Tayyaara, Tayyaraat	*airplane*	طائرة
Tayyib	*kind; good-natured*	طيّب
Tayyib!	*Okay!*	طيّب!
tazkara, tazaakir	*ticket (n)*	تذكرة
tazyeet	*lubrication*	تزييت
te'eel	*heavy; thick (dense)*	ثقيل
Teen	*mud*	طين
teena, teen	*fig*	تينة
TeHeena	*sesame paste*	طحينة
Teir, Teyoor	*bird*	طائر
Teloo9	*climbing; exit from*	طلوع
ter9a, tera9	*canal (fresh water)*	ترعة
teransh, teranshaat	*slice (n)*	ترنش
terbaas, tarabees	*bolt (n, for lock)*	ترباس
termometr	*thermometer*	ترمومتر
thaqaafa	*culture*	ثقافة
thawra	*revolution (uprising)*	ثورة
thowwaar	*revolutionaries*	ثوّار
ti9baan, ta9abeen	*snake*	ثعبان
Tibaa9a	*printing*	طباعة
Tibbi	*medical*	طبّي
Tibq el aSl	*identical*	طبق الأصل
timsaaH, tamaseeH	*crocodile*	تمساح
timsaal, tamaseel	*statue*	تمثال
tizkaar, tizkaraat	*memento*	تذكار
Toh' en-nagaah, aTwaa' en-nagaah	*lifebuoy*	طوق النجاة
tohm	*garlic*	ثوم
Tohoor	*circumcision*	طهور
tonsi, tawansa	*Tunisian*	تونسي
Tooba, Toob	*brick*	طوبة
Tool	*length*	طول
Tool 9omri	*all my life*	طول عمري
Tool en-nahaar	*all day long*	طول النهار
toonis	*Tunis(ia)*	تونس
toota, toot	*berries*	توت
tor, teraan	*bull*	ثور
Tor'a, Tor'aat	*corridor*	طرقة
torgoman, torgomanaat	*translator; interpreter*	ترجمان

torkeya	*Turkey*	تركيا
Toromba, Torombaat	*pump (n)*	طرمبة
Torshi	*pickles*	طرشي
treng, trengaat	*track suit*	ترنج
tufaaHa, tufaaH	*apple*	تفاحة
tuHfa, tuHaf	*masterpiece*	تحفة
tuhma, tuhamm	*charge (n, accusation)*	تهمة
turaab	*dust (n)*	تراب

U

ufuqi	*horizontal (adj);*	أفقي
	landscape (adj, picture)	
ughneyya, aghaani	*song*	أغنية
el umam el muttaHida	*the United Nations*	الأمم المتحدة
umm, ummahaat	*mother (n)*	أم
umma, umam	*nation*	أمة
umniya, amaani	*wish (n)*	أمنية
unboobit et-tanaffus	*snorkel (n)*	أنبوبة التنفس
untha, inaath	*female*	أنثى
urdoni, urdoniyeen	*Jordanian*	أردني
el urdunn	*Jordan*	الأردن
usra, usarr	*family*	أسرة
usToora, asaaTeer	*legend (myth)*	أسطورة

W

wa't, aw'aat	*time (n, of day)*	وقت
wa9d, wu9ood	*promise (n)*	وعد
waa'if	*standing; not working*	واقف
waadi, widyaan	*valley*	واد
waaDiH	*clear; unambiguous*	واضح
waagib, wagibaat	*duty (n, obligation)*	واجب
waaHa, waaHaat	*oasis*	واحة
waaqe9i	*realistic*	واقعي
waasi9	*wide; loose (adj, baggy)*	واسع
waathiq (min nafso)	*sure (of himself)*	واثق (من ‚نفسه)
waaTi, waTyeen	*low; base (adj)*	واطئ
el waD9	*status; position*	الوضع
il wadaa9!	*Farewell!*	الوداع
waDHeefa, waDHaayif	*job*	وظيفة
wafaah, wafeyyaat	*death*	وفاة
wafd, wofood	*delegation (n)*	وفد
wafy, awfeya	*loyal (n)*	وفي
waga9, awgaa9	*pain*	وجع

wagaaha	smartness (appearance)	وجاهة
wagba, wagabaat	meal	وجبة
waHdaani	lonely	وحداني
wahmi	unreal	وهمي
wakr, awkaar	den	وكر
waksa, waksaat	calamity	وكسة
wala Haaga	nothing	ولا حاجة
wala waaHid	nobody	ولا واحد
walaa9a, wala9aat	lighter (n, for cigarettes, etc.)	ولاعة
walad, awlaad	boy	ولد
walaw	even though, even if	ولو
waleyy el 'amr, awaleyaa' el 'omoor	guardian or parent	ولي الأمر
walla	or	ولا
wara	behind	ورا
wara' el bardi	papyrus	ورق البردي
wara' el ghaar	bay leaves	ورق الغار
wara'a, awraa'	paper (n, document, etc.)	ورقة
wara'it shagar, wara' shagar	leaf	ورقة شجر
waram, awraam	lump; tumor	ورم
warda, ward	flower (n, rose, etc.)	وردة
wareed, awrida	vein (anatomy)	وريد
warneesh	varnish	ورنيش
warraani	back (adj, rear)	وراني
warsha, wirash	workshop	ورشة
warTa	predicament	ورطة
wasaakha, wasakhaat	dirt; filth	وساخة
waseela, wasaayel	method	وسيلة
waseem	handsome	وسيم
waseeT, wosaTaa'	intermediary	وسيط
waSfa, waSfaat	recipe	وصفة
washm	tattoo	وشم
waSi, awSiyaa'	guardian	وصي
waSl, woSoolaat	receipt	وصل
watad, awtaad	peg (for tent, etc.); stake (e.g. wooden)	وتد
waTani, waTaniyeen	patriotic; national	وطني
wazeer, wozara	minister (government)	وزير
wazn, awzaan	weight (n)	وزن
wedn, wedaan	ear	ودن
weDoo'	ritual wash (Islamic)	وضوء

weHish	bad	وحش
weSeyya, waSaaya	will (inheritance)	وصية
wi-kamaan	and also	وكمان
widdi	amicable	ودّي
wikaala, wikalaat	agency (n)	وكالة
wil9a	flame	ولعة
wilaada, wiladaat	birth (n)	ولادة
wilaaya, wilaayaat	state (region)	ولاية
el wilaayaat el muttaHida	the United States	الولايات المتحدة
winsh, ewnaash	winch (n)	ونش
wiraathy	hereditary	وراثي
wirk, weraak	thigh	ورك
wisaam	medal	وسام
wish, weshoosh	face (n, anatomy)	وش
wisikh	dirty; filthy	وسخ
wisT	waist; middle; amid	وسط
wizza, wizz	goose	وزّة
wuSool	arrival	وصول

Y

yaakhod gawla	tour (v, visit)	ياخد جولة
yaakhud	take (v)	يأخذ
yaakul	eat (v)	يأكل
yaa'oot	ruby (n)	ياقوت
yadawi	manual (adj, by hand)	يدوي
yafTa, yofaT	sign (n, display board)	يافطة
yahoodi, yahood	Jew(ish)	يهودي
yakht, yukhoot	yacht	يخت
el yaman	Yemen	اليمن
yamani, yamaniyeen	Yemeni	يمني
yasmeen	jasmine	ياسمين
yathiq	trust (v)	يثق
ye'aabil	meet (v)	يقابل
ye'addar	estimate (v)	يقدّر
ye'addim	introduce; prioritize	يقدّم
ye'aggar	hire out (v); rent (v); lease (v)	يأجّر
ye'akkid	confirm (v)	يوكد
ye'akkil	feed (v)	يأكّل
ye'allil	reduce (v)	يقلل
ye'assim	divide (v)	يقتسم
ye'aTTa'	cut (v); tear (v)	يقطع
ye'bal	accept (v)	يقبل

ye'fil	shut (v)	يقفل
ye'lee	fry (v)	يقلي
ye'ool	say (v); tell (v)	يقول
ye'ra	read (v)	يقرأ
ye'til	kill (v)	يقتل
ye9aamil	treat (v, behave towards)	يعامل
ye9addi	cross (v, e.g. road)	يعدّي
ye9addil	adjust (v)	يعدل
ye9allim	teach (v)	يعلم
ye9ayyaT	cry (v, weep)	يعيط
ye9idd	count (v, add)	يعدّ
ye9mil	do; make (v)	يعمل
ye9oom	swim (v); float (v)	يعوم
ye9ooz	want (v)	يعوز
ye9raf	know (v)	يعرف
ye9riD	show (v); offer (v)	يعرض
ye9rog	limp (v)	يعرج
ye9tezir	apologize	يعتذر
ye9zim	invite (v)	يعزم
yeb'a	become	يبقى
yeb9at	send	يبعث
yeb9at bil-bareed	mail (v, letters, etc)	يبعث بالبريد
yebaadil	exchange (v)	يبادل
yeballagh	inform (v)	يبلّغ
yebaTTal	quit (v)	يبطل
yebee9	sell (v)	يبيع
yebla9	swallow (v)	يبلع
yebni	construct (v)	يبني
yeboSS	look (v, see)	يبصّ
yebtedi	start (v); begin (v)	يبتدي
yeDaayi'	harass (v)	يضايق
yedakh-khan	smoke (v)	يدخّن
yedardish	chatter (v)	يدردش
yedawwar	search (v); start (motor, etc.)	يدوّر
yeDayya9	lose (v, misplace)	يضيّع
yeddi	give (v)	يدّي
yedeer	run (v, operate)	يدير
yedfa9	pay (v)	يدفع
yeDHak	laugh (v)	يضحك
yedill	guide (v); direct (v)	يدل
yedoob	melt (v); dissolve (v)	يذوب
yedoor	turn (v, go around)	يدور
yeDrab	beat (v, hit)	يضرب

yeDris	study (v, a subject)	يدرس
yeDumm	join (v, connect)	يضم
yeegi	come (v)	ييجي
yefaaSil	haggle (v)	يفاصل
yefaDDal	prefer (v)	يفضل
yefakkar	think (v, consider)	يفكر
yefDal	stay (v); remain (v)	يفضل
yefham	understand (v)	يفهم
yefoot (9ala)	pass (by someone, v)	يفوت (على)
yeftekir	remember (v); think (v, assume)	يفتكر
yegarrab	try (v); sample (v)	يجرّب
yegeeb	obtain (v); bring (v)	يجيب
yeghanni	sing (v)	يغنّي
yeghaTTi	cover (v)	يغطّي
yeghayyar	change (v, clothes, etc.)	يغيّر
yeghish	cheat (v)	يغش
yeghli	boil (v, heat)	يغلي
yeghra'	drown (v)	يغرق
yeghsil	wash (v)	يغسل
yegorr	tow (v); drag (v)	يجز
yegri	run (v, jog)	يجري
yeH'in	inject (v)	يحقن
yeHaarib	fight (v); go to war against	يحارب
yeHaawil	try (v)	يحاول
yeHarrak	move (something else)	يحرّك
yeHassin	improve (v)	يحسّن
yeHawwil	turn (v); transform; transfer (money, etc.)	يحوّل
yeHess	feel (v)	يحس
yeHgiz	reserve (v); book (v)	يحجز
yeHibb	love (v); like (v)	يحب
yeHill (mushkila)	resolve (v, a problem)	يحلّ (مشكلة)
yeHinn	long for (v, miss)	يحن
yeHlam	dream (v)	يحلم
yeHlaq	shave (v); cut (hair)	يحلق
yeHoTT	put (v)	يحط
yeHra'	burn (v)	يحرق
yehrab	escape (v)	يهرب
yehris	mash (v)	يهرس
yeHSal	happen (v)	يحصل
yeHsib	calculate (v)	يحسب
yeHtaag	need (v)	يحتاج

yekammil	complete (v)	يكمل
yekarrar	repeat (v)	يكرر
yekassar	break (v, smash)	يكسّر
yekbar	grow (v, in size, age, etc)	يكبر
yekhaaf	fear (v)	يخاف
yekhabbaT	knock (, on door, etc.)	يخبط
yekhallaS	finish (v)	يخلص
yekhalli	keep (v, retain)	يخلّي
yekheff	recover (from illness)	يخفّ
yekhli	vacate (v)	يخلي
yekhrig	direct (v, a movie, etc.)	يُخرج
yekhrog	exit (v); go out	يخرج
yekhsar	lose (v, opp. win)	يخسر
yekhSim	deduct (v)	يخصم
yekhtaar	choose (v); select (v)	يختار
yekhtefi	vanish (v)	يختفي
yekrah	hate (v)	يكره
yeksab	win (v)	يكسب
yekshif	uncover (v)	يكشف
yektib	write (v)	يكتب
yekwi	iron (v)	يكوي
yel9ab	play (v)	يلعب
yelaa'i	find (v)	يلاقي
yelbis	wear (v)	يلبس
yeliff	turn (v, go around); wrap (v)	يلفّ
yelmaH	spot (v, see)	يلمح
yelmis	touch (v)	يلمس
yemdaH	compliment (v)	يمدح
yemeen	right (opp. left)	يمين
yemill	bore (of); lose interest	يملّ
yemkin	maybe	يمكن
yemla	fill (v); fill out	يملأ
yemlik	own (v); possess (v)	يملك
yemsaH	wipe (v); erase (v)	يمسح
yemshi	walk (v)	يمشي
yemshi naHyit	walk towards	يمشي ناحية
yemshi wara	walk behind	يمشي وراء
yemsik	hold (v); catch (v)	يمسك
yemurr (9ala)	pass (by) (v)	يمرّ (على)
yen9ish	refresh (v)	ينعش
yenaadi	call (v, summon)	ينادي
yenaam	sleep (v)	ينام
yenazzam	organize (v)	ينظم

yendam	regret (v)	يندم
yenDamm	join (v, enroll)	ينضم
yenfegir	burst (v); explode (v)	ينفجر
yengaH	succeed (v, opp. fail)	ينجح
yenoTT	jump (v)	ينط
yenqiz	save (v); rescue (v)	ينقذ
yensa	forget (v)	ينسى
yenwi	intend (v)	ينوي
yenzif	bleed (v)	ينزف
yenzil es-soo'	go to market	ينزل السوق
yeqarrar	decide (v)	يقرر
yeraa'ib	watch (v, observe)	يراقب
yerabbi	breed (v, animals); bring up (children)	يربي
yeraHHal	deport (v)	يرحل
yerattib	arrange (v)	يرتب
yerbuT	tie (v)	يربط
yerfid	fire (v, terminate employment)	يرفد
yerfuD	refuse (v)	يرفض
yerga9	return (v)	يرجع
yerka9	kneel (v)	يركع
yerkin	park (v, cars, etc.)	يركن
yermi	throw (v)	يرمي
yerodd	reply (v)	يرد
yerooH	go (v)	يروح
yersim	draw (v, illustrate)	يرسم
yes'al	ask (v)	يسأل
yesaa9id	help (v); assist (v)	يساعد
yesaafir	travel (v)	يسافر
yeSadda'	believe (v)	يصدق
yeSallaH	fix (v)	يصلح
yeSalli	pray (v)	يصلي
yesallif	lend (v)	يسلف
yeSammim	design (v); insist (v)	يصمم
yeSanna9	make (v); manufacture (v)	يصنع
yesarrakh	scream (v)	يصرخ
yeSbogh	dye (v)	يصبغ
yeseeb	leave (v, abandon)	يسيب
yesh-Hin	charge (v, battery, etc.)	يشحن
yesHa	wake (v)	يصحى
yeshaawir	wave (v, with hand); point (v, with finger)	يشاور

yesHab	*pull (v); withdraw (v, cash, etc.)*	يسحب
yeshagh-ghal	*run (v, operate)*	يشغّل
yesheel	*remove; lift; carry*	يشيل
yeshidd	*pull (v); attract (v)*	يشدّ
yeshimm	*smell (v)*	يشم
yeshmal	*includes*	يشمل
yeshoof	*see (v)*	يشوف
yeshrab	*drink (v)*	يشرب
yeshraH	*explain (v)*	يشرح
yeshteki	*complain (v)*	يشتكي
yeshteri	*buy (v)*	يشتري
yeshtim	*curse (v, abuse verbally)*	يشتم
yeskun	*live (v, dwell)*	يسكن
yesma9	*listen (v); hear (v)*	يسمع
yesmaH	*allow (v); permit (v)*	يسمح
yesoo'	*drive (v, car, etc.)*	يسوق
yeSoom	*fast (v)*	يصوم
yesta9gil	*hurry (v); expedite (v)*	يستعجل
yesta9mil	*use (v)*	يستعمل
yeSTaad	*hunt (v)*	يصطاد
yeSTaaD samak	*fish (v)*	يصطاد سمك
yestafragh	*vomit (v)*	يستفرغ
yestagimm	*relax (v)*	يستجم
yestakshif	*explore (v)*	يستكشف
yestanna	*wait (v)*	يستنى
yestarayyaH	*rest (v)*	يستريح
yestelim	*receive (v)*	يستلم
yet9ab	*tire (v)*	يتعب
yet9allim	*learn (v)*	يتعلّم
yetabbil	*marinate (v); season (v)*	يتبّل
yeTahhar	*disinfect (v)*	يطهّر
yeTalla'	*divorce (v)*	يطلّق
yeTbukh	*cook (v)*	يطبخ
yeTeer	*fly (v)*	يطير
yeTfi	*extinguish (v); switch off*	يطفئ
yetgawwiz	*marry*	يتزوج
yetHarrak	*move (v, oneself)*	يتحرّك
yetkallim	*talk (v); speak (v)*	يتكلّم
yetkhaani'	*quarrel (v)*	يتخانق
yetkhayyil	*imagine (v)*	يتخيّل
yetHarrak	*move (v, oneself)*	يتحرّك
yeTla9	*climb (v); exit (v)*	يطلع
yeTlub	*request (v)*	يطلب

yeTlub bit-tilifoon	*dial (v)*	يطلب بالتليفون
yetmanna	*hope (v)*	يتمنى
yetmarran	*train (v)*	يتمرّن
yetmatta9	*enjoy (v)*	يتمتّع
yeTrud	*eject; throw out*	يطرد
yetSawwar	*imagine (v); be photographed*	يتصوّر
yetshankil	*trip (v, stumble)*	يتشنكل
yetteSil	*contact (v, phone, etc.)*	يتّصل
yetzaH-la'	*slip (v, lose footing)*	يتزحلق
yewaafi'	*agree (v)*	يوافق
yewaDDab esh-shanTa	*pack (v) a bag*	يوضّب الشنطة
yewaffar	*save (v, economize)*	يوفّر
yewarri	*show (v, display)*	يورّي
yewaSSal	*connect (v); deliver (v)*	يوصّل
yewga9	*hurt (v)*	يوجع
yewSal	*arrive; reach (v)*	يوصل
yewSif	*describe (v)*	يوصف
yezaakir	*study (v)*	يذاكر
yezawwid	*increase (v); add to (v)*	يزوّد
yezbuT	*set (v, clock, motor, etc.)*	يضبط
yezo'	*push (v)*	يزق
yezoor	*visit (v)*	يزور
yezra9	*plant (v)*	يزرع
yibaTTal	*refrain from (v)*	يبطّل
yo'-9od	*sit (v)*	يقعد
yo'a9	*fall (v, tumble)*	يقع
yo'af	*stand (v, opp. sit)*	يقف
yo'mur	*order (v, demand)*	يأمر
yodkhol	*enter (v)*	يدخل
yokhrom	*pierce (v)*	يخرم
yor'oS	*dance (v)*	يرقص
yughma 9aleih	*faint (v, pass out)*	يغمى عليه

Z

za9eem, zo9ama	*leader*	زعيم
za9faraan	*saffron*	زعفران
za9laan	*unhappy; sad; upset*	زعلان
za9tar	*thyme*	زعتر
zaabiT, zubbaaT	*officer (military)*	ضابط
zaat nafso	*itself; himself*	ذات نفسه
zabaadi	*yogurt*	زبادي
zabzaba, zabzabaat	*vibration; frequency (radio, etc.)*	ذبذبة

zaffa	wedding procession	زفة
zaghab	down (n, feathers)	زغب
zaghrooTa, zaghareeT	trill	زغرودة
zaHma	crowd(ed); congestion	زحمة
zahra, zuhoor	rose	زهرة
zaki	clever; intelligent	ذكي
zalabaTTa	shaved head	زلبطة
zalaTa, zalaT	pebble	زلط
zamaan; min zamaan	a long time ago	زمان؛ من زمان
zaman	time (n, era, etc.)	زمن
zambalik	spring (in watch, etc.)	زمبلك
zanb, zonoob	guilt	ذنب
zarafa, zaraaf	giraffe	زرافة
zareef, zoraaf	quaint; amusing	ظريف
zarf, ezrof	envelope	ظرف
zarf, zoroof	circumstance	ظرف
zatoona, zatoon	olive (fruit)	زيتونة
zawya, zawaya	angle (n); prayer corner	زاوية
zayy	like (similar to)	زيّ
zebda	butter	زبدة
zebeeba, zebeeb	raisin	زبيب
zeena	decorations	زينة
zeit, zuyoot	oil	زيت
zemeel, zomala	colleague	زميل
zeyaara, zeyaraat	visit (n, trip)	زيارة
zeyada	more; extra	زيادة
zeyba'	mercury	زيبق
zhaahir	apparent; showing (visible)	ظاهر
zibaala	trash (n); litter	زبالة
zift	tar	زفت
zilzaal, zalaazil	earthquake	زلزال
zinzaana, zanazeen	cell (prison)	زنزانة
ziraa9a	agriculture (n)	زراعة
zo'aa'	alley	زقاق
zoh', azwaa'	manners; taste (style)	ذوق
zohr	throat	زور
zokaam	congestion (nose)	زكام
zolm	injustice	ظلم
zommaara, zamameer	wind instrument	زمّارة
zoraar, zaraayer	button (n)	زرار (زر)
zuboon, zabaayen	client	زبون
zukhrufi	ornamental	زخرفي
zumurrud	emerald (n)	زمرد

Words beginning with the letter 9ein

9a'd, 9o'ood	*contract*	عقد
9a'l, 9o'ool	*reasoning; sensibility*	عقل
9a'leyya, 9a'leyyaat	*mentality*	عقلية
9a'raba, 9a'aarib	*scorpion*	عقربة
9aadi	*common (adj, normal); ordinary*	عادي
9aadil	*fair (just)*	عادل
9aadim	*exhaust (n, fumes)*	عادم
el 9aadra	*the Virgin Mary*	العذراء
9aag	*ivory*	عاج
9aagiz, 9agaza	*disabled*	عاجز
9aalam	*world*	عالم؛دنيا
9aali	*high (tall)*	عال
9aali eS-Soht	*loud*	عالي الصوت
el 9aameyya	*colloquial language*	العامية
9aarif	*knowledgeable*	عارف
9aaSifa, 9awaaSif	*storm (n)*	عاصفة
9aaSima, 9awaaSim	*capital (city)*	عاصمة
9aaTil, 9aTleen	*unemployed*	عاطل
9aazib, 9uzzaab	*bachelor*	عازب
9aazil Tibbi	*condom*	عازل طبي
9abaaya, 9abayaat	*cloak*	عباءة
9abdu	*His (i.e. God's) slave*	عبده
9abeeT, 9obT	*stupid*	عبيط
9abqari, 9abaqra	*genius*	عبقري
9adaala	*justice (n)*	عدالة
9adad, a9daad	*number; digit*	عدد
9aDala, 9aDalaat	*muscle*	عضلة
9adasa, 9adasaat	*lens*	عدسة
9adawa, 9adawaat	*enmity*	عداوة
9addaad, 9addadaat	*meter (electricity, taxi fare, etc.)*	عداد
9adeel	*brother-in-law*	عديل
9aDHeem	*great (adj, marvelous)*	عظيم
9aDma, 9aDm	*bone*	عظمة
9ads	*lentils*	عدس
9adwa	*contagion*	عدوى
9afia	*wellbeing; vigor*	عافية
9afreet, 9afareet	*ghost; imp; mischievous child, etc.*	عفريت
9afsh	*furniture*	عفش

9afwan!	You're welcome!; Don't mention it!	عفوا!
9agabi!	I'm amazed!	عجبي!
9agala, 9agal	bicycle; wheel	عجلة
9ageeb	wonderful	عجيب
9ageena	dough	عجين
9agooz, 9awageez	elderly; old (person)	عجوز
9agwa	pressed dates paste	عجوة
9agz	disability; shortfall	عجز
el 9aks	the opposite, reverse	العكس
9ala	on	على
9alaama, 9alamaat	sign (n, mark)	علامة
9alal aakher	maximum	على الآخر
9alam, a9laam	flag	علم
9alashaan	because	علشان
9aleel el bakht	unlucky (adj)	قليل البخت
9amaleyya, 9amaleyyaat	operation	عملية
9amali	practical	عملي
9amm, 9imaam	uncle (paternal)	عمّ
9amma, 9ammaat	aunt (paternal)	عمة
9amoodi	vertical	عامودي
9amrit motor	engine overhaul	عمرة موتور
9anbar	ambergris	عنبر
9anbar, 9anaabir	ward (hospital)	عنبر
9and; 9andi	have; I have	عند؛ عندي
9aneef	violent	عنيف
9ankaboot, 9anaakib	spider	عنكبوت
9ara'	sweat	عرق
9arabeyya, 9arabeyyaat	car	عربية
9arabi	Arab(ian)	عربي
9arabi; el 9arabi	Arabic language	العربي
9arD, 9urooD	performance; show (n); offer (n)	عرض
9arD azyaa'	fashion show	عرض أزياء
9areeD	wide	عريض
9arees, 9irsaan	bridegroom	عريس
9aroosa, 9araayes	bride; doll	عروسة
9arsh, 9oroosh	throne	عرش
9aSab, a9Saab	nerve	عصب
9asal	honey	عسل
9aSeer, 9aSaayin	juice	عصير
9aSfoor, 9aSafeer	sparrow	عصفور
9asha	dinner	عشاء

9ashee'a, 9ashee'aat	*mistress*	عشيقة
9askari	*military (adj)*	عسكري
9askari, 9asaakir	*soldier*	عسكري
9aSr	*era*	عصر
el 9aSr	*afternoon*	العصر
9aSri	*modern, contemporary*	عصري
9ataba, 9atabaat	*doorstep*	عتبة
9atee	*ancient*	عتيق
9aTf	*kindness*	عطف
9aTlaan	*out of order*	عطلان
9atma	*darkness*	عتمة
9atshaan	*thirsty*	عطشان
9awwaama	*rubber ring; houseboat*	عوامة
9ayyaan, 9ayyaneen	*ill; sick (person)*	عيان
9ayyil, 9yaal	*child; infant*	عيل
9ayyina, 9ayyinaat	*sample (n, small example)*	عينة
9aza	*mourning event*	عزاء
9azaab	*torture (n)*	عذاب
9eed, a9yaad	*feast (n)*	عيد
9eed el 9ummaal	*Labor Day*	عيد العمال
9eed meelaad	*birthday*	عيد ميلاد
9eib, 9eyoob	*shame, disgrace; fault*	عيب
9ein, 9uyoon	*eye (n, anatomical); water spring*	عين
9eish	*bread*	عيش
9elmi	*scientific*	علمي
9esh-sha, 9eshash	*hut*	عشة
9esh-shit feraakh, 9eshash feraakh	*hencoop*	عشة فراخ
9eyaali	*juvenile (adj)*	عيالي
9ezba, 9ezab	*farm (n)*	عزبة
9ezooma, 9azaayem	*banquet*	عزومة
9idda	*tools*	عدّة
9idwaan	*aggression*	عدوان
9ifish	*trashy*	عفش
9igga	*omelet (variety of)*	عجة
9igl, 9ogool	*calf*	عجل
9ilaa'a, 9ila'aat	*relationship*	علاقة
9ilaag	*therapy; remedy; cure*	علاج
9ilaawa, 9ilawaat	*pay rise*	علاوة
9ilba, 9ilab	*box (n)*	علبة

9ilbit kabreet	*match-box*	علبة كبريت
9ilm el maSreyyaat	*Egyptology*	علم المصريات
9imaara, 9imaraat	*apartment block*	عمارة
el 9imaara	*architecture*	العمارة
el 9inaaya el murakkaza	*intensive care*	العناية المركزة
9inab	*grapes*	عنب
9inadi	*stubborn*	عندي
9inwaan, 9anaween	*address (n, mail)*	عنوان
9ir', 9oroo'	*vein*	عرق
9ir'soos	*licorice*	عرقسوس
9iraa'i, 9iraa'iyyeen	*Iraqi*	عراقي
el 9iraaq	*Iraq*	العراق
9iryaan, 9iryaneen	*unclothed*	عريان
9iSaaba, 9iSabaat	*gang*	عصابة
9iTr, 9oToor	*perfume*	عطر
9iyaada, 9iyaadaat	*clinic (doctor's)*	عيادة
9izaal	*moving house*	عزال
9la-shaan khaaTir	*(for the) sake (of)*	خاطر (علشان خاطر)
9o'd, e9-'aad	*necklace*	عقد
9o'da, 9o'ad	*knot; complex (n)*	عقدة
9oDweyya	*membership (n)*	عضوية
9oDwi	*organic*	عضوي
9okkaaz, 9okkazaat	*walking stick*	عكّاز
9omaan	*Oman*	عمان
9omaani, 9omaaniyyeen	*Omani*	عماني
9omda, 9omad	*mayor*	عمدة
9omla, 9omlaat	*currency (money, etc.)*	عملة
9omoola, 9omoolaat	*commission (percentage fee)*	عمولة
9omoomi	*public*	عمومي
9omr, a9maar	*lifetime; age*	عمر
9omra	*pilgrimage to Mecca (outside season)*	عمرة
9ood, e9waad	*oud (lute-like instrument)*	عود
9osr haDm	*indigestion*	عسر هضم
9oTl	*breakdown (n, malfunction)*	عطل
9ozr, a9zaar	*excuse (n)*	عذر
9yaaT	*weeping*	عياط

PHRASEBOOK CONTENTS

EGYPT: THE COUNTRY

Getting Started

When you first land, you may notice one or
two language oddities, such as people saying
"Welcome in Egypt" instead of "Welcome to
Egypt" when they greet you. This is a result
of literal translation from Arabic into
English. So now if you read it on a sign, or
hear it from a local, you can smile
knowingly.

More than likely, you will find that Egyptians,
generally speaking, welcome tourists
cheerfully. They have seen many. Perhaps it's
a good idea to be prepared and arm yourself
with a small "Getting Started" pack of
essential words and expressions. We will build
on them as we progress along the chapters.

hello
أهلاً
ahlan

yes
أيوه
aywah

no
لا
la'a

please

من فضلك

min faDlak

thank you

شكراً

shukran

maybe

يمكن

yemkin

certainly

أكيد

akeed

tomorrow

بكرة

bokra

sorry (m/f)

آسف/آسفة

aasif/aasfa

goodbye

مع السلامة

ma9as salaama

Where?

فين؟

fein?

Here!

هنا!

hena

Over there!

هناك!

henaak

If you had a window seat in a space ship and looked downwards you would see Egypt in the North Eastern corner of Africa. It would look like a huge expanse of desert, but it has one very thin squiggly green line going through it, ending in a triangle in the Northern tip as it meets the Mediterranean Sea. That would be the Nile valley and the Nile delta.

To the East you would see the Red Sea, separating Egypt from Jordan and the Kingdom of Saudi Arabia. The North of the Red Sea seems to be making the "victory" sign with two "fingers." The "finger" further away from Egypt is the Gulf of Aqaba, shared by Egypt, Israel, and Jordan. The closer "finger" is the Gulf of Suez. The space between these two fingers is the Sinai Peninsula.

If you look really close you'll see an almost straight line of blue water going North from the the tip of the Gulf of Suez towards the Mediterranean Sea. That would be the Suez Canal, dug by hand over ten years between 1859 and 1869.

Egypt

مصر

maSr

the Nile Valley

وادي النيل

waadi enneel

the [Nile] Delta

الدلتا

ed-delta

the Suez Canal

قناة السويس

qanaat es-suweis

Sinai

سيناء

seena

the Red Sea

البحر الأحمر

el baHr el aHmar

the Northern region

بحري

baHari

the Southern region

قبلي

ibli

Some Cities and Towns

city	river
مدينة	نهر
madeena	nahr
town	lake
بلد	بحيرة
balad	buHeira
port	coast
ميناء	ساحل
meenaa	saaHil

We would like to visit ...

عاوزين نزور ...

9awzeen nezoor ...

Aswan and Abu Simbel

أسوان وأبوسمبل

aswaan wabu simbil

Damanhour

دمنهور

damanhoor

El Ein es-Sukhna

العين السخنة

el 9ein es-sokhna

Are you from ...

أنتو من ...

entu min ...

Tanta?

طنطا؟

TanTa?

El Mahalla?

المحلة؟

el maHalla?

Alexandria?

اسكندرية؟

eskendereyya?

My grandfather was born in ...

جدي مولود في ...

giddi mawlood fi ...

Asyut

أسيوط

asyooT

Port Said

بور سعيد

bor sa9eed

Minya

المنيا

el menia

Our grandmother comes from ...

جدتنا من ...

giddetna min ...

Beni Suef

بني سويف

banisweif

Sohag

سوهاج

sohaag

May I...

ممكن ...

momkin ...

see your home?

أشوف بيتكم؟

ashoof beitkom

see (meet) the family?

أشوف العيلة؟

ashoof el 9eila

Show me ...

وريني ...

war-reeni ...

on the map

على الخريطة

9alal khareeTa

on the screen
على الشاشة
9alash-shaasha

the photo album
ألبوم الصور
alboom eS-Siwar

Some Cairo Landmarks

Most Egyptians refer to the city of Cairo as
maSr even though its official name is
al qaahira. It's the largest city in Africa and
one of the most populous in the world. The
Islamic centre of the city is the oldest part,
and it gets newer in a ripple-effect as you
leave the centre. The pyramids and sphinx
are several thousand years older, but they are
in Giza, which is technically outside the
modern city of *al qaahira* as you head out
west by north-west towards Alexandria.

Our house is in Cairo.
بيتنا في مصر.
beitna fi maSr

I'm traveling (m/f) to Cairo tomorrow.
أنا مسافر/مسافرة مصر بكرة.

We are from Cairo.
إحنا من مصر.
eHna min maSr

city center	ring road ("circular")
وسط البلد	الدائري
wisT el balad	*ed-daa'eri*
agricultural road	desert road
الطريق الزراعي	الطريق الصحراوي
eT-Taree' ez-zeraa9i	*eT-Taree' eS-SaHraawi*

Here are some landmarks and names you're likely to hear around Cairo:

Tahrir Square
ميدان التحرير
meedaan et-taHreer

Ramses station
محطة رمسيس
maHaTTit ramsees

Heliopolis
مصر الجديدة
masr eg-gedeeda, or *heliobolis*

Nasr City
مدينة نصر
madeenit naSr

Zamalek
الزمالك
ez-zamaalik

Maadi

المعادي

el ma9aadi

Doqqi

الدقي

ed-do'-'ee

Mohandeseen

المهندسين

el mohandeseen

Sixth of October bridge

كوبري ٦ أكتوبر

kobri settaktobar

The 6th of October 1973 (which fell on the 10th of Ramadan in that year) was the day the Egyptian army crossed over the Suez Canal to retake it from the Israeli army. This eventually lead to a peace treaty between the two states and the return of Sinai to the Egyptians. The late president Anwar El Sadat masterminded this phase of Egyptian history. He was eager to immortalize the occasion, and also to bring prosperity to the average man on the street. Sadat began an ambitious plan to create new towns in the desert in the hope they would attract industry and new communities. The names given to these new towns were not exactly ground-breakingly imaginative.

Sixth of October city

مدينة ٦ أكتوبر

madeenit settaktobar

Tenth of Ramadan city

مدينة العاشر من رمضان

madeenit el 9aashir min ramaDaan

Sadat city

مدينةالسادات

madeenit es-saadaat

We saw ...

... شفنا

shofna ...

    the tower

    البرج

    el borg

    the citadel

    القلعة

    el al9a

    Mohamed Ali mosque

    جامع محمد علي

    gaami9 meHammad 9ali

We spent the day ...

... قضينا اليوم

aD-Deina el yohm ...

in the museum
في المتحف
fil matHaf

in Kerdasa
في كرداسة
fi kerdaasa

in Saqqara
في سقارة
fi sa'aara

That's me and Tom ...
ده أنا وتوم ...
dah ana wi toom ...

by the pyramids
عند الهرم
9and el haram

beside the Sphinx
جنب أبو الهول
ganb abul-hohl

That's mom and dad ...
دول ماما ويابا ...
dool mama wi baba ...

in Tahreer Square
في ميدان التحرير
fi meedaan et-taHreer

in Khan el Khalili

في خان الخليلي

fi khan el khalili

Last night they took us to ...

امبارح بالليل خدونا ...

embaariH bil-leil khadoona ...

the new opera house

الأوبرا الجديدة

el obera eg-gedeeda

the sound and light show

الصوت والضوء

eS-Sowt wiD-Dow'

We bought ...

اشترينا ...

eshtareina ...

some souvenirs (gifts)

شوية هدايا

shewayyit hadaaya

papyrus

ورق البردي

wara' el barda

a brass tray

صينية نحاس

Seneyya naHaas

Up and Down We Go

I was in ...

أنا كنت في ...

ana kont fi ...

> Sharm El Sheikh
>
> شرم الشيخ
>
> *sharm esh-sheikh*

> Dahab
>
> دهب
>
> *dahab*

> Nuweiba
>
> نويبع
>
> *nuweiba9*

> Taba
>
> طابا
>
> *Taaba*

Our friends went to ...

أصحابنا راحوا ...

aS-Habna raaHu ...

> Hurghada
>
> الغردقة
>
> *el gharda'a*

Al Quseir

القصير

el 'oSeir

St Catherine's monastery

دير سانت كاترين

deir santa katreen

We will go to Luxor on Monday.

حنروح الأقصر يوم الأثنين.

HanrooH lo'Sor yohm-litnein

The following towns were named after various rulers of Egypt, all of whom were descendants of the great dynasty builder Mohamed Ali Pasha. They are all situated along the Suez Canal and are linked to it in one way or another. The Canal is one of the biggest businesses in Egypt, one of the biggest employers, and one of the largest sources of revenue for the state.

Port Fouad

بور فؤاد

bor fu'aad

Port Tawfik

بور توفيق

bor tawfee'

Port Said

بور سعيد

bor sa9eed

Ismailia

الإسماعيلية

el esma9al-leyya

Alexandria has a clear European flavor and heritage. Just look at these names of areas around the city.

Stanley Bay

ستانلي باي

estal-li

Laurent

لوران

luraan

San Stefano

سان استفانو

san istefano

Bianchi

بيانكي

bianki

Miami

ميأمي

miaami

Bacchus

باكوس

bak-koos

Gianaklees

جناكليس

janaklees

Camp de Cesar

كمب شيزار

kambi-shezaar

Victoria

فيكتوريا

faktoria

EGYPT: THE PEOPLE

Broadly speaking, Egyptians have an agreeable dusky skin color. In coastal towns, in desert communities and in Upper Egypt people are more tanned. Their eyes tend to be brown and expressive, and facial hair is quite common among men. It is also noticeable how Egyptian men and women walk with their backs straight.

It is not unusual in Egypt for two male friends to hug and kiss each other when they meet, or for two female friends to walk in the street holding hands. This is not a sign of sexual orientation. Egyptians are quick to laugh because they'll instinctively look for the funny side of absolutely anything.

Some Features

the Egyptians
المصريين
el masri-yeen

an Egyptian man
واحد راجل مصري
waaHid raagil masri

an Egyptian woman
واحدة ست مصرية
waHda sitt masreyya

A tall boy ...
ولد طويل ...
walad Taweel ...

    with a tawny complexion
    أسمر
    asmar

    with a completely shaved head
    حالق راسه زلبطة
    Haali' raaso zalabaTTa

    a little overweight
    سمين شوية
    semeen shewayya

The girl was ...
البنت كانت ...
el bint kaanit ...

    thin
    رفيعة
    rofay-ya9a

    with brown hair
    شعرها بني
    sha9raha bonni

    wearing glasses
    لابسة نظارة
    labsa naDDaara

head	chest
رأس	صدر
saar	*Sidr*
hair	arm
شعر	ذراع
sha9r	*deraa9*
eyebrow	elbow
حاجب	كوع
Haagib	*koo9*
eye	hand
عين	إيد
9ein	*eed*
nose	finger
مناخير	صباع
manakheer	*Sobaa9*
ear	abdomen/stomach
ودن	بطن
wedn	*baTn*
neck	leg
رقبة	رجل
re'aba	*rigl*
shoulder	heel
كتف	كعب
kitf	*ka9b*

An elderly man ...
راجل كبير ...
raagil kebeer ...

with a mustache
بشنب
bishanab

whose beard is gray ("white")
ذقنه بيضاء
da'no beyDa

with broad shoulders
بأكتاف عريضة
bik-taaf 9areeDa

That lady over there ...
الست اللي هناك دي ...
es-sitt illy henaak di ...

the one wearing a wig
اللي لابسة باروكة
illy labsa barooka

the one with the baby
اللي معاها بيبي
illy m9aha bebee

with a gold tooth
أم سنة دهب
omm sinna dahab

Body in Language

Among Egyptians, some parts of the body are used to express certain ideas, meanings or sentiments. For example:

My hand is itching!
(I may be getting some money soon.)
إيدي بتاكلني!
eedi bitakolni

My eye is fluttering!
(I feel something momentous coming up.)
عيني بترف!
9eini bit-riff

It's a twist of the heel! (It's very near.)
دي فركة كعب!
di farkit ka9b

By my mustache! (I swear by my mustache!
Of course it helps your credibility if you
have a mustache, but it is not strictly necessary.)
وشنبي!
wishanabi

Here's my chin!
(It's not going to happen! And you can punch
me right here on my chin if it does.)
آدي ذقني!
aadi da'ni

My knees were unhinged! (I was so terrified I couldn't stand up properly.)

رکبي سابت!

rokabi saabit

Put a summer watermelon in your stomach! (Rest assured!)

حط في بطنك بطيخة صيفي!

Hott fi baTnak baT-Teekha Seifi

My intestines were in a chaotic heap. (I was really anxious.)

مصاريني كركبت.

maSareeni karkebit

One ear made of mud, the other of dough! (I am pretending not to be involved in this situation – nothing to do with me!)

ودن من طين وودن من عجين!

wedn min Teen wi wedn min 9ageen

Titles You Too Can Use

Men:

أستاذ *ostaaz*

Standard respectful title that precedes someone's name ("ostaaz Ahmad"/"ostaaz Ismail"); suggests person is educated, urban, and of medium-to-low influence; it is also the title of school and university teachers, lawyers, middle managers, and similar.

أخ *akh*
Literally "brother"; ironically, it suggests there's a distance between speaker and person addressed; use it when you don't know the other person's name.

عم *9amm*
Literally "brother of one's father"; use it for the elderly; warm and respectful.

كابتن *cabtin*
Captain; used for young men you don't know; suggests person has not too much going for him at the moment, but that he could perhaps become a sports personality, or something, one day. Maybe.

حاج *Hagg*
A name given to a muslim male who has been to Mecca in Saudi Arabia to perform the pilgrimage, which is considered a huge blessing.

بيه *beih*
Relic from Ottoman Empire days but still used today; officially respectful title that follows someone's name ("Ahmad Beih" / "Ismail Beih"); well above *ostaaz* in influence and authority.

باشا *baasha*
Pasha; another relic from Ottoman Empire days,

but it is the preferred title today; use it when you
want to suck up to someone or massage their
ego in order to get something done.

Women:
هانم *haanim*
Probably another relic Ottoman title; suggests
reverence and respect; you don't get much
higher unless you are royalty.

أختي *okhti*
Literally "my Sister"; warmer and friendlier than
akh above; very useful indeed if you don't know
which of the following two titles to use.

مدام *madaam*
Based on the French, Madame; suggests she is
mature, serious and worthy of respect. She is
probably someone's wife, so be polite: no
touching, staring, winking, etc!

مزمزيل *mazma-zeil*
Based on the French, Mademoiselle, but
obviously a mouthful and a half to pronounce if
you are an Egyptian who doesn't speak French;
suggests she's young and eligible.

حاجّة *Hagga*
The title of a muslim woman who has been to
Mecca in Saudi Arabia to perform the pilgrimage.

Here are some more titles that are used in a professional context:

أسطى *osTa*
Suggests someone is a skilled, urban craftsman; used for drivers, plumbers, carpenters, car mechanics, and similar.

معلم *me9allim*
Suggests a senior figure, such as a whole-saler in a rural-orientated pursuit; used for fruit and vegetable merchants, butchers, and owners of popular tea houses.

متر *metr*
Headwaiter; also, informally, for lawyers.

باشمهندس *bash-mohandis*
Used for engineers and architects, or someone whose job is unclear but who seems important; also used by adults to address a young boy who looks like he may grow up to be an engineer, (he wears glasses, for example). Girls, on the other hand, don't get called *bash-mohandisa* until they have actually got an engineering degree and are working as one.

ريس *rayyis*
Broad term for "boss" or foreman; also for a navigator on a Nile boat.

قبطان *obTaan*
A distortion of "Captain," as in commander of a ship; used mostly in ports and coastal towns to describe someone who once worked on any kind of boat in any capacity whatsoever.

Searching for Mo

I am ...
أنا ...
ana ...

a university lecturer
أستاذ في الجامعة
ostaaz fig-gam9a

a chemistry teacher
أستاذ كيمياء
ostaaz kemya

She is the coach of the swimming team.
هي مدرِّبة فريق السباحة.
heyya modarribit faree' es-sebaaHa

My uncle is a captain of a submarine.
خالي قبطان غواصة.
khaali obtaan ghawwaaSa

I am looking for ...
أنا بادور على ...
ana badawwar 9ala ...

Idris, the doorman
عم إدريس البواب
9amm idrees el-bawwaab

Ibrahim, the plumber
أسطى ابراهيم السباك
osta ibraheem es-sabbaak

Sayyid, the electrician
أسطى سيد الكهربائي
osta sayyid, ek-kahrabaa'i

Hanafi, the carpenter
الحاج حنفي النجار
el Hagg Hanafi en-naggaar

Where is Ameen, the butcher?
فين المعلم أمين الجزار؟
fein el me9allim ameen, eg-gazzaar?

Can you send me ...
ممكن تبعتولي ...
momkin teb9atooli ...

Abdo, the ironing guy?
عبده المكوجي؟
9abdo, el makwagi?

Omm Ahmad, the cleaner?
أم أحمد بتاعت التنظيف؟
ommaHmad, betaa9it et-tanDeef?

Aziz, the trash collector?
عزيز الزبال؟
9azeez ez-zabbaal?

Are you the ...

أنت ...

enta ...

painter/decorator?

النقاش؟

en-na'-'aash?

upholsterer?

المنجد؟

el menaggid?

seamstress?

الخياطة؟

el khayyaaTa?

partner	colleague
شريك	زميل
shereek	zemeel
manager	deputy
مدير	نائب
modeer	naayeb
superviser	assistant
مشرف	مساعد
moshrif	mosaa9id
apprentice	consultant
صبي	استشاري
sabi	istishaari

Can you repair cell phones?

تعرف تصلح موبايلات؟

te9raf teSallaH mobaylaat?

Do you know ...

تعرف ...

te9raf ...

a good driver?

سواق كويس؟

sawwaa' kowayyis?

a clever cook?

طباخ شاطر؟

Tabbaakh shaaTir?

a first class tailor?

ترزي درجة أولى؟

tarzi daraga oola?

Yes, of course I do! Mo is the best!

أيوه طبعا أعرف! محمد أحسن واحد!

aywah, Tab9an a9raf mo aHsan waaHid

The name Mohammed is the most popular name in Egypt. It almost seems like half the population is called Mohammed. Nicknames for Mohammed include Mo, Hamaada, and Hamaam.

WEATHER AND NATURE

Talk about the Weather

Winter days in Egypt are generally short and mild. It does get chilly after sunset and through the night. You will get bursts of rain and wind lasting a day or two, but it gets mild again after these bursts have passed.

Fall is generally the best time to go to Egypt because the weather is moderate and on its best behavior. It is predictable and it doesn't play tricks, as it can do in spring.

Summer is hot and humid but you can be physically active early in the morning or late in the afternoon and early evening.

In spring the weather is pleasant enough, but Egypt gets an unwelcome visitor called the "khamaseen" winds. These are gusts of wind that fill the air with sand and dust, which is no fun. The weather remains dusty and unsettled for a day or two then it rains a little, and the weather goes back to being pleasant.

Today, the weather is ...

النهاردة الجو ...

en-naharda eg-gaw ...

> beautiful!
>
> جميل!
>
> gameel

terrible! ("tar-like"!)

زي الزفت!

zayy ez-zift

very cold!

برد جداً!

bard giddan

deathly hot!

حر موت!

Harr moot

winter	climate
الشتاء	الطقس
esh-sheta	*eT-Ta's*
fall	weather
الخريف	الجو
el khareef	*eg-gaww*
spring	temperature
الربيع	درجة الحرارة
er-rabee9	*daragit el Haraara*
summer	degrees centigrade
الصيف	درجات منوية
eS-Seif	*daragaat me'a-weyya*

The humidity is high.

الرطوبة عالية.

er-reTooba 9alya

There isn't a breeze!

مافيش نسمة!

mafeesh nesma

The weather is going to turn.

الجو حيقلب.

eg-gaww Haye'lib

One of the features of Egyptian Arabic which sometimes surprises people is how someone in Aswan, for example, might say "The world is hot!" when it is hot in Aswan. Or someone in Damietta might say, "The world is crowded!" when the street he is walking through, in Damietta, is crowded, and so on. Egyptians just use "the world" as an expression to mean "the immediate environment around me as I experience it right here, right now this minute!"

The world is raining! (It's raining in our village.)

الدنيا بتمطر!

ed-donya betmaTTar

The world is "ice"! (It's a little cold today.)

الدنيا ثلج!

ed-donya talg

The world is "on fire"! (I'm a bit hot.)

الدنيا نار!

ed-donya naar

Be Prepared

I would like to buy ...
عاوز أشتري ...
9awiz ashteri ...

> gloves
> جوانتي
> *gewanti*

> a scarf
> كوفية
> *kofeyya*

> a heater
> دفاية
> *daffaaya*

> a blanket
> بطانية
> *baTTaneyya*

We will need ...
حنحتاج ...
HaneHtaag ...

> an electric fan
> مروحة كهرباء
> *marwaHa kahraba*

an umbrella
شمسية
shamseyya

swimming trunks
مايوهات
mayohaat

Turn the air conditioner on.
شغّل التكييف.
shagh-ghal et-takeef

Open the window.
افتح الشباك.
eftaH esh-shebbaak

Shut the door.
اقفل الباب.
e'fel el baab

You will find me ...
حتلاقوني ...
Hatla'ooni ...

under the blankets
تحت البطاطين
taHt el baTaTeen

by the pool
جنب البيسين
ganb el beseen

The Calendar

January
يناير
yanaayir

July
يوليو
yul-yu

February
فبراير
febraayir

August
أغسطس
aghosTos

March
مارس
maaris

September
سبتمبر
sebtember

April
أبريل
abreel

October
أكتوبر
oktohbar

May
مايو
maayu

November
نوفمبر
nofimber

June
يونيو
yun-yu

December
ديسمبر
disember

Forces of Nature

There's a pharaonic calendar that is particular
to Egypt. It is a little obscure in modern,
urban circles, but many farmers still use
it today when discussing weather conditions
and farming cycles. The two most famous

months in this calendar are *Tooba*, notorious for its cold nights, and *Amsheer*, the month of dust storms. Everyone will have heard of at least these two.

Fishermen in Egypt's coastal Mediterranean towns also use this calendar. A spell of rough sea, wind and rain is called a *nawwa* by the fishermen. Each *nawwa* has a name and a known duration. So, through experience, the fishermen know when to rush back if they are at sea, and when to stay put if they are on dry land.

The sea is rough.
البحر هايج.
el baHr haayeg

The waves are high.
الموج عالي.
el mohg 9aali

Did you feel...
حسيتو ...
Hasseitoo ...

    the earthquake?
    بالزلزال؟
    biz-zilzaal?

    the tremor?
    بالهزة؟
    bil hazza?

thunder	gof
رعد	ضباب
ra9d	Dabaab
lightning	high winds
برق	ريح
bar'	reeH
flood	clouds
سيل	سحاب
seil	saHaab
current	rain
تيار	مطر
tayyaar	maTar
storm	tsud
عاصفة	تراب
9aaSifa	toraab

The Spring Celebration

Shamm en-neseem ("smelling the breeze") is a traditional, one-day Egyptian family holiday dating back to ancient times. Egyptians usually celebrate it on a Monday around early April by going out on picnics in the great outdoors to enjoy nature and the improved weather. Some will go on boat rides on the river, to the zoo, or out by the pyramids, but for the vast majority any green area will do.

The picnics traditionally consist of lettuce, scallion (spring onion), salted fish, and multi-colored hard-boiled eggs. There is an element of luck at play because the weather could be pleasant for the picnic, or not.

Where will you (pl.) smell the breeze?

حتشموا النسيم فين؟

Hatshemmo en-neseem fein?

We will rent a boat.

حنأجر مركب.

Han'ag-gar markib

We will need two cars.

حنحتاج عربيتين.

HaneHtaag 9arabey-yetein

Shall we go to ...

نروح ...

nerooH ...

Magda's farm?

عزبة ماجدة؟

9ezbet magda?

Ayman's new chalet?

الشاليه الجديد بتاع أيمن؟

esh-shahleih eg-gedeed betaa9 ayman?

The Universe and All That

sun
شمس
shams

moon
قمر
'amar

star
نجمة
negma

planet
كوكب
kawkab

crescent
هلال
hilaal

full moon
بدر
badr

the Earth
الأرض
el arD

the Universe
الكون
ek-kown

gravity
الجاذبية
eg-gazebbeyya

eclipse of the sun
كسوف الشمس
kesoof esh-shams

eclipse of the moon
خسوف القمر
khesoof el-'amar

LET'S MEET IN ARABIC

Most tourists will want to meet and interact with the local residents when they visit a country. It adds insight, depth and injects flavor into the trip. Sometimes the language and culture are quite different and it seems daunting at first. However, once you take the plunge most locals will show appreciation and a willingness to rejoice and celebrate our shared humanity. Egypt is no different. And, while people in Egypt speak Arabic, they are also fluent in the language of laughter. Of course you shouldn't celebrate our shared humanity to the point where you lose site of your handbag, or get separated from your camera or phone.

Hello!

أهلا!

ahlan

My name's Michael.

أنا اسمي مايكل.

ana ismee maikil

What's your name? (formal, masc.)

اسم حضرتَك ايه؟

ism HaDritak eih?

What's your name? (formal, fem.)

اسم حضرتِك ايه؟

ism HaDritik eih?

What's your name? (informal, masc.)

اسمَك ايه؟

ismak eih?

What's your name? (informal, fem.)

اسمِك ايه؟

ismik eih?

Who are you? (formal, masc./fem.)

مين حضرتَك/حضرتِك؟

meen HaDritak/HaDritik?

Who are you? (informal, masc./fem.)

أنتَ/أنتِ مين؟

enta/enti meen?

Who are these people?

مين الناس دول؟

meen en-naas dool?

Who is this (masc./fem.)?

مين ده/دي؟

meen dah/dee?

These people are with us.

الناس دول معانا.

en-naas dool ma9aana

Have we met before?

احنا اتقابلنا قبل كده؟

eHna et'abelna 'abl kida?

The Family, Too!

Are you with your mother?

أنتَ مع والدتك؟

enta ma9a waldetak?

I am with my husband.

أنا مع جوزي.

ana ma9a gohzi

This is my wife.

دي مراتي.

dee meraati

These children are with me.

الأولاد دول معايا.

el-awlaad dool ma9aaya

You are similar to my brother.

أنتَ زي أخويا.

enta zayy akhooya

You remind me of my sister.

أنتِ بتفكريني بأختي.

enti betfak-kareeni b'okhti

My father is over there.

أبويا هناك.

abooya hinaaak

My grandfather was here during the war.

جدي كان هنا في الحرب.

giddi kaan hina fil Harb

Where Are You From?

We're from ...

احنا من ...

eHna min ...

> the U.S.
> أمريكا
> *amreeka*

> Britain
> بريطانيا
> *biriTaanya*

> Australia
> أستراليا
> *ostoralia*

> Canada
> كندا
> *kanada*

I am German and my wife is Swiss.

أنا ألماني و مراتي سويسرية.

ana almaani wi meraati swisreyya

I am Mexican and my husband is Spanish.

أنا مكسيكية وجوزي أسباني.

ana maksikeyya wi gohzi asbaani

Are you (masc.) from Alexandria?

أنتَ من إسكندرية؟

enta misken-dereyya?

Are you (plural) from Aswan?

أنتو من أسوان؟

entu min aswaan?

France	China
فرنسا	الصين
faransa	*eS-Seen*
Spain	Japan
أسبانيا	اليابان
asbanya	*el yabaan*
Norway	India
النرويج	الهند
en-nirweeg	*el hind*

How Long?

When did you arrive?

وصلتوا إمتى؟

waSaltu emta?

How many days ago?

من كام يوم؟

min kaam yohm?

a week [or] two

أسبوع، أسبوعين

osboo9, osboo9ein

two [or] three months

شهرين، ثلاثة

shahrein, talaata

a year or more

سنة أو أكثر

sana aw aktar

Are you (fem) coming tomorrow?

أنتِ جاية بكرة؟

enti gayya bokra?

when?

إمتى؟

emta?

in an hour or two

بعد ساعة أو ساعتين

ba9d saa9a aw saa9tein

What day is it today?

النهاردة إيه؟

ennaharda eih?

Monday	Sunday
الاثنين	الأحد
letnein	el-Hadd
Tuesday	yesterday
الثلاثاء	امبارح
et-talaat	embaariH
Wednesday	today
الأربعاء	النهاردة
larba9	ennaharda
Thursday	tomorrow
الخميس	بكرة
el khamees	bokra
Friday	the day after
الجمعة	tomorrow
eg-gom9a	بعد بكرة
	ba9d bokra
Saturday	
السبت	
es-sabt	

Next week is better for us.

الأسبوع الجاي أحسن لنا.

el osboo9 eg-gayy aHsan lenaa

I'll see you (masc.) next Friday.

أشوفك يوم الجمعة الجاي.

ashoofak yohm eg-gom9a eg-gayy

Let's have lunch together Wednesday.

يـاللا نتغدى سوا الأربـع.

yalla netghadda sawa larba9

Sorry, I must go now.

آسـف، لازم أمشي دلوقتي.

aasif, laazim amshi delwa'ti

We'll wait five more minutes.

حنستنى كمـان خمس دقائق.

Hanestanna kamaan khamas da'aayi'

The best time is now!

أحسن وقت هـو دلوقتي!

aHsan wa't howwa delwa'ti

I don't want anything right now.

أنا مش عاوز حاجة دلوقتي

ena mish 9aawiz Haaga delwa'ti

Just a moment.

لحظة واحدة.

laHza waHda

Some other time.

وقت تـاني.

wa't taani

At the appropriate time.

فـي الوقت المنـاسب.

wa't monaasib

day	second
يوم	ثانية
yohm	sanya
week	minute
أسبوع	دقيقة
osboo9	de'ee'a
month	hour
شهر	ساعة
shahr	saa9a
year	a quarter of an hour
سنة	ربع ساعة
sana	rob9 saa9a
century	half an hour
قرن	نص ساعة
qarn	noSSe saa9a
a long time ago	
من زمان	
min zamaan	

It's still early. Stay a bit longer!

لسه بدري. خلليكو شوية!

lissa badri. khaleeko shewayya

We're very late. We must run!

اتأخرنا. لازم نجري!

et'akh-kharna. laazim negri

He came to us ...
جالنا ...
galna ...

in the middle of the day
في عز النهار
fee 9ezz en-nahaar

in the middle of the night
في عز الليل
fee 9ezz el-leil

around sunset
ساعة المغرب
saa9et el maghreb

How Many?

I only understand a couple of words.
أنا بافهم كلمتين بس.
ana bafham kelmetein bass

I don't understand anything at all.
أنا مش فاهم حاجة خالص.
ana mish faahim Haaga khaaliS

What's going on ("the story") exactly?
إيه الحكاية بالضبط؟
eih el Hekaaya beZ-Zabt

I don't know how many.
ماعرفش كام.
ma9rafsh kaam

There's two of us.
إحنا اثنين.
eHna itnein

Approximately, it's about …
تقريباً، حوالي …
ta'reeban, Hawaali …

    five hundred meters
    خمسميت متر
    khomsomeet metr

    six years
    ست سنين
    sittes-neen

    nine thousand pounds
    تسع تلاف جنيه
    tesa9 talaaf geneih

I'd like (masc./fem.) …
أنا عاوز/عاوزة
ana 9aawiz/9awza …

    eight of each
    ثمانية من كل واحدة
    tamanya min koll waHda

the first and the second

الأول والثاني

el awwil wit-taani

only the last one

آخر واحد بس

aakhir waaHid bass

Give us ...

إدينا ...

eddeena ...

a dozen

دستة

dasta

a roll

لفة

laffa

three tubes

ثلاث أنابيب

talat anabeeb

It will be about ...

حيكون حوالي ...

Haykoon Hawaali ...

one thousand a month

ألف في الشهر

alf fesh-shahr

four times a year

أربع مرات في السنة

arba9 marraat fes-sana

a kilo a day

كيلو في اليوم

keelo fil yohm

Short, Sharp Expressions

Get out!

اطلع برة!

eTla9 barra

Get in!

ادخل جوه!

edkhol gowwa

Enough!

كفاية!

kefaaya

No, my dear! (masc./fem.)

لا ياحبيبي/لا ياحبيبتي!

la yaHabibi/la yaHabibti

Exactly like that!

بالضبط كده!

beZ-Z-abt keda

Impossible!

مش ممكن!

mesh momkin

Unbelievable!

مش معقول!

mesh ma9-'ool

Thief!

حرامي!

Haraami

Well done!

برافو عليك!

bravo 9aleik

Shame on you!

اخص عليك!

ekhS 9aleik

Everything!

كل حاجة!

koll Haaga

Nothing!

ولا حاجة!

wala Haaga

Come immediately!

تعالوا حالاً!

ta9aalu Haalan

I don't know.

ماعرفش.

ma9rafsh

Short Blunt Expressions

To say, "I disapprove!"

This is any talk! (This is haphazard and not very well planned.)

ده أي كلام!

dah ayy kalaam

This is boiling eggs! (This has been done quickly and without attention to detail.)

ده سلق بيض!

dah sal' beiD

To say, "It'll never happen!"

In the apricot (season)!

في المشمش!

fil mishmish

Meet me then!

ابقى قابلني!

eb'a 'abelni

When you see your earlobe! (reflection in mirror doesn't count)

لما تشوف حلمة ودنك!

lamma teshoof Halamit wednak

To say, "I agree totally!"

The eye of reasonableness! (It is absolutely right.)

عين العقل!

9ein el 9a'l

Right is with you!

معاك حق!

ma9aak Ha'

To say, "It's a certainty!"

One hundred, one hundred! (percent)

مية مية!

meyya meyya

For sure!

أكيد!

akeed

To say, "I'll do anything for you!"

My neck! (I'll put my neck on the line for you!)

رقبتي!

re'abti

My eyes are for you!

عينيا لك!

9enayya leek

To say, "It's nothing to do with me!"

And what's in it for me?

وأنا مالي؟

wana maali?

I have no invitation.

ماليش دعوة.

maleesh da9wa

I neither part-own the ox nor the flour. (as in a traditional mill)

لا ليا في الطور ولا في الطحين.

laleyya fiT-Tor wala fiT-Teheen

To say, "Get lost!"

Get disconnected from me!

حل عني!

Hill 9anni

Show us the width of your shoulders (from the back, as you go)!

ورينا عرض أكتافك!

warreena 9arD ketaafak

Push your bicycles! (Imaginary bikes, but that's the point!)

زق عجلك!

zo' 9agalak

To say "There's no hope!"

There's no benefit (in continuing).

مافيش فايدة.

mafeesh fayda

Lock this subject up.

سك عالموضوع ده.

sokk 9al-mawDoo9 dah

Forget (it)!

انسى!

ensa

Let it (him) go!

سيبك منه!

seebak mennoh

To say, "I am in a bad mood right now!"

I am possessed by a hundred "Afreets"!
(demons or genies)

راكبني ميت عفريت!

rakebni meet 9afreet

I am not alert for you right now!

أنا مش فايقلك دلوقتي!

ana mish faaye'lak delwa'ti

I can't stand the flies on my face!

أنا مش طايق دبان وشي!

ana mish Taaye' debbaan wish-shi

To say, "@#*@#*@!!"

I will destroy your houses!

أنا حاخرب بيوتكو!

ana Hakhrib beyotko

I will make them collapse on your heads!

أنا حاطربقها على دماغكو!

ana Hatarba'ha 9ala demaghko

I'll send you all to jail!

أنا حاسجنكو!

ana Hasgenko

Note that someone who is sulking and in a bad mood is described as "pouting a mouth," *Daarib booz* in Arabic. If they are really, really angry, they are described as "pouting two mouths," *Daarib boozein*!

Social Interaction

At Someone's Wedding

Every wedding must have a *zaffa* or else it is not a proper wedding. And every *zaffa* must be very loud indeed or else it is not a proper *zaffa*. The *zaffa* is the procession that announces to the world, and beyond, that this woman in white and that man in black are now married.

A *zaffa* has to include a *fer'a* (band) of men who can't sing very well, thumping local percussion instruments, including the *tabla* (drums) and the traditional *dofoof* that look like giant tambourines. I believe the thumping surface is made from the lining of goats' stomachs. Add an assortment of wind instruments if the family is well off.

Leading these processions from the front is usually a belly dancer who more or less determines the pace. Usually she will hog the limelight, and bask in the flashlights from multiple digitals cameras and phones. A *zaffa* will normally move excruciatingly slowly, but if the belly dancer is booked to go to another *zaffa* after this one, there'll be a spring in her step.

Do you (pl.) know...

انتو تعرفوا ...

entu te9rafu ...

>the bride?

>العروسة؟

>el 9aroosa?

>the groom?

>العريس؟

>el 9arees?

Are you (pl.)...

انتو ...

entu ...

>(from the) family?

>من العيلة؟

>min el 9eila?

>their friends from work?

>أصحابهم من الشغل؟

>aS-Haabhom mesh-shoghl?

>their neighbors?

>جيرانهم؟

>geraanhom?

Her dress is very elegant!

فستانها شيك قوي!

fustanha sheek awi

pink ribbon
شريطة بمبة
shereeTa bamba

white candle
شمعة بيضاء
sham9a beiDa

colored candy
ملبس ملون
melabbis melawwin

basket of flowers
سبت ورد
sabat ward

lots of colors
ألوان كثير
alwaan keteer

lots of lights
أنوار كثير
anwaar keteer

lots of kids
عيال كثير
9iyaal keteer

boy in a sailor suit
ولد صغير لابس بحار
walad soghayyar
laabis baH-Haar

girl in a blue dress
بنت لابسة فستان أزرق
bint labsa fustaan
azra' faatiH

belly dancer
رقاصة بلدي
ra'aaSa baladi

Is this the mother of the bride?
دي أم العروسة؟
dee omm el 9aroosa?

I wonder if there'll be food?
ياترى فيه أكل؟
yaa-tara fee akl?

Are you with the band? (masc./fem.)

أنت مع الفرقة؟

enta/enti ma9al fer'a?

What? I can't hear anything!

إيه؟ أنا مش سامع حاجة!

eih? ana mish saami9 Haaga

Marking the Passage of Time

Some occasions in the life of an Egyptian family are marked by the passage of time, like birth, death, and marriage. Note how the name of the occasion is linked to the time it marks.

birthday

عيد ميلاد

9eed milaad

There's an Arabic version of that famous birthday song, "Happy birthday to yoooo ..." and the Arabic lyrics are sung to the same tune. Like most birthdays everywhere, kids run around, scream and eat cake while the parents get a mild headache.

Sebou: a week after birth

السبوع

es-suboo9

One week after birth, the baby is put in a sieve on the floor while the mother crosses over it seven times while being extra careful not to step on it. An elderly relative tells the baby to be good when it grows up.

wedding anniversary
عيد الجواز
9eed eg-gawaaz
(Not observed by everyone because it is
considered an import – which it is.)

the four Thursdays after death
الخمسان
el khemsaan

forty days after death
الأربعين
el arbi9een

death anniversary
السنوية
es-sanaweyya

Hospital Visit

Opportunities to have real fun in a hospital
are usually limited. Yet we may still have to
go there sometimes, perhaps to visit a friend
who has just had their tonsils removed or a
colleague who has just had a baby. Here are
some phrases you may hear or use.

Do you know the visiting times?
تعرفوا مواعيد الزيارة؟
te'rafoo mawa'eed ez-zyaara

We are looking for Georgina Thompson.

إحنا بندور على جورجينا تومسون.

eHna bendaw-war 9ala jorjeena tomsen

Which way to the maternity section?

قسم الولادة منين؟

'ism el welaada menein

Your friend (masc./fem.) is ...

صاحبكم/صاحبتكم ...

SaHibkom/SaHbetkom ...

at the Italian hospital

في المستشفى الإيطالي

fil mostashfa el eeTaali

on the new ward

في العنبر الجديد

fil 9anbar eg-gedeed

over there, third room on the left

هناك، ثالث أوضة على الشمال

hinaak, taalit ohDa 9ash-shimaal

through here, first suite on the right

من هنا، أول جناح على اليمين

min hina, 'awwil genaaH 9al-yemeen

the last door, at the end of this corridor

آخر باب في آخر الطرقة دي

aakhir baab, fi aakhir eT-Tor'a dee

on the floor above. Take the elevator.

في الدور اللي فوق. خذوا الأسانسير.

fid-dohr illy fow'. khodol asanseir

on the floor below. Here are the stairs.

في الدور اللي تحت. السلم أهه.

fid-dohr illy taHt. es-sellim aho

You've got another basket of flowers, Eddie.

جالك سبت ورد ثاني يا إدي.

gaalak sabat ward taani ya eedee

There's a man outside with a bouquet, Lisa.

فيه راجل برة معاه بوكيه ياليزا.

feeh raagil barra ma'aah bookeyh ya leeza

They will remove ...

حيشيلوا ...

Ha-ysheelo ...

the stiches

الغرز

el ghoraz

the cast

الجبس

eg-gebs

The doctor said ...

الدكتور قال ...

ed-doctoor aal ...

it's a simple procedure with local anaesthetic

دي عملية بسيطة بالبنج الموضعي

dee 9amaleyya baseeTa bil-bing el mawde9i

the anaesthetist will give her a general
anaesthetic

دكتور البنج حيديلها بنج كلي

doctoor el bing Ha-yiddilha bing kolli

he can go home tomorrow or the day after

ممكن يروح بكرة أو بعده

momkin yerawwaH bokra aw ba9do

medicine	patient
دواء	مريض
dawa	mareeD
injection	operation (surgery)
حقنة	عملية
Hu'na	'amaleyya
blood	operating room
دم	أوضة العمليات
damm	ohDit el 9amaleyyaat
bone	nurse (fem.)
عظمة	ممرضة
aDma	momarriDa

What To Say and When

You've been invited to someone's house for a
meal and you want to show your appreciation:

Your cooking can drive one insane! (fem.)
(because it's so delicious)

طبيخك يجنن!

Tabeekhik yegannin

May your hand be safely protected! (fem.)
(so you can cook some more)

تسلم إيدك!

teslam eedik

May your prosperity last! (masc.)
(so you can continue to be generous)

دام عزّك!

daam 9ezzak

The hosts may then say:

(Eat) with contentment and health.

بالهنا والشفا.

bel hana wish-shefa

A colleague is showing you a photo of his
wife and kids:

Such is the will of God!
(and He has willed them to be lovely)

ما شاء الله!

maa-shaa' Allah

May God protect them.
ربنا يحميهم.
rab-bena yeHmeehom

May God keep them for you.
ربنا يخلليهم لك.
rab-bena yekhal-lihom lak

The colleague may then say:

May God protect you.
الله يحفظك.
Allah yeHfazak

A colleague tells you that his father has
passed away:

May the remainder be in your life.
(he died too soon, and may the years he should
have lived, but hasn't, be added to your life)
البقية في حياتك.
el ba'eyya fi-Hayaatak

"Pull your strength." (Be strong.)
شد حيلك.
shidd Heylak

What To Say and Where

At the hairdresser/barber
عند الكوافير/الحلاق
9and ek-kwaafeer/el Hallaaq

Please …
... من فضلك
min faDlak …

> tidy up here a little
> وضّب هنا شوية
> *waDDab hina shwayya*

> cut this
> قص ده
> *oSS dah*

> remove all those
> شيل كل دول
> *sheel kolli-dool*

> cut the ends only
> قص الطروف بس
> *oSS eT-Toroof bass*

I want my hair …
... أنا عاوز شعري
ana 9aawiz sha9ri …

very short

قصير جداً

oSayyar giddan

short from the back

قصير من ورا

oSayyar min wara

like this

كده

kida

even length

طول واحد

Tool waaHid

Cut the sides and back.

قص الجناب ومن ورا.

oSS eg-genaab wimin wara

I want (masc./fem.)...

عاوز/عاوزة

9aawiz/9awza

to wash my hair

أغسل شعري

'aghsil sha9ri

to choose a color

أختار لون

akhtaar lohn

At the shirtmaker/tailor

عند القمصانجي/الترزي

9and el qumSaangi/et-tarzi

Some women arrange to have made-to-measure belly-dancing costumes made for them in Egypt. For men, having fitted Egyptian cotton shirts made in Egypt makes good commercial sense. Both men and women can have the flowing robes called *galabeyya* made as well, in fine cotton for summer and in wool for winter.

Take my measurements.

خذ مقاساتي.

khod ma'asaati

Show me the fabric.

وريني القماش.

wer-reeni el 'omaash

This one's nice. How much is it per meter?

ده حلو. بكام المتر؟

dah Helw. bekaam el metr?

How many meters will it take?

ده يأخذ كام متر؟

da yaakhod kaam metr?

What's your ("hand") fee/charge?

أجرة إيدك كام؟

ogrit eedak kaam?

plain	loose
سادة	واسع
saada	waasi9
with a pattern	tight
منقوش	ضيق
man'oosh	Dayya'
collar	an opening here
ياقة	فتحة هنا
yaa'a	fatHa hina
waist	by the shoulder
وسط	عند الكتف
wisT	9and ek-kitf
short sleeve	above the elbow
نص كم	فوق الكوع
noSS komm	foh' ek-koo9
long sleeve	below the knee
كم طويل	تحت الركبة
komm Taweel	taHt er-rokba
buttons	an evening dress
زراير	فستان سهرة
zaraayir	fustaan sahra

When will it be ready?

يجهز إمتى؟

yeghaz emta?

Is it possible before that?

ممكن قبل كده؟

momkin 'abl kida?

Can you send them to the hotel?

ممكن تبعتهم الفندق؟

momkin teb9at-hom el fondo'?

red (masc./fem.)	black (masc./fem.)
أحمر/حمراء	أسود/سوداء
aHmar/Hamra	*eswid/sohda*
blue (masc./fem.)	white (masc./fem.)
أزرق/ زرقاء	أبيض/بيضاء
azra'/zar'a	*abyaD/beida*
green (masc./fem.)	yellow (masc./fem.)
أخضر/خضراء	أصفر/ صفراء
akhDar/khaDra	*aSfar/Safra*
brown	purple
بني	بنفسجي
bonni	*banaf-segi*
gray	pink
رمادي	بمبة
romaadi	*bamba*
light	dark
فاتح	غامق
faateH	*ghaami'*

At the Bazaar

في السوق

fis-soo'

The temptation to spend money increases when one travels, and this money is probably the backbone of the tourism industry at a micro level. Many store owners and specialist craftsmen depend on tourist dollars to keep a traditional craft alive, or an old shop open.

Do you make these here?

بتعملوا ده هنا؟

bete'melo dah hina?

Did you prepare all this?

انتوا جهزتوا كل ده؟

entu gah-heztu kol dah?

Are you teaching your son?

إنت بتعلم ابنك؟

enta bet9allim ibnak?

Are they working...

هم بيشتغلوا ...

homma beyeshtaghalo ...

with brass?

بالنحاس؟

bel naHaas?

with mother-of-pearl?

بالصدف؟

beS-Sadaf?

with silver?

بالفضة؟

bel faDDa?

Is this made...

ده معمول ...

dah ma9mool...

of glass?

من الإزاز؟

min el 'izaaz?

of gold?

بالدهب؟

bid-dahab?

wool	cotton
صوف	قطن
Soof	*oTn*
leather	silk
جلد	حرير
geld	*Hareer*

How do you color it?

إزاي بتلوّنوه؟

ezzay betlaw-winooh?

It looks very beautiful.

شكله جميل خالص.

shakloh gameel khaaliS

They are as soft as silk.

دي ناعمة زي الحرير.

dee na9ma zayy el Hareer

We would like to buy two.

عاوزين نشتري اثنين.

9awzeen neshteri etneyn

Could you put ... on it?

ممكن تحط عليها ...

momkin teHoTT 9aleyha ...

my name

اسمي

ismi

my daughter's photo

صورة بنتي

Soorit binti

my husband's name

اسم جوزي

ism gohzi

Can you wrap this one?

ممكن تلف دي؟

momkin teliff dee?

It looks very delicate.

شكلها رقيقة خالص.

shaklaha ra'ee'a khaaliS

I'm worried about putting it in my suitcase ...

أخاف أحطها في شنطتي ...

akhaaf aHoTTaha fi shanTeti

    in case it gets broken

    لحسن يتكسر

    laHsan yetkessir

    in case it gets damaged

    لحسن يبوظ

    laHsan yebooZ

    in case it gets bent

    لحسن يتثني

    laHsan yetteni

Can I pay with this card?

ممكن أدفع بالكارت ده؟

momkin adfa9 belkart dah?

FOOD SHOPPING

The Vegetable Market

سوق الخضار

soo' el khoDaar

Open-air fruit and vegetable markets have a rawness about them, and it's not just in the produce. It's in the aromas, colors, sounds, displays and general human vibrancy. An airconditioned, sanitized and manicured supermarket cannot replicate this. There is also the cleverness of the vendors who appear to know each individual orange or tomato intimately, even if to you the display appears random. They also know how to sell you two and a half of something when you only need one.

Weigh for us two kilos of...

أوزن لنا اثنين كيلو ...

ewzin lena itnein kilo ...

> ripe tomatoes
> قوطة مستوية
> *ooTa mesteweyya*

> small cucumbers
> خيار صغير
> *khiyaar soghayyar*

> green (bell) peppers
> فلفل أخضر
> *filfil akhDar*

celery	spinach
كرفس	سبانخ
karafs	sabaanikh

sweet potatoes	okra
بطاطا	بامية
baTaaTa	bamya

peas	zucchini
بسلة	كوسة
besella	kohsa

lettuce	carrots
خس	جزر
khass	gazar

scallions	eggplant
بصل أخضر	باذنجان
baSal akhDar	betingaan

cabbage	potatoes
كرمب	بطاطس
koromb	baTaaTis

Find us ...

شوف لنا ...

shuflena...

a nice bunch of parsley

حزمة بقدونس حلوة

Hezmit ba'doonis Helwa

a fresh bunch of coriander

حزمة كزبرة طازة

Hezmit kozbara Taaza

two big bulbs ("heads") of garlic

رأسين ثوم كبار

raasein tohm kobaar

Aren't there any onions except for those?

مافيش بصل غير ده؟

mafeesh baSal gheir dah?

The Fruit Guy

الفكهاني

el fakahaani

Are these apples American or Syrian?

التفاح ده أمريكاني ولا سوري؟

et-toffaaH dah amreekani walla soori?

Are these oranges for juicing?

ده برتقال للعصير؟

dah borto'aan lil 9aSeer?

Find us a sweet watermelon.

شوف لنا بطيخة مسكَّرة.

shuflena baTTeekha mesakkara

Yesterday's bananas were tasteless.

الموز بتاع امبارح مالوش طعم.

el mohz betaa9 embaariH maloosh ta9m

pineapple	dates
أناناس	بلح
ananaas	balaH
grapefruit	strawberry
جريب فروت	فراولة
grib-feroot	farawla
lemon/lime	figs
ليمون	تين
lamoon	teen
cantaloupe	apricots
شمام	مشمش
shammaam	mishmish
pomegranate	plums
رمان	برقوق
rommaan	bar'oo'
grapes	guava
عنب	جوافة
9enab	gawaafa
peaches	mango
خوخ	منجة
khohkh	manga

Prickly pears are called "prickly figs" in Egypt (*teen shohki*). Remember to always let the vendor handle and peel them for you! It's a special skill because they use a knife so sharp it can split a hair.

Seedless grapes are called "girlie grapes" (*9enab banaati*)!

At the Butcher's
عند الجزار
9and eg-gazzaar

beef
لحمة بقري
laHma ba'ari

mature beef
لحمة كندوز
laHma kandooz

veal
لحمة بتللو
laHma betello

mutton
لحمة ضاني
laHma Daani

lamb
ضاني صغير
Daani Soghayyar

chicken

فراخ

feraakh

sausages

سجق

sogo'

fillet

فللتو

feletto

slices

ترنشات

teranshaat

cubes

مكعبات

moka9-9abaat

ground meat

لحمة مفرومة

laHma mafrooma

We'd like something suitable ...

... عاوزين حاجة تنفع

9awzeen Haaga tenfa9 ...

> for (making) soup
> للشوربة
> *lesh-shorba*

for a barbecue

لباربيكيو

lebarbikyoo

for the cat

للقطة

lel oTTa

We want to cook ...

عاوزين نطبخ ...

9awzeen neTbokh ...

roast beef

روزبيف

rozbeef

oxtail

عكاوي

9akaawi

calves' liver

كبدة بتللو

kebda betello

Please remove ...

من فضلك شيل ...

min faDlak sheel ...

the fatty bits

الدهن

ed-dehn

the bones
العظم
el 9aDm

the head
الرأس
er-raas

chicken leg	shoulder of mutton
ورك فرخة	كتف ضاني
wirk farkha	*kitf Daani*
chicken livers	tongue
كبد فراخ	لسان
kebad feraakh	*lisaan*
chicken breast	leg of lamb
صدر فرخة	فخذة ضاني صغير
Sidr farkha	*fakhda Daani Soghayyar*

Can I put it in the freezer for a week?
ممكن أحطه في الفريزر أسبوع؟
momkin aHoTTo fil freezar osboo9?

Is this enough for six?
ده يكفي ستة؟
dah yekaffee setta?

From the Grocer

من البقال

mil-ba'-'aal

"Baladi" bread (Egyptian wholemeal flat bread)

عيش بلدي

9eish baladi

Syrian flat bread

عيش شامي

9eish shaami

baguette

عيش فينو

9eish feeno

sliced bread

عيش توست

9eish tost

cheese

جبنة

gibna

butter

زبدة

zebda

black olives

زيتون أسود

zatoon eswid

green olives

زيتون أخضر

zatoon akhDar

yogurt

زبادي

zabaadi

rice

رز

rozz

macaroni

مكرونة

makarohna

spaghetti

مكرونة اسباجيتي

makarohna spagitti

salt

ملح

malH

black pepper

فلفل

filfil eswid

mixed spices

بهارات

boharaat

Margaret wants a can of ...

مارجريت عايزة علبة ...

margareet 9aiza 9elbit ...

tuna

تونة

toona

corned beef

بولوبيف

bulobeef

sardines

سردين

sardeen

tomato paste

صلصة طماطم

salsit TamaTim

What's left is to get a bottle of ...

فاضل نجيب إزازة ...

faaDil negeeb izaazit ...

olive oil

زيت زيتون

zeit zatoon

vinegar

خل

khall

ketchup

كتشب

ketshab

Don't forget to buy a jar of ...

ماتنساش تشتري برطمان

matensaash teshteri barTamaan ...

jam

مربى

merabba

mustard

مسطردة

mosTarda

honey

عسل

9asal

pickles

طرشي

Torshi

Please, how much is ...

لو سمحت، بكام ...

lau samaHt, bekaam...

a kilo?

الكيلو؟

ek-keelo?

one of them?

الواحدة؟

el waHda?

a pair?

الجوز؟

eg-gohz?

a dozen?

الدستة؟

ed-dasta?

a (small) box?

العلبة؟

el 9ilba?

a (large) box?

الصندوق؟

es-sandoo'?

a bag?

الكيس؟

ek-kees?

How much do I owe you?

كام الحساب؟

kaam el Hisaab?

Can someone ...

ممكن حد ...

momkin Hadd ...

help me carry?

يشيل معايا؟

yesheel ma9aaya?

take them to the car?

يوديهم العربية؟

yewaddee-hom el 9arabeyya?

take them upstairs?

يطلعهم فوق؟

yeTalla9-hom foh'?

Fruit Juice Shops

محلات العصير

maHallaat el 9aSeer

A common sight in the streets of Egypt are the fresh fruit juice shops. Traditionally, these will have a sugar cane squeezer, which looks a bit like a torture device from a medieval dungeon designed to make you renounce anything and everything.

The sugar cane is passed through the narrowest of gaps between two huge spiked metal drums that are turning in opposite directions. The guy then collects the flattened canes from the other side of the drums, bends them over once, then returns them back through the same narrow space to squeeze the last possible drop of juice out, before discarding the pulp. The juice flows downwards onto ice, then out of the machine through a nozzle to a waiting jar.

The juice is poured, usually from a height of an outstretched arm, into glasses. The pouring from height gives it a frothy head. Sugar cane juice is sweet, but not sickly sweet – an acquired taste, nonetheless.

Please, one ... juice
من فضلك، واحد عصير ...
min faDlak, waaHid 9aSeer ...

sugar cane
قصب
aSab

orange
برتقال
borto'aan

mango
منجة
manga

guava with lemon
جوافة بالليمون
gawaafa bil-lamoon

banana with strawberry
موز بالفراولة
mohz bil-farawla

pomegranate

رمان

rommaan

juice cocktail

عصير كوكتيل

9aSeer kukteel

in the blender

في الخلاط

fil khallaaT

without ice

من غير ثلج

min gheir talg

without sugar

من غير سكَّر

min gheir sokkar

Cooking tip

Ta'leyya – a secret weapon in the Egyptian kitchen. Take something simple, bland, or boiled, add *ta'leyya* and that same something suddenly explodes into life and becomes all singing, all dancing.

Ta'leyya is crushed garlic with dry coriander, fried lightly and then a little vinegar is added. Aromatic and flavorful.

Eating Out and About

Food fans who grow up in Egypt develop a mental catalog of where might be the best place to buy a fresh "X" in season, or where the best "Y" comes from, and where to eat the tastiest "Z." Here are some flashes in the pan of my mental food catalog.

Pockets of Fish

With a river, several lakes, and two coasts, Egypt was destined to offer a wide variety of fish and seafood. Some towns became known for certain dishes, but that's not to say you can't get these exact same dishes elsewhere as well. The fish is grilled, fried, baked, or dry-cured in salt depending on its suitability.

Before you sit down to a fish meal, you're likely to be asked to choose the fish you want to eat. You'll either be escorted to an impressive display on ice deep in the belly of the restaurant, or a waiter will bring you some samples on a tray. Broadly speaking, fish is not cheap. So at this point it's worth your while to ask about the price per kilogram and how much each fish weighs.

Once seated, you'll probably be served a finely chopped mixed salad, fresh bread, a sesame paste called *TeHeena*, and lots of pickles, some of which will be hot, as in full of chili. Rice is also served. The traditional "fish rice" is cooked with fried onion and tomato, which gives it a deep reddish brown color and a brilliant flavor.

We'd like to try ...

عاوزين نجرب ...

9awzeen negarrab ...

the salted fish from Rosetta

الفسيخ بتاع رشيد

el feseekh betaa9 rasheed

the baked fisherman's dish from Port Said

السمك الصيادية بتاع بور سعيد

es-samak es-Sayyadeyya betaa9 bor sa9eed

the big prawns of Abu Qeer

الجمبري الكبير بتاع أبو قير

eg-gambari ek-kebeer betaa9 abu'eer

the fish roe from the lakes

البطارخ بتاعت البحيرات

el baTaarekh betaa9et el buHeiraat

the grilled grey mullet from Suez

البوري المشوي بتاع السويس

el boori el mashwi betaa9 es-suweis

the sole from lake Qaroon in Fayyoom

سمك بحيرة قارون في الفيوم

samak buHeiret Qarron fil fayyoom

prawns and crab by the sea in Alexandria

جمبري وكابوريا على البحر في اسكندرية

gambari wekaboria 9albaHr feskendereyya

eel ("snake fish")

سمك تعبـان

samak te9baan

Waiter, is this type better grilled or fried?

يـا متر، النوع ده أحسن مشوي وللا مقلي؟

ya metr, en-now9 dah aHsan mashwi walla ma'li?

Is the squid cooked in tomato sauce?

الكلمـاري مطبوخ بصلصـة الطمـاطم؟

el kalamari maTbookh biS-SalSit eT-TamaaTim?

Can we have one more plate of "fish rice"?

ممكن واحد رز سمك كمـان؟

momkin waaHid rozz-samak kamaan?

No onion in the salad, please.

بلاش بصل في السلطة من فضلك.

balaash baSal fis-salaTa, min faDlak

I'll try the octopus in garlic.

أجرب الأخطبوط بـالثوم.

agarrab el ekhTabooT bet-tohm

How much is a kilogram of lobster?

بكـام كيلو الاستـاكوزا؟

bekaam kilol-estakoza?

How much would one of these weigh?

الواحدة تطلـع قد إيه؟

el waHda tet-la9 add eih?

Rural Feasts

Some farmers still use rural Egyptian methods of cooking in primitive clay ovens and traditional earthenware. They burn wood or other organic fuels and use natural ingredients to add an unmistakable flavor to the food. Many restaurants try to recreate the atmosphere of a farmer's kitchen in order to capture the aromas and flavors of the Egyptian countryside. When it works, it is a real treat.

We'd like to taste the rural pastry...
... عاوزين ندوق الفطير المشلتت
9awzeen nedoo' el feTeer el meshaltet ...

> with white cheese from Mansura
> مع جبنة بيضا من المنصورة
> *ma9gebna beyDa mil-mansoora*

> with strong, extra mature cheese
> بـالمش
> *bel-mish*

> with honey
> بـالعسل
> *bel-9asal*

We'd like to try...
... عاوزين نجرّب
9awzeen negarreb ...

oven-baked clay pot of okra with mutton
طاجن البامية باللحمة الضاني
Taagin bamia bel-laHma eD-Daani

oven-baked pot of rice, meat, and milk
البرام البلدي بالرز واللحمة
el beraam el baladi ber-rozz wil-laHma

grilled pigeon/stuffed pigeon
حمام مشوي/حمام محشي
Hamaam mashwi/Hamaam maHshi

tray of flat pastry with ground meat
صينية الرقاق باللحمة المفرومة
Seneyyet er-ro'aa' bel-laHma el mafrooma

green leaf soup with rabbit
ملوخية بالأرانب
melokh-kheyya bel-araanib

chicken with thyme
فراخ بالزعتر
feraakh bez-za9tar

I'll have the stuffed vegetables.
أنا حآخذ المحشي.
ana Haakhod el maHshi

I love spinach very much.
أنا بأحب السبانخ جداً.
ana baHibb es-sabaanikh giddan

Pot of mixed vegetables with veal, please.

طاجن تورلي باللحمة البتللو، من فضلك.

Taagin torli bel-laHma el betello, min faDlak

We'll have the tray of potatoes with meat.

حنآخذ صينية البطاطس باللحمة.

Hanaakhod Seneyyet el baTaaTis bel-laHma

I want my (main) dish with ...

أنا عاوز طبقي مع ...

ana 9aawiz Taba'ee ma9a ...

plain white rice

رز أبيض سادة

rozz abyaD saada

vermicelli rice

رز بالشعرية

rozz besh-sha9reyya

French fries

بطاطس محمرة

baTaaTis meHammara

traditional (finely chopped mixed) salad

سلطة بلدي

salaTa baladi

steamed vegetables

خضار مسلوق

khoDaar masloo'

Urban Delights

Some food formulas work well in a big city setting. They are served quickly, are expected to be tasty, and are often reasonably priced.

الكباب *kabaab*

Kabaab is sold at a *kababgi* or *Haati*. It is tasty, marinated cubes of mutton, grilled on charcoal and served on a bed of chopped parsley. Authoritative-looking cooks often man the grill that is usually visible to the customers. Seeing the grill is an integral part of the experience, but more importantly, you can also smell the kabaab half a mile down the road which can be quite compelling if you're hungry.

Kabaab is sold and priced by the kilogram, so you can always work out how much you are likely to pay. Salad, fresh bread, *TeHeena* and pickles are usually served. In addition, some *kababgis* offer *gargeer*, which is a green leaf similar to rocket and watercress.

Nine and a half out of every ten people who go to a *kabaabgi* go there to eat kabaab, but sometimes someone may go there to eat a different dish. You are likely to find baked mutton shanks, known as *mohza*, or vegetables baked in the oven with chunks of meat and served with rice.

A kilo of mixed kabaab, please.

كيلو كباب مشكّل من فضلك.

kilo kabaab meshakkil, min faDlak

Include some extra cutlets!

وضّب الرَّيَش!

waDDab er-reyash

Don't include fatty bits!

بلاش الملبّس!

balaash el melabbis

Do you have mutton shanks or veal shanks?

فيه موزة ضـاني أو موزة بتللو؟

fee mohza Daani aw mohza betello?

الكشري *koshari*

Another urban favorite is *koshari*, a quick, economic, filling, no-frills meal made up of rice, short-cut macaroni, chickpeas, vermicelli, lentils and fried onions. There are two bottles on every table, one containing a chili and tomato sauce, the other a garlic, vinegar and herb concoction that adds zest and tang to the dish.

One koshari, and make it special.

واحد كشري وصلّحه.

waaHid koshari wi SallaHo

No fried onions.

خـالي الورد.

khaali el ward

An additional small portion.

واحد كمـالة.

waaHid kemaala

الفول *fool* (fava beans)

Fool is probably the most popular food item in Egypt. Traditionally, it is cooked over a tiny flame overnight in a clay pot with an onion added for flavoring. It is nutritious, filling, cheap and very flexible because there's about a hundred and one ways of preparing it, depending on how ambitious one feels. Another aspect of its flexibility is that it can be eaten for breakfast, lunch or dinner.

The most basic way of preparing *fool* is just to add oil ...

fool with oil

فول بالزيت

fool bez-zeit

You could add lemon ...

فول بالزيت والليمون

fool bez-zeit wil-lamoon

cumin ...

فول بالزيت والليمون الكمون

fool bez-zeit wil-lamoon wik-kammoon

tomatoes ...

فول بالزيت والليمون الكمون والطماطم

fool bez-zeit wil-lamoon wik-kammoon wiT-TamaaTim

Add ... well, the list goes on. It includes eggs, ground meat, garlic, cheese, sausages, green peppers, pastrami, to name a few.

فلافل/طعمية falafel/Ta9meyya

Falafel are basically crushed *fool* flavored with garlic and parsley. They are fried and eaten hot. They are also known as *Ta9meyya*.

كبدة اسكندراني kebda eskandaraani

"Alexandrian" liver is chopped and fried with onion, tomato and chili.

فطير feTeer

FeTeer is a huge, thin pastry that is folded several times over. It can be prepared with either sweet or savory fillings. There is an element of showmanship in its preparation as the cook hurls and whirls the dough into the air several times to make it thinner.

فاكهة fakHa (fruit)

Fresh fruit is often available from roadside carts.

These figs come from el-Alamein.

التين ده من العلمين.

et-teen dah min el alamein

The fig season is August and September.

موسم التين أغسطس وسبتمبر.

moosim et-teen oghosTos wi sebtember

The tastiest melons come from Ismailia

أحلى شمام من الإسماعيلية

aHla shammaam min el esma9aleyya

Egyptian strawberries are small and very sweet.

الفراولة المصري صغيرة وحلوة قوي.

el farawla el maSri Soghayyara wi Hilwa awi

Hindi and Alfonse are delicious types of mango.

الهندي والألفونس أنواع لذيذة من المنجة.

el hindi wil-alfons anwaa9 lazeeza min el manga

For Starters and Afters

We're two (people).

احنا اثنين.

iHna itnayn

Can we have that table?

ممكن التربيزة دي؟

momkin el-tarabeyza dee?

Waiter!/Waitress!

لو سمحت!/ لو سمحتي!

lau samaHt!/lau samaHti!

Is there a menu in English?

فيه منيو بالانجليزي؟

feeh menu bel-ingeleezi?

The check, please!

الحساب من فضلك!

el Hisaab min faDlak

TRAVEL AND ACCOMMODATION

Egypt can be an attractive destination for business opportunities or for memorable family vacations. There is something there for nearly everyone. Someone may choose to go and visit the sites or enjoy the beaches and sunshine, and another may want to take advantage of the relatively modest labor costs.

Most visitors will arrange accommodation well before they travel. Egypt has several airports and nearly all category of hotel, from five stars all the way down to a single candle.

Business Trip: Arrival

This is a business trip.

دي زيارة عمل.

dee zeyaarit 9amal

We have been to Egypt before.

زرنا مصر قبل كده.

zorna masr abli keda

Two days here and two in Kuwait.

يومين هنا ويومين في الكويت.

yohmein hena we yohmein fik-kuweit

The purpose of the trip is...

الغرض من الرحلة هو ...

el gharaD min er-reHla howwa ...

to visit a factory

زيارة مصنع

zeyyarit maSna9

to visit a hospital

زيارة مستشفى

zeyyarit mostashfa

business meetings

اجتماعات عمل

egtima9aat 9amal

We have a stand at the fair.

عندنا جناح في المعرض.

9andena genaaH fil-ma9raD

We have an invitation from ...

عندنا دعوة من ...

9andena da9wa min ...

the partners

الشركاء

esh-shoraka

the ministry

الوزارة

el wizaara

the distributor

الموزع

el muwazzi9

A representative will ...
فيه مندوب ...
fee mandoob ...

> organize the visa
> حينظّم الفيزا
> *HaynaZZam el viza*

> take us from the airport
> حيأخذنا من المطار
> *Hayakhodna min el maTaar*

> help us through customs
> حيساعدنا في الجمارك
> *Haysaa9edna fig-gamaarik*

Business Trip: Hotel

Shall we meet ...
نتقابل ...
net'aabil ...

> at eight thirty?
> الساعة ثمانية ونص؟
> *es-saa9a tamanya wi noSS?*

> for breakfast?
> على الفطار؟
> *9alal feTaar?*

> in the lobby?
> في اللوبي؟
> *fil-loobi?*

hotel	desk
فندق	مكتب
funduq	maktab
room	meeting room
غرفة	غرفة اجتماعات
ghorfa	ghorfit egtima9aat
key	business center
مفتاح	مركز الأعمال
muftaaH	markaz el a9maal
bathroom	internet access
حمَام	وصلة انترنت
Hammaam	waSlit internet

Who will take us to the office tomorrow?

مين حيأخذنا المكتب بكرة؟

meen Hayakhodna el maktab bokra

Robert will bring samples of ...

روبرت حيجيب عينات من ...

robirt Haygeeb 9ayyinaat min ...

the US product

المُنتَج الأمريكاني

el montag el amreekani

the competitive brand

الصنف المنافس

eS-Sanf el monaafis

the European version
النسخة الأوروبية
en-noskha el orobeyya

Jack will show you ...
جاك حيوريكم ...
jaak Haywar-reekom ...

the price list
قائمة الأسعار
'aymit el as9aar

the most recent invoices
آخر فواتير
aakhir fawateer

Veronica is responsible for all ...
فيرونيكا مسئولة عن كل ...
veronika mas'oola 'an koll ...

the packaging
التغليف
et-taghleef

the shipping documents
أوراق الشحن
awraa' esh-shaHn

the insurance
التأمين
et-ta'meen

box/boxes	ship
صندق/صناديق	سفينة
Sandu'/Sanadee'	safeena
bottle/bottles	shipping
إزازة/أزايز	شحن
'izaaza/'azaayiz	shaHn
sack/sacks	cargo
شوال/شولة	شحنة
shewaal/shewela	shoHna
container	tracking
كونتينر	متابعة
konteenar	motab9a

Will we have time for ...

حيكون فيه وقت لـ...

Hakoon fee wa't li ...

some quick sightseeing?

سياحة سريعة؟

seyaaHa saree9a?

a round of golf?

شوية جولف؟

shewayyit golf?

buying souvenirs?

نشتري تذكارات؟

neshteri tezkaaraat?

I must see the pyramids, Hassan!

لازم أشوف الأهرام يا حسن!

laazim ashoof el ahraam, ya Hassan!

Money Talks

Does the budget allow (this)?

الميزانية تسمح؟

el meezaneyya tesmaH?

What are the other expenses?

إيه المصاريف الثانية؟

eih el maSareef et-tania?

These costs are ...

التكاليف دي ...

et-takaleef di ...

> reasonable
>
> معقولة
>
> *ma'oola*

> a little higher than my estimate
>
> أعلى شوية من تقديري
>
> *a9la shwayya min taqdeeri*

We have to think about the taxes.

لازم نفكر في الضرايب.

laazim nefak-kar fiD-Daraayib

Profits are excellent this year.

الأرباح ممتازة السنة دي.

el arbaaH momtaaza es-sanaadi

There is a margin to cover ...

فيه هـامش يغطي ...

fee haamish yeghaTTi ...

any extras

أي زيادات

ayy ziyaadat

the guarantee

الضمـان

eD-Damaan

Leave these considerations ...

سيب الاعتبارات دي ...

seeb el i9tibaraat di ...

for the accountant

للمحـاسب

lil-moHaasib

for the board

لمجلس الإدارة

limaglis el idaara

for the future

للمستقبل

lil-mosta'bal

account	report
حساب	تقرير
Hesaab	taqreer
statement of accounts	invoice
كشف حساب	فاتورة
kashf Hesaab	faatoora

Pleasure Trip: Arrival

Most families with very young children will go to Egypt as part of a group, and they would go there primarily for the beaches. Once the kids are older and tougher they can cope with and enjoy the rigors of visiting the pyramids, temples, and tombs.

The tour guide will be ...
الدليل حيكون ...
ed-daleel Haykoon ...

at the arrivals hall
في صـالة الوصول
feSaalit el woSool

wearing a special cap
لابس كاب مخصوص
laabis kaab makhSooS

carrying a sign

شايل يافطة

shaayil yafTa

All the bags will be on this bus.

كل الشنط حتكون على الأوتوبيس ده.

koll esh-shonaT Hatkoon 9ala otobees dah

The blue mini bus is for Sunshine Resort.

الميني باص الأزرق لصن شاين ريزورت.

el meeneebaaS el azra' lesunshaain rezort

We're staying ...

إحنا قاعدين ...

eHna a'deen ...

in Giza

في الجيزة

fig-geeza

with friends

مع أصحابنا

ma9aS-Habna

at our relatives'

عند قرايبنا

9and arayebna

The hotel is in the city center.

الفندق في وسط البلد.

el fondo' fe-wusT el balad

furnished apartment	yacht
شقة مفروشة	يخت
sha''a mafroosha	yakht
villa	house boat
فيللا	عوامة
filla	9awwaama
room	youth hostel
أوضة	بيت الشباب
ohDa	beit esh-shabaab
tent	student hostel
خيمة	بيت الطلبة
kheima	beit eT-Talaba

Pleasure Trip: Hotel

We booked a room ...

حجزنا أوضة ...

Hagazna oDa ...

with an extra bed

بسرير زيادة

besereer zyaada

on the ground floor

في الدور الأرضي

fed-dohr el arDi

by the swimming pool

على حمام السباحة

9ala Hammaam es-sebaaHa

with a small bathroom

بحمام صغير

be-Hammaam soghayyar

that has a wide balcony

فيها بلكونة واسعة

feeha balakohna was9a

air conditioning	balcony
تكييف	بلكونة
takeef	*balakohna*
twin beds	sea view
سريرين	على البحر
sereerein	*9alal baHr*
extra blanket	garden view
بطانية زيادة	على الجنينة
baTTaneyya zyaada	*9alag geneina*
soft pillow	kids' playground
مخدة طرية	ملعب الأطفال
mekhadda Tareyya	*mal9ab el aTfaal*
another towel	activity
فوطة كمان	نشاط
fooTa kamaan	*nashaaT*

We can walk to ...

ممكن نمشي لغاية ...

momkin nemshi leghaayit

the bazaars

البازارات

el bazaraat

the beach

البلاج

el belaaj

the funfair

الملاهي

el malaahi

Can we book ...

ممكن نحجز ...

momkin neHgiz ...

a massage appointment?

ميعاد للمساج؟

ma9aad lil masaaj?

a babysitter?

بيبي سيتر ؟

bibiseetar ?

a birthday cake?

تورتة عيد ميلاد ؟

tortit 9eed meelaad ?

We need an umbrella and four chairs.

محتاجين شمسية وأربع كراسي.

meHtageen shamseyya we arba9 karaasi

beach towel	rubber ring
فوطة بلاج	عوامة
fooTit belaaj	*9awwaama*
beach bag	flip-flops
شنطة بلاج	شبشب زنوبة
shanTit belaaj	*shibshib zannooba*
cream	sunglasses
كريم	نظارة شمس
kereim	*naDDaarit shams*
hat	sun stroke
برنيطة	ضربة شمس
borneiTa	*Darbit shams*

Ring the bell.

اضرب الجرس.

eDrab eg-garas

Press the button.

دوس الزرار.

doos ez-zoraar

Draw the curtains.

اقفل الستارة.

e'fil es-setaara

Moving Around

train	seat belt
قطر	حزام الأمان
'aTr	hezaam el amaan
station	brakes
محطة	فرامل
maHaTTa	faraamil
car	driver
عربية	سواق
9arabeyya	sawwaa'
taxi cab	platform
تاكسي	رصيف
taksee	raSeef
bus	tourist class
أوتوبيس	درجة سياحية
otobees	daraga seyaaHeyya
ferry	first class
معدية	درجة أولى
me9addeyya	daraga oola

highway

طريق سريع

Taree' saree9

square

ميدان

meedaan

tunnel

نفق

nafa'

bridge

كبري

kobri

traffic

مرور

moroor

The Nile

Nile cruises in Southern Egypt are famous for the breathtaking views. The boats seem to glide smoothly along the river because there are no waves. Life on both banks goes on as you sail by, and it looks like the scenery and activities have not changed very much since the time of the pharaohs. The air is fresh and clean and the colors are vivid. It's a treat to the senses, so if you go to Egypt, don't miss it.

The Nile cruise is two days.

رحلة النيل يومين.

reHlit en-neel yohmein

We stop at the temples for three hours.

حنقف عند المعابد ثلاث ساعات.

Hano'af 9and el ma9aabid talat sa9aat

Tourism and the Social Agenda

As an emerging economy, Egypt receives help from the international community in several areas. One of these areas is monitoring and controling the impact of mass tourism on the environment. There are several programs to protect areas and species, as well as programs to create employment opportunities and offer training in tourism and other relevant industries.

Our area of specialty is the environment.

مجال تخصصنا هو البيئة.

magaal takhaS-SoSna howwa el bee'a

We try to help with ...

بنحاول نساعد في ...

benHaawil nesaa9id fee ...

environmental development

التطور البيئي

et-taTawwur el bee'i

environmental planning

التخطيط البيئي

et-takhTeeT el bee'i

environmental management

الإدارة البيئية

el idaara el bee'eyya

We are an organization that provides …

إحنا منظمة بتقدّم ...

eHna monaZZama bet'ad-dim …

    environmental services

    الخدمات البيئية

    el khadamaat el bee'eyya

    consultancy on environmental matters

    استشارات في شؤون البيئة

    esteshaaraat fee she'oon el bee'a

    financial assistance

    مساعدات مالية

    mosaa9adaat maaleyya

We work with women to …

إحنا بنشتغل مع الستات علشان ...

eHna beneshtaghal ma9es-settaat 9alashaan …

    teach them new skills

    نعلمهم مهارات جديدة

    ne9alimhom maharaat gedeeda

    improve family health

    نحسّن صحة الأسرة

    neHassin SeHHit el osra

    increase their incomes

    نزود دخلهم

    nezawwid dakh-lohom

orphans	poverty
أيتام	الفقر
aytaam	el fa'r
widows	illiteracy
أرامل	الأميّة
araamil	el ommeyya
divorced women	disease
مطلّقات	المرض
moTallaqaat	el maraD
the disabled	birth control
المعاقين	تحديد النسل
el mo9aqeen	taHdeed en-nasl

These animals are ...

الحيوانات دي ...

el Haywanaat dee ...

under threat of extinction

مهددة بالإنقراض

mohad-dada bel enqeraaD

not in their natural habitat

مش في بيئتها الطبيعية

mish fee bee'et-ha eT-Tabe9eyya

looking healthy and lively

فيها صحة وحيوية

feeha SiHHa wi-Hayaweyya

STUDY HARD

Many students from all over the world go to Egypt on trips related to their studies or to their hobbies and interests. These trips may last anywhere between a few days and a whole academic year or two. Those studying Arabic, Egyptology, archeology, history, Islamic art, architecture or theology at Al Azhar University could stay even longer.

We are studying ...
احنا بندرس ...
eHna benedris ...

Egyptology
المصريات
el maSriyaat

Arabic
عربي
9arabi

Islamic studies
الدراسات الإسلامية
ed-deraasaat el islaameyya

art history
تاريخ الفنون
tareekh el fenoon

literature
الآداب
el aadaab

history
التاريخ
et-tareekh

economics
الاقتصاد
el eqteSaad

art
الفنون
el fenoon

Middle East Studies
دراسات الشرق الأوسط
derasaat esh-sharq
el awsaT

humanities
العلوم الإنسانية
el 9eloom el
insaaneyya

Eastern languages
اللغات الشرقية
el-loghaat esh-
sharqeyya

social sciences
العلوم الاجتماعية
el 9eloom el
igtemaa9eyya

Islamic history
التاريخ الإسلامي
et-tareekh el islaami

architecture
هندسة المعمار
handasit el me9maar

I am in the ...
أنا في ...
ana fee ...

    first year
    أول سنة
    awwil sana

second year
ثاني سنة
taani sana

final year
آخر سنة
aakhir sana

My degree is in ...
شهادتي في ...
shahad-ti fee ...

political science
العلوم السياسية
el 9eloom es-seyaaseyya

sociology
علم الاجتماع
9ilm el igtimaa9

anthropology
الأنثروبولوجيا
el anthropologia

I specialize in ...
تخصصي في ...
takhaS-SoSi fee ...

marine biology
الأحياء المائية
el aHyaa' el maa'eyya

enviromental studies

دراسات البيئة

deraasaat el bee'a

organic farming

الزراعة العضوية

ez-zeraa9a el 9oDweyya

I'll take it next semester.

حآخذه الترم الجاي.

Hakhdo et-tirm eg-gayy

Are you coming to the lecture?

حتيجوا المحاضرة؟

Hateego el moHaDra?

I'll search in the library.

حادور في المكتبة.

Hadawwar fil maktaba

My tutor ...

المدرس بتاعي...

el modarris betaa9i ...

is great!

هايل!

haayel

is tough!

جامد!

gaamid

is boring!

ممل!

momill

student	Al Azhar University
طالب	جامعة الأزهر
Taalib	*gam9it el azhar*
institute	The American University
معهد	الجامعة الأمريكية
ma9had	*eg-gam9a el omrikeyya*
academy	post-graduate
أكاديمية	دراسات عليا
akademeyya	*derasaat 9olyaa*
university	master's degree
جامعة	ماجستير
gam9a	*majesteir*
Cairo University	doctorate
جامعة القاهرة	دكتوراة
gam9it el qaahira	*doktohraah*
Ein Shams University	thesis
جامعة عين شمس	رسالة
gam9it 9ein shams	*risaala*

Have A Dig

I have a scholarship to study archeology.

عندي منحة لدراسة علم الآثار.

9andi menHa lederaasit 9ilm el aathaar

We're going on a trip ...

رايحين رحلة ...

rayHeen reHla ...

to the excavation site

لموقع الحفريات

li mawqi9 el Hafreyyaat

to the tombs

للمقابر

lil ma'aabir

to the temples

للمعابد

lil ma9aabid

to the valley

للوادي

lil waadi

We will be near ...

حنكون جنب...

Hankoon ganb ...

Karnak temple

معبد الكرنك

ma9bad ek-karnak

Habu temple
معبد هـابو
ma9bad haboo

El Gorna village
قرية القرنة
qaryit el gorna

Our group ...
مَجموعتنا ...
magmoo9-etna ...

is based outside the valley of the Kings
موجودة برة وادي الملوك
mawgooda barra waadi el mulook

is based beside the valley of the Queens
موجودة جنب وادي الملكات
mawgooda ganb waadi el malikaat

is staying on the west bank
قاعدين في البر الغربي
'adeen fil barr el gharbi

Egypt is like one enormous graveyard that has
been divulging its treasure bit by bit over the
centuries. Particular locations in the Nile
Valley keep reappearing in the news every
time a new discovery is made.

Luxor	El Fayyoum
الأقصر	الفيوم
lo'Sor	el fayyoom

Dahshoor	the oases
دهشور	الواحات
dah-shoor	el waHaat

Saqqara	Siwa
سقارة	سيوة
sa'-aara	seewa

Isna	El Dakhla
إسنا	الداخلة
esna	ed-dakhla

Idfu	El Kharga
إدفو	الخارجة
edfu	el kharga

Tel El Amarna	El Farafra
تل العمارنة	الفرافرة
tallel 9amarna	el farafra

Arabic To Me

I wish I could learn ...
نفسي أتعلم ...
nifsi at9allim ...

the Arabic language
اللغة العربية
el-lugha el 9arabeyya

Arabic calligraphy
الخط العربي
el khaTT el 9arabi

hieroglyphics
الهيروغليفي
el heero-ghleefi

Arabic poetry
الشعر العربي
esh-shi9r el 9arabi

This is suitable ...
ده مناسب
dah monaasib ...

for beginners
للمبتدئين
lil mob-tadi'een

for your level
لمستواك
li mostawaak

for the intermediate level
للمستوى المتوسط
lil mostawa el motawasseT

We need some ...

عاوزين شوية

9awzeen shewayyit ...

extra activities

نشاط زيادة

nashaaT zeyaada

handwriting exercises

تمرينات كتابة

tamreenat ketaaba

spoken practice

تدريبات شفوية

tadreebat shafaweyya

I must ...

أنا لازم ...

ana laazim ...

study for the test

أراجع للإمتحان

araagi9 lil emtiHaan

finish this paper

أخلص الموضوع ده

akhallaS el mawDoo9 dah

concentrate on the plurals

أركز على الجمع

arakkiz 9ala el gam9

He always ...

هـو دايماً ...

howwa dayman ...

carries his dictionary

شايل القاموس بتاعه

shaayil el qamoos betaa9u

writes down his observations

بيكتب ملاحظاته

beyektib molaHazaato

asks questions

بيسأل أسئلة

beyes'al as'ila

It's better if we ...

أحسن لو ...

aHsan lau ...

try to speak Arabic

نحاول نتكلم عربي

neHaawil netkallim 9arabi

read about the subject first

نقرأ عن الموضوع الأول

ne'ra 9an el mawdoo9 el awwil

study

نذاكر

nezaakir

the alphabet
الأبجدية
el abgadeyya

word
كلمة
kelma

sentence
جملة
gomla

line
سطر
saTr

paragraph
فقرة
faqra

page
صفحة
SafHa

grammar
قواعد
qawaa9id

verb
فعل
fi9l

noun
اسم
ism

adjective
صفة
Sefa

dialect
لهجة
lahga

spoken
العامية
9ammeyya

colloquial
الدارجة
darga

classical Arabic
الفصحى
al fusHa

Modern Standard
Arabic (MSA)
العربية المعاصرة
el 9arabeyya el
mo9aSra

She's improved! She started reading ...

اتحسنت! ابتدت تقرأ ...

etHas-sinit! ebtadit te'ra ...

the novels of Naguib Mahfouz

روايات نجيب محفوظ

rewayaat nageeb maHfooz

the plays of Tewfik El Hakeem

مسرحيات توفيق الحكيم

masraHey-yaat tawfee' el Hakeem

They were listening to the songs of ...

كانوا بيسمعوا أغاني ...

kaanu beyesma9u aghaani ...

Omm Kolthoum

أم كلثوم

omm kolsoom

Abdul Haleem Hafez

عبد الحليم حافظ

9abdel Haleem Haafez

It's useful to watch the old movies of ...

مفيدة الأفلام القديمة بتاعت ...

mofeeda el aflaam el 'adeema betaa9it ...

Omar Shariff

عمر الشريف

9omar esh-shereef

Islamic Studies

We're students at al Azhar University.
إحنا طلبة في جامعة الأزهر.
eHna Talaba fee gam9it el azhar

I came with them from Malaysia.
أنا جيت معاهم من ماليزيا.
ana geit ma9ahum min malizia

He's originally from Nigeria.
هو أصلا من نيجيريا.
howwa aSlan min nijeria

Are there many students from Indonesia?
فيه طلبة كثير من اندونيسيا؟
fee Talaba keteer min indonesia?

After I graduate, ...
بعد ما أتخرج ...
ba9d ma at-kharrag, ...

I will teach Arabic in Ghana
حادرّس عربي في غانا
Hadarris 9arabi fee ghaana

I will become an Imam in Baku, Azerbaijan
حابقى إمام في باكو، أذربيجان
Hab'a imaam fee baaku, azerbayjaan

I will open a school for refugees
حافتح مدرسة للاجئين
HaftaH madrasa lil lage'een

God	alms
الله	زكاة
Allah	zakaah
prophet	fasting
رسول	صيام
rasool	Siyaam
the Koran	pilgrimage
القرآن	حج
al-qur'aan	hajj
prayer	feast/eid
صلاة	عيد
Salaah	9eid

There are several important mosques in the old Islamic part of Cairo named after Islamic figures. These include *sidna el Hussein*, named after one of the grandsons of the prophet Mohammed; *es-sayyida Zeinab*, named after the grandaughter of the prophet Mohammed; *es-sayyida Aisha*, named after an eighth-century descendant of the prophet Mohammed; and *Amru ibn el 'aaS*, named after the commander of the Muslim army that conquered Egypt.

PLAY HARDER

What a Sport!

Visitors and residents find that Egypt is a good place for sports and outdoor pursuits because the weather is agreeable most of the time.

soccer	golf
كورة	جولف
kohra	*golf*
tennis	gymnastics
تنس	جمباز
tenis	*gombaaz*
hockey	track and field
هوكي	ألعاب القوى
hoki	*al9aab el qowa*
basketball	javelin
باسكت	الرمح
baskit	*er-romH*
volleyball	physical fitness
فولي	لياقة بدنية
foli	*lyaaqa badaneyya*
squash	weights
اسكواش	حديد أثقال
eskiwaash	*Hadeed ath'aal*

You'll find her...

حتلاقيها ...

Hatla'eeha ...

> in the gymnasium
>
> في الجيم
>
> fij-jeem

> in the sauna
>
> في الساونا
>
> fis-sawna

> at the stables
>
> في الاسطبل
>
> fil esTabl

These are my exercises ...

دي تمريناتي ...

di tamreenati ...

> daily
>
> كل يوم
>
> *kolli-yohm*

> three times a week
>
> ثلاث مرات في الأسبوع
>
> *talat marraat fil osboo9*

> whenever I get the chance
>
> كل ماتجيني فرصة
>
> *koll mat-geeni forSa*

I always start with …

أنا دايماً ابتدي بـ …

ana dayman abtedi bi- …

> warming up the muscles
>
> تسخين العضلات
>
> *taskheen el 9aDalaat*

> exercises to loosen up the muscles
>
> تمرينات فك العضلات
>
> *tamreenat fakk el 9aDalaat*

> floor exercises
>
> تمرينات أرضية
>
> *tamreenaat arDeyya*

Egyptian Sunshine Games

I prefer a light jog.

أنا بأفضل جري خفيف.

ana ba'faD-Dal garyy khafeef

Stan and I play soccer every Friday.

أنا وستان بنلعب كورة كل يوم جمعة.

ana wi staan benel9ab koora koll yohm gom9a

They are members of the equestrian club.

هم أعضاء في نادي الفروسية.

humma a9Daa' fee naadi el foroseyya

She trains at the rowing club.

هي بتتمرن في نادي التجديف.

heyya betet-marran fee naadi et-ta'deef

referee	defender
حكم	مدافع
Hakam	modaafi9
coach	ball
مدرب	كورة
modarrib	kohra
team	bat/racket
فريق	مضرب
faree'	maDrab
club	net
نادي	شبكة
naadi	shabaka
attacker	whistle
مهاجم	صفارة
mohaagim	Soffaara

Jimmy and Ahmad went to the shooting club.

جيمي وأحمد راحوا نادي الرماية.

jimmy wi aHmad raHoo naadir-remaaya

In the Eid vacation, we can ...

في أجازة العيد ممكن...

fee agaazit el 9eed, momkin ...

go diving in Raas Mohammed

نغطس في رأس محمد

neghTas fee raas meHmmad

take out the sailing boat in el Gouna

نآخذ المركب الشراعي في الجونة

naakhod el markeb esh-sheraa9i fig-goona

go fishing in Marsa Alam

نصطاد سمك في مرسى علم

neS-Taad samak fee marsa 9alam

She is the club captain in ...

هي كابتن النادي في ...

heyya kabtin en-naadi fee ...

judo

الجودو

ej-joodoo

karate

الكاراتيه

ek-karaateih

kung fu

الكونج فو

ek-kungifoo

Sorry, captain, I forgot my ...

آسف يا كابتن أنا نسيت ...

aasif ya kabtin, ana neseet ...

gloves

الجوانتي

eg-gewanti

racket

المضرب

el maDrab

bathing suit

المايوه

el maayoh

A hundred push-ups so you remember tomorrow!

مية ضغط علشان تفتكر بكرة!

meyya Daght 9alashaan tefteker bokra

championship	relay
بطولة	تتابع
beToola	*tatabo9*
competition	freestyle
منافسة	حرة
monafsa	*Horra*
contest	butterfly
مسابقة	فراشة
mosab'a	*faraasha*
tactics	breaststroke
تكتيكات	صدر
takteekaat	*Sidr*
instructions	backstroke
تعليمات	ظهر
ta9leemat	*Dahr*

Banana Skin Moments

People who love sports hate injuries. It's sad when you train hard for four years, dreaming of glory and a medal in the Olympic games, then slip on a bar of soap as you shower on the morning of your event.

He twisted his knee in the gym.

لوى ركبته في الجيم.

lawa rokbeto fij-jeem

She fell in the shower after the match.

وقعت في الدش بعد الماتش.

we'-'et fid-dush ba9d el matsh

It is just ...

ده ...

dah ...

> a mild concussion
>
> ارتجاج بسيط
>
> *irtegaag baseeT*

> an allergy
>
> حساسية
>
> *Hassaseyya*

> a virus
>
> فيروس
>
> *vayroos*

I feel a little dizzy.
أنا دايخ شوية.
ana daayekh shwayya

I'll go for a check up.
حاروح أعمل كشف.
HarooH a9mil kashf

I'll go to bed early.
حنام بدري.
Hanaam badri

I'll check the blood pressure.
حاقيس ضغط الدم.
Ha'ees Daght ed-demm

Here, I have a ...
هنا، عندي ...
hina 9andi ...

    pain
    وجع
    waga9

    rash
    حكة
    Hakka

    bleeding
    نزيف
    nazeef

Two days ago, ...
من يومين ...
min yohmein ...

I slipped on the stairs
اتزحلقت على السلم
etzaHla't 9ala es-sillim

I got a stomachache
جالي مغص
gali maghaSS

I vomited
رجّعت
ragga9t

The wound is ...
الجرح ...
eg-garH ...

deep
عميق
9amee'

infected
ملوث
molawwass

superficial
سطحي
saT-Hee

hip	joints
حوض	مفاصل
HohD	mafaaSil
thigh	cartilage
فخذ	غضروف
fakhd	ghaDroof
knees	wrist
ركب	رسغ
rokab	risgh
foot	collar bone
قدم	عظمة الترقوة
'adam	9aDmit et-terqoo-wah
cramp	rib
تقلص	ضلع
taqal-loS	Dil9
hernia	ribcage
فتاء	قفص صدري
fitaa'	afaS Sadri

Doctor, you need to know ...

يا دكتور، لازم تعرف ...

ya doktoor, laazim te9raf ...

   that I have a heart condition

   إن عندي مشكلة في القلب

   enn 9andi mushkila fil 'elb

that I am diabetic

إن عندي السكَّر

enn 9andi es-sokkar

that I am pregnant

إني حامل

enni Haamil

that I suffer from asthma

إن عندي ربو

enn 9andi azma

that I am allergic to penicillin

إن عندي حساسية للبنسلين

enn 9andi Hassaseyya lil-bensileen

fractured/broken	swollen
مكسور	وارم
maksoor	waarim
infected	painful
ملوث	موّلم
molawwass	mu'lim
inflamed	burnt
ملتهب	محروق
moltahib	maHroo'
sterile	sprained
معقم	مجزوع
mo9aqqam	magzoo9

First, we will need ...

أولا حنحتاج ...

awalan, HaneHtaag ...

an x-ray

أشعة

ashe9-9a

a urine test

تحليل بول

taHleel bohl

You will need ...

حتحتاج ...

Ha-teHtaag ...

physiotherapy

علاج طبيعي

i9eebaT gaale9

tnemtaert resal

علاج بالليزر

9elaag bel-leezar

complete rest

راحة تامة

raaHa taamma

I am much better now, thanks.

أنا أحسن كثير دلوقتي، شكراً.

ana aHsan keteer delwa'ti, shokran

Printed in the USA
CPSIA information can be obtained
at www.ICGtesting.com
JSHW012034030124
54747JS00017B/490